THE INDOMI7

Truths of Trauma, Trials, and Triumphs

Keynu Scott

THE INDOMITABLE QUEEN: A MEMOIR

TRUTHS OF TRAUMA, TRIALS, AND
TRIUMPHS

Author Photo: Branden Adams Photography

Cover Design: Angelia Vernon Menchan

Makeup: Amari Angelique

Props: Weldon Bonds Studio

THE INDOMITABLE QUEEN: A MEMOIR

Truths of Trauma, Trials and Triumphs

Author Keynu Scott

Disclaimer:

This memoir is based upon a true story. It reflects the author's present recollections of experiences over time. All names have been changed to protect the identity of the characters.

Publisher:

Honorable MENCHAN Media L.L.C.

Angelia Vernon Menchan

Email: acvermen@yahoo.com

www.angeliavernonmenchan.com

This memoir is a riveting story based on Ms. Scott's memories and recollections. The publisher is unable to verify or corroborate the contents.

Angelia Vernon Menchan

DEDICATION

God, I can't thank you enough. Your faithfulness and mercy to a sinner like me has been so overwhelming. God you kept me through all of my lowest of times. Thank you for your everlasting love and always showing me that you have the final say and you're in control.

Kysen, I couldn't imagine life without you.
You are my light, you are my happiness, and I am very proud to call your handsome self my son. Your smile, your laugh, and your random hugs and kisses keep me going. I wouldn't trade you for anybody in the world. Everything I do is for you. I'm going to make sure you have the best life possible and try my best to give you a childhood you don't have to heal from. Keep being the bright and beautiful boy that you are. I'll always believe in you and have your back no matter what. I love you!

TITLE MEANING

INDOMITABLE

in·dom·i·ta·ble

/inˈdämədəb(ə)l/

adjective

1. impossible to subdue or defeat.

Similar: Invincible, Unconquerable, Courageous

Example: "A woman of indomitable spirit."

Why did the author name herself "The Indomitable Queen"?

After all of the obstacles set before her and the many times she wanted to completely give up, she didn't. She adapted to her circumstances and maintained a courageous spirit.

She crowns herself as a queen because throughout her struggles she had an insurmountable amount of strength. The trauma and trials she faced took a lot of strength and she mastered it.

PREFACE

Life hasn't always been easy for me. I've had many ups and plenty downs, more downs than I ever imagined. Some changed me for the good, some for the bad, but to be honest, I wouldn't change any of it. It has formed who I am today and it has made me stronger in ways I never thought possible. I have a different outlook on life now and I'm striving to get better every day. Trials and tribulations can come after me, but they'll never knock me down to the point where I won't get back up. I'm a survivor, the true definition of one, and now I'm here to tell my story. This is my story, my feelings, all being exposed for my healing. I hope the obstacles and pain I endured is an inspiration for others to overcome any obstacles they are faced with and also speak out on it. We all have a story, some big and some small. Don't stay silent, speak the truth, your truth that is. Go through it, grow through, and glow through it.

TABLE OF CONTENTS

1: Childhood   Page 8

2: All Grown Up   Page 20

3: Dating and Relationships   Page 26

4: Signing my life over   Page 35

5: Military, Marriage, & Mess   Page 44

6: Arrest & Adultery   Page 102

7: Divorce & Drama   Page 126

8: Motherhood Mattered More   Page 243

9: New Beginnings   Page 249

10: Not My Baby!   Page 264

11: Reflections   Page 315

12: Healing and Growth   Page 337

Cast of Characters

Deidra- Mom
Marquise -Dad
Bryna- Mack's Babymama
Madison- Ex Girlfriend
Mack- Husband
Faith- Wife
Moesha- Mistress
Tamesha- Mother In Law
Correll- Father In Law
Sherry- Correll's Fiance
Mir- Son

CHAPTER ONE: Childhood

On December 19, 1991, I was born to my mother Deidra and my father Marquise. They named me Faith. I was a precious baby with caramel skin and pretty curly hair. I came into the world a little over nine months after my parents were married. I was my parents' only child they had in common. Before I was born, my mother had my sister with her ex-boyfriend and my father had my brother with his ex-wife. My sister is 11 years older than me and my brother is 7 years older than me which made me the baby of the family. I don't remember anything about my infant and toddler years until I was about 4 or 5 years old.

I grew up in Ocala, Florida in a three-bedroom blue vinyl siding house in the suburbs of the Silver Springs Shores area. It was a nice house that sat by itself but as the years passed, construction workers began adding houses on the side of our house and across the street from it. We had a large backyard however, there were no outdoors toys back there for me to play with. There was a garage attached to the house that my dad stored all of his auto tools, lawn mower, and miscellaneous things stored in. My dad used to hunt for land turtles where he would catch them, gut and clean them, and prepare them to be cooked. It was a popular meal in my house served with a side of white rice and vegetables. I had no idea what was it was particularly, I just knew my dad had caught it and cooked it. Of course as a child I was always told to eat what was set in front of me. I didn't have a choice but to do so or else I would go hungry that day. My parents had a ritual when it came to breakfast and dinner time. Breakfast had to be consumed in the morning time which would consist of bacon, eggs, and grits and dinner had to be consumed before it got dark. Some meals they would cook were spaghetti, fried chicken with fries, catfish and tilapia fish, pork chops, rutabaga with rice and vegetables, meatloaf, hamburger, and sometimes corned beef and cabbage. Those are just a few of the meals I recall because they cooked it so often. There was only one type of seasoning that I knew they used and it was Tony Chachere's Creole seasoning. They used that seasoning on everything so much that I became familiar with the taste of it and vowed when I got older I would have a variety of seasonings and flavors not just one. After dinner, my mother and father would either go to their bedroom and rest which meant for me that I could watch TV in the living room or find something to do in my room. Often times on Sunday nights before my mom had to go to work on Monday morning, my mom would do my hair just about every week. I would sit on the floor on top of a sofa pillow while she brushed and combed my hair applying hair grease thoroughly as she was getting ready to either braid it into cornrows or pigtails with bows and barrettes. I was so tender headed and sensitive to the touch that I would scream and cry for my mother to take it easy on my hair. Sometimes she would yell at me, "Girl hush I ain't hurting you" and other times she would get frustrated and say, "Okay well you can walk around with your hair all over your head." I had to suck it up, squirm through the pain, and anxiously wait as my mother finished my hair. I didn't want to walk around with my hair all over my head looking nappy and bring attention to myself for others to laugh and bully me so I complied. My mother and my father both worked so when they did, I had to go to my grandma's house. My grandmother owned her own home daycare so she kept me for years. I would always be excited going to my grandma's house because there were other kids to play with as well as my cousins. I don't recall my parents doing many activities with me that were kid friendly and involved interactions with other kids outside of daycare. They had only taken me to Disney World, the zoo, and circus once and occasionally I would be taken to a neighborhood playground but it wasn't often that I got to enjoy being a kid in a public play setting. Most of my time as a kid was spent inside the house and sometimes outside of the house in the front yard when they had time to keep a close eye on me. I recall the tricycle my parents had bought for me. It was red and shiny and had a fanny pack attached to the front of it. It became my favorite outdoor activity. You couldn't tell me a thing once I really got the hang of riding it. I didn't really like being indoors much so this made me really happy being able to play with it. I preferred being on the go. I was such a busy body little girl with not a care in the world.

I remember my parents owned one vehicle and it was a gray two-door Pontiac Grand-Am. I hated that car. I felt so squished in the back of it. I was excited when it ran out of commission and my parents bought a white Ford Explorer. I loved that SUV. It had plenty of space for me to move around without feeling cramped. I wanted to go everywhere in it and let me tell you I was so proud to get in and step out of it, you would've thought it was mine. I would tell everybody I came in contact with that my parents had bought a new car. My parents were finally able to pack my tricycle in the trunk of it so we could go to the nearest park and ride our bikes for hours. They had their own bikes too. I enjoyed riding alongside them and playing racing games to see who could ride their bike the fastest. Of course with my little bodied self, I couldn't pick up a lot of speed, but I certainly did try. There were a lot of days and times where I wanted to spend time with just my mom and sometimes just my dad. My mother was accepting of it and our alone time together would be riding bikes together down to the end of our neighborhood street or simply taking a walk or jog. We also would go to Dollar Tree very often too and it became a ritual of ours. I enjoyed going to that store because everything was a dollar and my mom allowed me to pick out everything that I wanted and didn't have to pay a lot for it. When it came to my dad he would always be busy doing something but it rarely included me. When he would get frustrated, he often told me, "I wish I never had you." My mother corrected him only once to my knowledge for saying that and other times she would remain silent. This is when my abandonment, rejection, and daddy issues began to develop. Marquise broke my heart before any other man ever could. My mother was nurturing to me but sometimes she would act very saddity when she got around certain people. Sometimes she would feed into how he acted to keep him calm and not lash out at her for taking up for me and going against his will or discipline towards me.

Marquise would mostly be getting high smoking weed and getting drunk or either going to my uncle's house to hang out with him on the other side of our town. I still remember each house my dad would go to get his baggies. He also enjoyed going to a nearby lake to catch fresh water fish called "bream". That was a hobby of his that he enjoyed doing alone. I recall the only time my dad was nice to me was when he was drinking. Other times he was very mean and seemed like every opportunity he had, I got my ass beat. My dad also had an R&B and gospel singing group that took up a lot of his time. The group of a few ladies and a couple of men would have rehearsals in our extra bedroom that was made into a computer and music room. He would lock the door and the group would chatter for a few before beginning to sing each of their parts of the songs. He even had a CD and case with the group name and their picture on it he passed out regularly when at church or in public places. He wanted to share what he thought was great music to the world and he was so proud. My dad has always had aspirations of being on tv shows such as "Sunday's Best" and "America's Got Talent" and would talk and fantasize about it quite often bragging about when he made it in the industry and how he would make sure I was financially taken care of in every way. He carried on this persona for several years throughout my childhood and it never happened. It was empty words with mediocre actions. He broke my heart when he didn't keep his word and I didn't know what the future held for me. He had built me up to believe I was going to be taken care of by him before I ever depended on another man. Eventually, I came to the realization that he was not a man of his word, one that could be trusted with words but because he was my father and at the time I saw him as faultless, I let whatever he said to me be taken in seriousness not realizing that he was just a smooth talker when he wanted to be.

My mother, Deidra would never interject when she knew my father wasn't telling the truth. She would go along with it or let it fall on deaf ears. As I started to get older, I became rebellious against some of my parents commands. I started to form my own opinions of things and my parents frowned upon and shamed me for having a voice that spoke differently than theirs. There was a time I recall that my mother had once had beat me with no clothes on when I did or said something she didn't like. It took years later for her to reveal to me that her stepmom did it to her too and she had scars to prove it. I remember when my mom would leave and go to the store or handle business after work, my dad would quickly go into the computer room, close, and lock the door. I never knew what he was doing until one day he forgot to lock the door and I sneakily walked in on him watching pornography with his eyes glued to the screen in amazement. I had to be eight or nine years old. When he realized I was in the room, He would suddenly click off to another screen and see what it was I wanted and yell at me, "Get out this room and go sit down somewhere." I also used to watch him look up escort services as well in the phone book. He would leave a place marker in the page to come back to later and forget to remove it. He forgot to remove it so it couldn't be traced by my mother who looked down upon it. When mother and I had alone time together I would tell her what I saw. I would even show her the internet history. She was often silent or in denial and didn't want to believe it even with the proof in her face. Watching my dad participate in these activities often gave me the notion that my dad was searching for another woman. Of course I didn't want him searching for another woman. He had my mother so I didn't understand his need to have two. When MySpace existed, he used to secretly inbox women and I would still figure it out because I knew his passwords until he caught on and changed it. My dad was a huge hypocrite and such a phony person. He would use social media as his platform to post bible scriptures as if he was a perfect Christian and holier than thou man but, behind closed doors he would attempt to lure women in by having Christian and some explicit conversations. He would excessively cuss, heavily drink, negatively speak and talk about me as a child, and whoop me when it was not always necessary. He was verbally abusive towards my mother when she went against his manipulation or commands.

   I recall when my dad and mom got into arguments frequently, my dad would tell my mother to go to their bedroom. He would close the door, lock it, and all I would hear is him yelling and screaming at her. I believe I heard hitting sounds and wails from my mother as well. I didn't understand then but, I understand now that my dad had a violent demeanor. On Sundays, we went to church and I dreaded going and sitting on the pew next to my mother while she listened to the sermon. I knew nothing about the scriptures and the message the pastor was preaching but I was always told by my mother, "Sit down, hush, and listen." as she chewed her Wrigley's gum. One Sunday each month at church, it was considered baptism day. My mother had told me to go up to the altar of the church one Sunday and tell them I would like to accept Jesus Christ as my lord and savior. I clearly remember getting baptized and how I held onto the glass of the baptism pool. I was scared and had a fear of drowning in water since when I was a younger child because on a couple of occasions I had a near-drowning experience. My pastor led me down to the water and I was baptized. I had no real understanding of what was going on but my parents told me that I was giving my life to Christ. I had no idea until later the true meaning of that. I was also a member in the church youth choir and sang the tune of a soprano. The choir director put me in the front of the choir which I did not like for some reason. I guess the older cool kids were in the back of the choir and I wanted to sing along next to them. As time went on, I grew bored with going to rehearsals and singing in the choir.

A few months later, I told my mother, "I do not want to be in the choir anymore." At first she kept trying to force me to go but, when she saw I wasn't putting the effort in towards singing anymore, she allowed me to stop going. I also did praise dancing which I was really shy about because I had no rhythm and did not know how to dance. I had self-esteem issues because I hadn't hit puberty like the other girls did causing me to be ashamed so I did not want to be in the spotlight. I did some acting but that grew old too. Honestly, I didn't want any type of role in church in front of a crowd due to my lack of confidence. When holidays came, all I did was recite speeches in front of the church, watch the crowd applaud, take a seat, and at the end of those services I would participate in kid activities and go home with my parents. After church, we would go to Dairy Queen and get ice cream and either go to the park or to my grandma's house. I loved and enjoyed going because I got to spend time with my grandparents. My granddad was my favorite. He watched TV with us, played games, and kept us entertained with his jokes. My grandma was also a good cook too, so I enjoyed going to eat whatever food she cooked. I didn't grow up in the house with any siblings my age so my cousins were the next closest to me. We played house, enjoyed rides in Grandma's blue Lincoln Town car running errands with her and especially when we would go to Sam's Club and sample the food. We also walked to the Lillian Bryant Park not too far from her house and got freeze cups, hot sausages, candy, hot fries, and pickles. My cousin Que and I had a serious addiction to all of these snacks and we both loved ice. Our granddad used to yell at my cousin and I each time we went to the icebox and was making a lot of noise. It was hilarious to us because we really tried to be sneaky and get ice while he was sleep and he would still hear us.

"Que, Faith, get out that fridge!" he would say. We would laugh hysterically as we ran back to the playroom my grandma had in the back for us. There was a tent, books, and portable games we would occupy ourselves with.

When I was of school age, I went to a magnet school. A magnet school is a public school offering special instruction and programs not available elsewhere, designed to attract a more diverse student body from throughout a school district. There were times my teachers would reach out to my mother and tell her about how I was coming along as a new student and at one point my mother came and observed me on some occasions to monitor my progress. My mother told me how much of a busy body I was in class and how it wasn't normal when all the other kids were sitting down doing what they were supposed to do. There was a time when my teacher scolded me for mixing my food together and she tried to make me eat it. My mother showed up at the school embarrassed and told the teacher because of her singling me out and treating me oddly that she was taking me out of the school. My parents then took me to a doctor, told them their concerns as well as what the teacher observed. At the age of kindergarten, I was diagnosed with ADHD and anxiety. I was prescribed Ritalin and Lexapro medicine which kept me calm and focused. Overtime, my mother saw a gradual change in my behavior both at school and home. When school ended, I would go to my grandma's house and wait for my parents to get off work and pick me up. When I did get home, I would complete my homework before being allowed to play. When I would take my homework back to school and the teacher graded it, I would have E's for Excellent and S's for satisfactory. I successful completed elementary school and was promoted to middle school.

Once I got to middle school that is when peer pressure and bullying came into play. Boys and girls my age were going out partying, having sleepovers, sex, and getting pregnant. My parents didn't allow me to participate in any of that. I felt sleepovers should've at least been allowed however, my mother didn't budge. She used to always say, "If you get pregnant, you're going to end up unmarried and on Section 8 getting food stamps and living in the projects." My mother said such negativity towards me as if she was in control of my future had that happened. In reality, she was projecting the lifestyle she ended up in. She got pregnant with my older sister by a man who she was not married to who was an alcoholic and he left her barefoot and pregnant in the projects and refusing to pay child support. My mother was using a situation of me wanting to enjoy my childhood and teen years to manipulate it to her own concerns she had with her past. I just thought it was absurd that I wasn't allowed to party nor attend sleepovers even if they were family. My mother didn't get along with my dads' side of the family for reasons unknown to me, and she started limiting the amount of time I was around my dad's side of the family. She claimed that they acted funny or acted like they were better than us. Although I was an innocent child and I had nothing to do with how she felt about them, she poisoned my mind to think negative about them which caused me to not ever have a real relationship with them. When I was around them at occasional family events, they definitely did treat me as if I did not belong. As a growing teen, I couldn't even hang with or talk to boys in person or on the phone. If I wanted to go to a friend's house, my mother had to talk to the parents first and make sure that there were no boys in the house even if it was their son, before she would allow me to stay. My mother always used to drill in my head, "If you get pregnant I'm kicking you out of the house."

I was told I was not allowed to have a boyfriend until I was eighteen and then that changed to when I get out of their house. I kept asking my parents to have one but they refused to let up. They were super strict and sheltered me from the outside world as much as possible. I was an average student in middle school. I got A's, B's, and C's just about each time progress and report cards were generated. There were a few times where my grades slipped especially in math. I was never good at Math. I looked forward to getting good grades because the church I was attending gave savings bonds for those who got good grades and that was motivation enough do well in school.

When my mom and dad were financially struggling, they would take and cash my savings bonds and made promises to pay back. As far as after school activities, I didn't get a chance to participate in sports or school field trips because my mother was on a budget, or if she couldn't keep a close eye on me she didn't allow me to go. She felt if I wanted to participate, that I should search for a job. I wasn't a sneaky or troubled teenager at all so I didn't understand why my mother was such a helicopter parent the way she was. She had to know every move that I made. I wasn't like any of the other girls I went to school with. I was different, much like an outcast.

I wasn't popular nor did I keep up with the latest clothing and hairstyles as much as everyone else. My mom was always on a budget and I was told to appreciate what I got. I either had a clip in ponytail or some braids which she sometimes would allow to stay in my hair until it got old and fuzzy then she would try to freshen it up using hair mousse instead of getting me a fresh hairstyle. I wasn't allowed to get any color in my hair at all because didn't want me to be too attractive and bring attention to boys at all. I wore nerdy looking glasses, my teeth were yellow, buck, and I had a gap so wide you could fit four quarters through it.

I was extremely self-conscious. I didn't feel pretty nor was I told by my parents that I was pretty on a regular basis which heightened my insecurities even more. I didn't get any attention from boys whatsoever. When I got to high school, nothing really changed. My mother and her views were the same. Puberty hadn't hit me yet. I was very flat-chested, had big feet, and sometimes my hair wasn't always a fresh style. I never got in any fights and when I got picked on and bullied and I would either stay silent or try to avoid those people altogether. My mother always told me if I ever got in fights that I would get whooped for it. Her suggestion was, "Pray to God and they'll leave you alone." So basically I couldn't defend myself for fear of getting in trouble at home. My attention towards guys increased and I had a couple of crushes but none of them liked me back because I wasn't their type of definition of "pretty and poppin." It bothered me a lot because I didn't fit in. I always wanted to feel like I belonged somewhere. Due to my mom prohibiting me from male contact, I had to readjust my focus back to my school work.

Academically, I did fine in 9th and 10th grade. When I reached the 11th and 12th grade, I struggled a lot, so much that my mother started letting me get help from tutor services online. She helped when she could but other times she was focused on her own academics and career. I managed to seek out fellow classmates and get help. Some of them also allowed me to cheat. I knew it was wrong but I did it anyway because I wanted to graduate and not be left behind. I remember right before graduation, I was bold enough to log in to my mother's school teacher email without her knowing pretending to be her and I sent my teacher a message asking her to help me pass my class so I can graduate on time. It wasn't the right thing to do but it did work, and I graduated on time in 2010 with the rest of my classmates. I ended up telling my mother after I graduated. When my mother realized we went to the same church as that teacher, my mother ended up telling her what I had done. Why? I don't know what purpose it served to tell her after I had already done it. If that lady was the type of teacher to be nasty, she could've somehow had my diploma reversed but thank God she didn't.

CHAPTER TWO: All Grown-up

After graduation, my mom gave me two options. I could go to school or work and give her half of my paycheck to stay in their house. My mother was always the one working and my dad could barely keep a job so she was trying to get money out of me to make up for what he wasn't doing and because she acted as if I was a burden. She saw at it as me paying her rent for living there. I didn't agree with her logic at all. I felt that I should be able to get on my feet so I could move out and not be dependent on them nor tolerate any more of their crap. I ended up going to school and working but I did not give her half of my check. I refused.

My parents and I started to not get along because I had a mind of my own and I did not agree with their views, early curfew, and their constant sheltering of me from reality. I started looking for apartments because I couldn't deal with either of them anymore. They were controlling and they tried to keep me from having a social life. I couldn't go to graduation bash, prom, or anything as it is so when I graduated I wanted to go out with friends and enjoy my life. At one point, I started threatening them to leave for the Army to get away from them and they begged and pleaded for me not to do that only because they wanted to have control over me and continue to watch my every move. I didn't go because I was afraid of dying while in service, bringing grief to my family and I didn't have a lot of knowledge or skills that I felt were compatible enough to go.

While I was in college, I wasn't focused at all. I mean come on, I had just graduated out of high school and wanted to have fun. You know the clubbing, drinking, and good sex type of fun. I wanted to be a part of the cool crew. I was taking four classes and it was too much for me at the time. I was failing terribly. Additionally, problems at home were gradually getting worse. The older I got the more my mind was developed and I rebelled even more against my parents. Can you believe they were still trying to whoop me with a belt at eighteen years old because I started standing up for myself and calling out their toxic behavior? They felt it was disrespectful but, in reality it was just correction of their wrong as parents.

I remember one day when I was sitting in the kitchen at the table minding my business, jamming to music, and playing on my phone, my dad came in and randomly knocked me upside my head. I guess he was frustrated or tired of me at the time. He had a really short temper all the time. I told my mother what he did and I went to my room contemplating what I should do next. I ended up calling the police and when they showed up, they asked what happened. I told them and they gave him the option to leave the house to avoid being arrested. My mother was angry because he had to leave the house. I didn't do or say anything to him to piss him off, he just did it randomly. I got tired of them doing and saying things to me without any repercussions for fear of getting whooped so when I turned 18 all of that accepting misbehavior went out the window for me. Later in the same year, my mother and father were having a dispute which resulted in the police being called and a restraining order being placed against my dad. I guess they were arguing about my nieces being at the house and my sister not picking them up on time and he wanted to have the freedom to do as he pleased without having to watch them. My mother and father exchanged words and got very loud. My dad decided to leave out the door, slamming it behind him, and took off in my mother's car. My sister ended up coming to get my nieces and my mother told her what happened. She had me use my car to transport her and my sister used her car to follow my dad to get her car back. Although, my parents were married, my mother tried to file her car as stolen but when she talked to police, they said it was joint property and they could not do it. They involved each of our immediate family members and it got nasty. My brother in law threatened to pull a gun on my dad if he did not give my mother her vehicle back. My mom felt so unsafe going back home that we stayed at my sister's house and then she got an apartment of her own and avoided contact with my dad for months. I used to cry because I didn't want my parents to not be together and everything was so chaotic.

Later that year, I got fed up with everything and I ended up moving to my own apartment after I got tired of getting into verbal disputes with my parents and them trying to shelter and have extreme control over me. They tried to manipulate me into staying with them and made empty promises that things would be different but I did not change my mind. I wanted my independence to do, say, and go as I please. After all, I listened to my parents talk so much crap about my brother and sister when they chose to leave their house for good instead of putting up with them and I got tired of that too. I see why both of them didn't want to live under my parent's roof anymore. They were way too controlling and invasive in our lives. My first townhouse was in a two bedroom income based neighborhood. My rent was very affordable and the area was safe. When I got settled in and allowed my parents to come and visit apartments I had, they would walk in, speak, and they did an inspection as if it was necessary for their approval to be heard. This continued every time I moved to a new place, my mom and dad examined and made slick remarks if it wasn't what they liked or if it was nicer than what they had. They walked in parts of my apartment they had no business even being in, just invading my entire privacy as an adult.

My parents were going through bankruptcy and foreclosure on the house I grew up in so of course because their daughter was living a life better than what they thought I should be living, the hate became more apparent. My mother has always been obsessed with taking pictures of my place to show and tell other people I moved out to either gloat or be messy. Family or church members, who never talked to me prior to moving out, were coming to me telling me things that they heard from my parent's mouth about how I was living and what I was doing in my life.

I was living a low-key life trying to figure out what I wanted to do next in life and for my parents to be parading my business out made me realize I shouldn't share with them. I hate that I thought I could trust them. I didn't know it then but my mother's continued lack of boundaries between her and I, a dynamic of over-involvement, overbearing, lack of privacy, and my individuality or a desire for independence seen as betrayal were clear signs of family enmeshment. Family enmeshment is enmeshment between a parent and child which often results in over-involvement in each other's lives so that it makes it hard for the child to become developmentally independent and responsible for her choices. Sometimes the effect this has on the parent and child relationship is not a positive one. It creates a codependent type of relationship where the child or adult child has difficulty making decisions in a relationship, has difficulty identifying their own feeling, difficulty communicating, valuing the approval of others more than self, and lacking trust in one's self causing poor self-esteem.

My sister has even made remarks about my mothers' ways and not being able to "hold water" meaning she can't keep in a secret and was telling my sister mine and other people's business. I hated that. My sister is a hater and a down talker of me as well. She has always been the type to listen to me talk about my business and have something negative to say but keep her business very private. Why? Because she wanted to know what I had going on so she could keep up or get ahead of me. She was in competition with me and although she tried to mask it, she was never good at doing so. My sister has never been there for me in any achievement of my life as an adult. Other than my high school graduation she never cheered me on, she just listened, watched, spoke negativity and instilled doubt and in me when I would tell her what my next best move was.

I used to try to be close to my mom as a growing adult. Of course because I was developing a lot more from every experience I encountered in life on my own, my mother and father would still share differences with me. They were stuck in their old ways of doing things. Often as a child and an adult, my parents collectively didn't know that me disagreeing with them is not a sign of disrespect, it's simply the fact that I don't think the same way they do. Disrespect is being impolite or lacking courtesy such as name-calling, sarcasm, and rolling eyes, belittling, or making fun. Disagreeing is having or expressing a different opinion. That is the difference. This was how she attempted to manipulate me to bow down to her and my father on what they agreed with or else I would get a beating. I didn't go as far as saying they were lying or not saying true things because that would get me one too. Whether we're the parent or the child, if something is not truthful and is not a fact, there's nothing wrong with respectfully disagreeing. We should get out of the mindset that because we had certain values, morals, or standards that were instilled in us as children growing up and now that we're adults we have to live by those same standards. No, that's not the case for everything. You have to be open-minded and do some self-development and research to see what aligns with the spirit within you. There have been times in my life both good and bad I desperately wanted my mother's validation. I looked at her as a mother and my friend that I could confide in but little did I know the things I would tell her, she would throwback in my face later if I disagreed with her. She wanted to have control over my views or opinions that differed from hers. Her response would usually be a cut and dry response or silence when it was an accomplishment of mine but sometimes when it came to the downfalls I shared, she contributed by adding more negativity instead of speaking positivity to keep my spirits high. She didn't share the same amount of happiness I did, she shared some slight happiness and envy. Why? Because who she said I would be as a young child, superseded what she ever thought or imagined.

To be honest, my mother has always been in comparison of my lifestyle to hers because I've always been in a better financial and living situation than her and my dad. There have been more times I can count that she and my dad have asked me for money, more than I have ever asked of them and I rarely asked since I've been out on my own at eighteen. My dad would be more dismissive when I would confide in him about an interaction with a male and seek advice. He would say, "Uh Huh, "Yeah" "Okay" but wasn't listening to me or my thoughts. His advice wouldn't be constructive criticism with positivity; it would be demeaning as if I should know things all on my own.

If there's one thing I can say, I learned a lot about how to manage life outside of my parents' home than I did while living with them. Their parenting was very dull and boring so when I got out on my own, I did a lot of self-teaching, sought out guidance from friends, and learning from books and the internet. My experiences, my upcoming and downfalls all taught me how to handle situations in the spur of the moment.

CHAPTER THREE: Relationships and Dating

I entered the dating scene at 18 years old shortly before I graduated high school. I became a popular girl who was well kept up and I had a lot of platonic guy friends. I met them all on MySpace because my parents were so strict I didn't have a social life outside of school and anyone I connected with I either attended school with them or met on social media. I started to become curious about relationships, sex, and all the cute stuff that comes along with it. Due to my dad not showing me a lot of love and attention as a child, I began to seek love and validation from every man I met. I wanted a man that would call me every day and text me back quickly to validate the feelings of inadequacy I would feel. I also wanted a man to make sure I was safe while at school and work. I wanted a man that would help me out when I needed financial support and give me money to go enjoy myself as well as alleviate the stress of doing everything alone. Someone who would pick me up from home and take me out on well planned and put together dates and adore every aspect of me. After all, I knew I was a good catch, a young woman who was willing to show love and help out the man I'm with if he wasn't all the way up to standards in some way, and I would guide him into being better so I expected the same in return. I needed love and affection and a man who would offer me reassurance about the way he feels about me and always make sure he never put another woman before or after me. I was looking for what my dad never gave me as a little girl. I used to want a man who had possessive qualities and was jealous of any man who tried to get my attention. I thought it was cute and signified how protective he was about me. I wanted a man that would fight for me if someone else disrespected or called me out of my name. I wanted my dad to meet a guy and give his way for them to date me. I wanted my father to screen the guy and tell me what he thought. I wanted to know the game guys play instead of being downed for having an interest in one. I remember how desperate for love I used to be. Any man that there was a mutual level of attraction with, I would bat my eyes at and flirt, even though I didn't even know how to flirt. I would giggle, smile, steal a few looks at him, and say a few words or two that I thought would catch his attention and heart. This method didn't work out well for me and I ended up running into men that were, popular men with a lot of options, some were emotionally unavailable, and a few were physically abusive and verbally abusive just like my father. I ended up getting hurt looking for the love I wanted. I didn't know my worth so I went through a big stage of promiscuity. It made me feel somewhat better about myself to be validated by guys using my body. It didn't matter how many times I got my heart broke, I still allowed a new guy to enter my life once one acted up. I pretty much became popular keeping up with the latest clothing and skin, tight clothes and hairstyles desperately seeking attention and satisfaction from a man. I didn't have any boundaries whatsoever. Anything that a guy said to me I took it at face value. I knew that I had good intentions so I thought they would see that I did and have them too. I didn't know it then but I became a girl that these guys saw simply as a sex symbol. There was never a long term commitment with them, it was always just talk. The ones I did sleep with, I automatically used to think they were mine and we were together but realistically the ones I'm speaking of were not even relationship ready. They never declared that we were exclusive, I just thought if we laid in bed together, kissed, went out here and there that it was official. Call me naive, gullible, and easy because that's exactly what I was. I started fantasizing how life would be with a man going on dates, getting married, having kids, living together and waking up next to each other. I don't know why I had that mind frame but that's what it was. I'm glad I grew out of that way of thinking. In my head, I was fairytale living. The love I saw on television is the love I thought I deserved and desired in every guy I met that showed me attention. It wasn't until I got my heartbroken many times placing the same expectations on each of them that I finally woke up. My first male encounter was when I was friends with this guy named Tyree. We used to talk all the time about everything. At first, I wasn't going to deal with him because at the time he had a baby mama and I always wanted to be involved with someone who had no kids. To me, it was less drama involved and I didn't have to worry about the insecurity of myself or the other woman. The more he and I talked we started to like each other. My parents let me use their Dodge Neon to get back and forth to work and when I wasn't at work, I would see Tyree. We would cuddle up, watch TV and caress each other. We started kissing and dry humping and soon after, he took me into his bedroom and we had sex. I did not know how to have sex at all so I let him take the lead. It hurt at first but it felt good once we got into it. We messed around a few times but eventually, it affected our friendship and it ended. In my mind, he wasn't supposed to be the one to take my virginity though. I had a crush on this guy named Smoke. He was a fine football player in high school that all the girls wanted. He was friends with my cousins and when I went to their house that's when I got a chance to see him. Other than those times, I would use the car my parents allowed me to use to go and see him at his house. We saw each other for about a month or so before one thing led to another and sex was had. Again, I still did not know about sex at all but my body was aching to have a piece of him so I let him take the lead. I would go to his football games and cheer him on and he'd look at me in the stands and smile. The next time we hung out, I started to pick up energy that Smoke was talking to someone else besides me because the text messages got slower and the phone calls did too. One day when we met at a park, I asked him if he was talking to someone else. He didn't confess to it but everything came to the light eventually. He was talking and getting serious with his ex-girlfriend's best friend. As time progressed, they were in a serious relationship and she got pregnant by him. I stopped talking to Smoke but he would occasionally have a conversation with me on MySpace still. Once that got old and I was no longer attracted to him. I took some time to be alone. We weren't in a relationship, but yet another situationship gone wrong. Months later, there was this twin named TJ and him and I started talking. A couple of times we went out of town to go to a mall and shop there. I remember us eating lunch at Burger King and we were talking about what our relationship status would be. He told me, "You can't have all of me but you could have half of me." I looked at him crazy because I was not into that type of stuff. I had also found out he was talking to another girl. Eventually she and I exchanged words online. When she got around him and had access to his phone, she would call me and tell me to leave him alone. I told her that I wasn't calling him and that he was always blowing my phone up. He was in his feelings one day and we were hanging out at his house before I found out about the other female and he told me something to the effect of, "You won't let me use your car, you won't give me no money, you won't let me fuck. You ain't good for nothing." Those words crushed me. He made me feel so unworthy because I wouldn't give up myself to him. I mean why the hell would I. I was just another girl to him meanwhile, he had a girlfriend, boo thang, or whatever she was to him. Even after he uttered these words to me he still blew my phone up for me to come to see him but I didn't budge much anymore. I had a few more guys that I associated with but I became too busy with work I didn't have time to spend with them. I'm going to fast forward past situationships, some I have forgotten about and some are not even worth mentioning. It was obvious to me I had an identity issue that I felt needed to be validated by a guy and it didn't work out how I was hoping it would. Finally, I had met a Jamaican guy with long dreads named CJ. He and I conversed every day and started seeing each other every day. I wasn't sure how it was going to begin and end especially because before meeting him I didn't have the best of luck with men but I took a chance anyway. I didn't have much luck because something was wrong me or I wasn't a good woman but because I made bad choices in partners. I didn't get a chance to know them, I just dived in head over heels hoping for the best not knowing their intentions had underlying motives then what they presented or appeared on their outer surface. Anyways, CJ was very comical and great in keeping my attention. From the first day we met, we saw each other every day and didn't grow tired of it. I was still living with my parents at the time and working at Target. My parents had a rule that I had to be home within 30 minutes of my shift but that barely ever happened. They would call and be angry because still at 18 years old they wanted to have a lot of control over my life and my associations with guys. You can call them helicopter parents because that's exactly what they are. Anyways, I and CJ started going on dates and when things got more serious that's when we talked about living together. We moved in our first apartment together when I was 19 years old and it was a great feeling. I felt secure and he did his part in making sure I did too. We went half on all the bills and at one point we worked at the same job together in close vicinity at a warehouse called Signature Brands. His uncle owned a seafood business and he knew seafood was the way to my heart. He used to get me a dozen blue crabs each week because he knew that made me very happy. I was working at Target for like a year or so and when I lost my job, his uncle allowed him and me to work at his seafood business together. After working at this point, I decided I needed more money and I wanted a career job. I was looking through listings of employment and came across a job at a sheriff's office working in a jail. CJ's aunt happened to be a Corrections Officer at the jail so he got permission from her for me to use her as a reference. The employment process took a year but I got hired on and I was so thankful for him and his aunt helping me. When I started employment at the jail, I was nervous and scared. Horror thoughts started going through my mind about what could happen while I was there.

"What if an inmate assaults me?"

"What if a crazy situation happens and I have to be on lockdown?"

"What if I'm too young to know the ins and outs of the jail and end up getting taken advantage of?"

"What if I don't like it, what am I going to do next?"

Those thoughts ran rapidly through my mind for a few weeks. I went through training of the control rooms and how to let an inmate and officer in and out the doors, I was trained on how to conduct the booking process when an officer brings in a new arrestee which included obtaining their file, entering charges, gathering their fingerprints and DNA, taking their mug shot, and the bonding out process. I also learned how to operate the switchboard phones when people called in inquiring about their loved ones. I conducted video visitation where families would come to see and communicate with an inmate via a video screen. I was taught how to monitor sessions and schedule visits, how to complete restraining orders, and child support purges.

I have to say my most memorable and favorite area of working inside the jail was in booking. There was never a dull moment. There were times when people would come in drunk and combative fighting the officers, some would be visibly high off drugs and alcohol, and refusing to do a strip search so the officer could make sure they weren't coming in the jail with contraband. It was also interesting to read through the police reports and run criminal history searches to find out what the inmate has done in their past. I also on a few occasions had to book in murderers and be face to face with them when they came through the door. At first, I was terrified and in shock that they were in close vicinity to me and I didn't have any form of weapon to use besides my hand, but I quickly adjusted and got over it realizing they are human as well and I had a lot of officers around to protect me in the event something occurred. On some occasions, I got a chance to communicate with the inmates in passing especially the regular ones who were always coming back month after month. They got used to seeing my face and I got used to seeing theirs and sometimes depending on the vibe or the energy I got from them, I would engage in small talk as to why they were there and try to figure out what the root cause of their behavior is. Some of them were doomed since their childhoods. Their mothers and fathers were not good examples to them and because what they saw was all they knew, they became a product of it. It was interesting to hear the stories and some I would give words of encouragement too. It was very weird when a few family members and classmates came through because I had to keep it professional yet the memory of knowing who they are just made it completely awkward. Sometimes when I would have downtime, I would listen to the radio of the patrol officers when they were giving a heads up on what type of case they were bringing in to the jail. I learned the NATO phonetic alphabet such as Alpha, Bravo, Charlie, etc. These were the zones of the pods were the inmates were housed. Working in the control room tower with inmates' right below me was quite interesting. I saw it all. Some men would purposely go to the shower and stare directly at me and that's when I figured they were masturbating. Some would try to get my attention just to say sweet nothings but I paid no attention to it. I was there for a job not to find a love connection and besides what can a guy in jail behind walls do for me when I have the freedom to go and do as I please after I exit those walls. The female inmates would sometimes engage in fights and they would engage in sneaky behavior behind their room doors such as girl on girl contact and when I realized what they were doing, of course, I had to report it. I have to say working at the jail is where I learned a lot about myself and other people. Being that I worked around a lot of con artists that had 24/7 to think of ways to get over on me and the officers, I had to be on guard and observant at all times. This is where my investigative traits started to kick in full force. I didn't want my job to be terminated for not paying attention to detail and being irresponsible had something major occurred. I developed great observation skills and there was nothing the inmates could do or say to get over on me. I never had any disciplinary action against me for not taking action on the forbidden behaviors of inmates. I made sure that the pod I worked in was always kept under control and I monitored the safety of the officers and kept it professional with the inmates. I used to be a workaholic there. Anytime someone would call out of work, I would stay and work overtime. Some days I worked my full 12-hour shift and other days I worked 16 or 18 hours. I kept this up for 2 years as long as overtime was offered and my checks always looked great. Outside of work, CJ and I would go out and enjoy our relationship together. I loved him. He made me feel like the best woman in the world as much as he adored me. We were together 2 years and had talked about engagement, marriage, and kids but he wanted us to get ourselves together first and give our relationship more time. Unfortunately, our relationship ended due to differences and I was also considering the military as well.

I was heartbroken at first and took it very hard because he was the first guy that truly made me feel like I was worth something but our differences were not reconcilable so it was a must we moved on. After we broke up, I continued working at the Sheriff's office and focusing on myself until I figured out that I was ready to end that career and venture off into something else.

CHAPTER FOUR: Signing My Life Over

After working at the Sheriff's Office for a few years, I grew very tired of the terrible leadership and no room for growth. I started looking at other avenues to create a good life for myself and my future family. At first, I started filling out online job applications in Tampa, Jacksonville, and Orlando and then I would travel there for additional testing. I did that for a few months, hoping to land a job and move away. Well, that didn't work out exactly how I wanted to and it was a tedious process. I revisited the thought of joining the military and researched all branches of services. I knew for sure I wasn't going to the Army or Marines. I set up an appointment to see an Air Force recruiter and do the practice test. When I showed up, there was no one in the office. I didn't waste any time trying to figure out what happened so I ended up going to the Navy office. I spoke with a recruiter and took the practice test. Considering I had been out of high school and college for 4 years, I didn't recall any of the academic material and I failed the test.

I went to Barnes and Noble and bought an Armed Services Vocational Aptitude Battery (ASVAB) book and started to study it. Math was the subject I needed the most improvement in. I couldn't grasp the concept of some of the harder math, so I decided to hire a tutor. We met a couple of times a week at the library and I started to do very well. About a month later, I felt ready to take the practice test again. I went back to the Navy recruiting office and got a better score. My recruiter scheduled me to take the real test. I took it and I passed.

I explored my options with the recruiter on how I wanted to enlist in the military and the date I wanted to leave. I wanted to leave as soon as possible but I knew that wasn't going to happen. For starters, I did not know how to swim so I started taking lessons at the YMCA. I was still scared of learning how to swim from childhood trauma because I almost drowned on a couple of occasions. I did not succeed in mastering swimming but I wasn't going to give up. I did start getting in the gym and doing PT exercise with the other potential Navy enlisters. My recruiter gave me my options on my processing date to see if I qualify for the military. I went to the Military Entrance Processing Command in Jacksonville and did all medical and assessments. I spent the whole day there and everything came out clear for me to move forward. I selected a suitable job as Aviation Maintenance Administration personnel and got a shipping date to go to boot camp. I told my parents what I had done and they were shocked. My entire family was shocked. I was still working at the Sheriff's office and they felt that I was already in a good position. I thought otherwise. They tried to convince me to stay and used scare tactics to deter me from joining the military. My sister had made remarks about me being sure I was making the right decision. She questioned me leaving Ocala, leaving my job at the jail, and pretty much all of my life choices I made in life to progress. I should've known that my family not going anywhere outside of our hometown, that they would have a small mind mentality of me leaving and going to do greater. It seemed to cause a lot of jealousy and envy towards me amongst my family but I didn't allow that to stop me. When my shipping date came around, my parents took me to Jacksonville, Florida to catch my flight to boot camp in Great Lakes, Illinois. It happened to be their wedding anniversary. I wished them well and went about my journey.

The night before I took flight, I was nervous and afraid of what things were going to be like. I knew I had to spend eight weeks in boot camp with little contact with my family and I had to pass the swim test. The morning came and for the first time, I took an airplane to Chicago. When I arrived in Chicago and got off the plane there was a group of others lined up and some sitting down waiting for the bus to take us to the Recruit Training Command where we would spend two months undergoing training to be mission ready. We had to be in complete silence on the bus and not use our cellphones. It was cool to be on this bus because I got to see snow for the first time too. When we arrived on the training grounds it was very cold and packed with snow. We got off the bus and were separated into groups. The process started where we were issued all of our gear and had to package up the items we came with and send them back home. Once all of this was done, I was sent to my division. We did regular physical training, uniform regulations, boot camp regulations, and drilled. During my entire time in boot camp, I was in shock mode. I felt like I wasn't achieving any of the learning at the same rate as everyone else was because I was stuck at the fact that I joined before completely analyzing what it was all about. I was always questioning my decision at that point and it didn't help that I was home sick. When it came time for our swim test, of course, I didn't pass on the first try. Even though I took swim lessons before, I tensed up when I got there. I had to go to the pool every day twice a day until I passed. I wasn't the only one, but it felt humiliating because as boot camp was about to end for me, I was still struggling with passing. The requirement was to do a 5 min prone float and any swim strokes from one side of the pool to the other in 12 feet of water. That was terrifying for me being that I had never been in more than 5 feet of water before. After going to the pool for 2 months, one day I made my mind up I was going to do it and there was no stopping me. I had 2 weeks to get it together before I would've been discharged from the Navy. I was sent to a remedial division to complete and pass the swim test. I went, I conquered, and passed it however I did not get a chance to walk across the graduation stage. I was depressed about that because I knew my parents were looking forward to coming and seeing me walk across so I knew I let them down.

Regardless, I graduated and was sent to a temporary processing unit to wait until I got a flight to go to Meridian, Mississippi for a training school. A few weeks later, I received my flight information and was sent on my way to Mississippi. When I got there it was very hot and humid. It looked very country and the training base was small. I had to wait about a month for a class to open up for my job title so in the meantime, I was assigned to monitor the quarterdeck building and serve as security for the barracks buildings. There were Marines on the base training with us as well and we shared duties with them. When I was able to get in a class and start training on my job for the fleet, my instructor was Marine and so were half of my classmates. I always had the mindset that Marines were "crazy" but little did I know there was one in particular in class that I would begin talking to. I don't know what it was about him but he was dark-skinned, pretty smile, and we were mutually attracted to each other. I used to adore his walk. I can't explain it except that he had a classy and cocky walk like he knew he had it going on and it was a turn on. We started off becoming acquainted pretty well and during our breaks and after class we would hang with each other and talk. When we went back to our barracks room, we would talk on FaceTime for hours and fall asleep on the phone. We talked about the future after we got out of school and everything seemed to be aligned with what we both wanted. However, the problem began when his two friends that we were in the class started to pick on me to him and he became engaged in it. It became very annoying and juvenile to me because he shouldn't let what his friends thought about my attractiveness get to him and allow it to interfere with his liking for me. I cut it off with him after a few months of tolerating and he blew my phone up every day. He would try to make hints to me at school to hit him up but I wouldn't. I was pissed off. Eventually, I told him how I felt and completely left him alone but you could tell he still felt some type of way about it. Months later, he apologized for his actions but the apology was way too late for me and I didn't care. The bond we had was great, but one thing I won't tolerate is childish behavior. He was a couple of years younger than me at the time so that did make a difference.

Little did I know the next guy I dated was going to change my life forever. I was still in training school and I remember I had taken a mirror selfie of myself in my barracks room and uploaded it to my Instagram. A few minutes later, I got a direct message from a guy named Mack. He asked me if I was at the same training school as he was and when I asked him why he told me because of the similar design and color of the window curtains. We both confirmed that we were on the same grounds. Mack told me where he usually hangs at and I told him the same. I went and scrolled through his Instagram page to see who he was and I saw a few of his pictures of his face. Mack was a photographer that took pictures of landmarks and people anywhere he would go. He then told me maybe we'd catch each other around and hang out. The next day after our conversation while I was sitting in class when I looked up at the door and, I saw him outside of my classroom mopping the floors of the building. A few hours later, I had gone outside to go use the bathroom and he was still doing the cleaning. I told him who I was and proceeded to go to the bathroom. Mack acted like he wanted to say something but was nervous too. After I came out of the bathroom he was mopping the floors near the vending machines. He watched me walk by and asked if he can take me on a date. I was surprised because not many guys these days directly ask to take you on a date. It's as if chivalry is barely a thing. I accepted his offer and he sent me his phone number on Instagram. From then we started talking every day on the phone, to Face Timing, and when we had free time we would hang out. We started going off base, going out to eat and getting hotels spending the day together having sex and watching TV. It felt way too good to be true. After a few dates, Mack made it known he wanted us to be together and I was somewhat okay with it. He appeared to be a charming and happy guy with a big bright smile. The first time we had sex he pounded on me as if I was a fresh piece of meat and I was irresistible. He then lay on top of me as we started kissing, he opened a condom and we began to have sex. He attempted a few times throughout our relationship to get me pregnant but I got a Plan B and then decided to get on birth control. This is the point when I should've stopped dealing with him because he was adamant to get me pregnant against my wishes not to do so because we weren't unmarried and I was unsure I would still like him or if the relationship would last once I got stationed in Japan for a few years. When we returned to school and others saw us together a lot they began to poke and make fun of him liking me. Some started to spread false rumors about me because they were jealous and he would bring it back to me. I told him I didn't want to hear any other stuff and if he continued I would stop talking to him. He stopped with the foolishness. His likeness for me became an obsession. Anytime he would see me in school he would yell out my last name so loudly. I was flattered and embarrassed at the same time. It was cute he was into me but annoying at the same time. Everyone had heard him and would laugh and tease me pointing out the obvious of him yelling my name. I rolled my eyes and kept it moving. When I made it to my room one day, I had found out that his room was across the courtyard at the top of the building and we could see each other if we looked out the window. We engaged in window games playing hide and seek while on the phone until it got dark and it was time for us to go to sleep and get ready for school the next day. Some days we would sit on the courtyard steps and talk about the future. One of those times we both felt a sense that we were meant to be together and made plans of the future. It felt right and at the same time, something didn't seem right to me. The good thing about him is he paid a lot of attention to detail with me. If a hair was out of place or if I had something on my face, he would take care of it. Mack's qualities were very gentleman like and I didn't have that before. Even with these things in mind, I started to feel a very disturbing stir in my body. It felt like everything was too good to be true and made me feel like I was in love. I didn't know it then but I wasn't in love nor was he in love, nor was he falling in love. I was being charmed and groomed into something I never imagine happened to be possible. At the time, I wasn't awakened by his character and reputation to put everything together. Unbeknownst I was falling into lust, deceit, and a trauma bond.

I also thought that maybe I was feeling insecure because of my bad past experiences. In reality, now, I believe these were the red flags that he was not the one but I went against my gut and entertained him, anyway thinking maybe that feeling would change. Mack and I would go and get hotel rooms and spend the day laid up in them ordering food, having sex, watching TV, and talking about the future. I recall one time we rented a car and left Mississippi for a day and a half to go to Pensacola on the beach and no one even noticed that we were gone but we enjoyed a day at the beach and eating seafood together basking in the newness of our relationship. We went grocery shopping there and spent the rest of the day stuffing our face and chilling at our hotel. We enjoyed our time away from the military lifestyle. We headed back to Mississippi and continued our normal military routine while still seeing each other. When Mack graduated class, he went back to his hometown in Philadelphia and I went back to mine in Florida, shortly after he left. Our relationship was at a standstill. We pretty much were on a break. He went back home and dealt with old females and I went back home and dealt with a guy that I used to talk to for a year on Skype before we both went to boot camp. He was living in Chicago when we first started talking and we had met through a future sailors group. That guy and I had a lot of chemistry and of course being he was in one state and I was in another and we finally had a chance to be around each other, we went out to eat, had drinks, and from there it went to the next level. The hotel room I was staying in for the night, I invited him inside, and we talked about how our boot camp experiences were, reminiscing on our old convos we used to have for hours, hugged each other in excitement before we got into the bed, watched TV and then began to have sex. When we were finished, we hung out for a little longer and then I prepared for a shower and the bed while he went back to his dorm room. I was honest about it with Mack; however, he was secretive and dishonest about his dealings with females back at home. Instead of admitting to what he had done, he took the stage and boohoo cried. He cried so loud and so hard and it was just unbelievable at this point. This man thought only one could play that game, but I showed him two can too. He never did admit to me what he did and with who but I found out much later in the year that he had been cheating our entire relationship with this chick he was running a lot of game on making her think she had a huge significance in being in his future as his girlfriend.

After this conversation of me confessing my dirt, we didn't talk for the rest of the day and then when the next day came about he said he would never do that to me and asked how could I. I mean the boy was carrying on as if he was innocent. He was not. We had talked about marriage before but I told him to let us take that off of the table at this point because with the amount of distance between us it was nearly impossible to keep us afloat any longer when we were headed to different parts of the world beginning our journey as Navy sailors. Instead, he insisted that he will get over it and we should still get married. I started to do a bit of downplaying by saying, "No, I don't deserve it and I don't think we should, etc." I was hoping he would confess his doing. He still did not budge. In spite of this, he brushed it off and we talked on the phone and tried to make plans to see each other at his duty station before I was due to go to mine in San Diego, California to sail to Japan. Mack bought a plane ticket and flew from Philadelphia, Pennsylvania to Tampa, Florida, we got a hotel and spent time together. He brought his camera with him and we went out on some dates and took professional photos of the city and of each other. It was a cute photo shoot showing off each other's camera skills. We had a great time together. The next day, he left and flew back to Philadelphia. Later that day, he told me he felt empty and needed to see me again. We had no idea when the next time would be because I was supposed to go overseas within a week. I ended up finding a cheap flight and we went half on it to meet him at his duty station in Virginia. We spent the day together, went to the mall, and got a hotel on the base and he mentioned that we were soul mates and he didn't want to miss out on having a life with each other. He talked of marriage bliss and kids and we had names picked out. At this moment, things were getting ready to change our lives forever. We were to go from being two to one, and forever be committed till death do us part. At least that's what it was supposed to be.

CHAPTER FIVE: Military, Marriage, and Mess

In August 2015, we went to the courthouse and got married. We recited the vows with the marriage officiator and there we were, Mr. Mack B & Mrs. Faith B. I was happy and so was he. Afterwards, we went to a festival near the beach enjoyed music, ice cream, and ate food together then went to the beach. Mack surprised me with the Michael Kors watch I always wanted. My eyes lit up in excitement. We didn't have rings at the time of the marriage ceremony and I didn't want us to be without them so we went to the Navy Exchange on base, got credit cards, and I bought him a wedding band and he bought me a ring. We smiled from ear to ear as we put them on each other's finger. Back to the hotel we went to end our night and prepare for me to fly home and fly to San Diego the next day. We said our goodbyes, cried, and couldn't wait until we saw each other again. When I got to San Diego, I was assigned to the USS Ronald Reagan aircraft carrier. I slept on the ship on a rack similar to the bunks they have in jail but a bit fancier. It was hard getting used to being so far away from everything I was once familiar with. I was hearing sounds of the aircraft taking off from the flight deck above my rack as well as other loud noises I couldn't identify. The food wasn't great at all. It was almost like jail food. I got a meal three times a day and sometimes I would get a midnight meal as well.

The workspace I was assigned to was all male. I was the only female, the only black female at that. I was starting to learn the duties of my job and got overwhelmed with the feeling of wanting to be near my husband. I started working on the process to get relocated with him, but my chain of command gave me a hard time and told me it would not be a fast process because I had just got into the military and they didn't want to get me transferred until I finished all 3 of my years of sea duty. I didn't take no for an answer because I knew it was possible and it was written in a Navy instruction manual that it could happen and no time frame was noted in it. Additionally, I was supposed to be receiving a housing allowance that would allow me to live off of the ship and into a house either on base or in the city. One of my leaders whom was a black Senior Chief typed a document in Microsoft Word to deny me which he did not have the approving authority or final authority to do so. The personnel department was responsible for handling it and the response I would've received from them would have been on a professional letterhead. This is when I began to have negative feelings towards my senior chief and I felt like I was being held captive from what I was entitled to. I went to the personnel department on the lower deck of the ship and tried to handle things myself. They gave me the runaround as well. So at this point, I knew my senior chief had communicated with them to convince them to be unhelpful to me and I didn't understand why. It wasn't hurting their pockets or causing them any type of inconvenience for me to go after what I desired.. I began to feel like my back was against the wall. The individuals that were supposed to help me were showing me they were against me. My mind was not focused on the ship and the mission at all. It was focused on being closer to Mack. I'll admit getting married early in the military was not the best decision I've made. My focus was not where it should've been because I couldn't separate the two. In my mind, I was really concerned about the amount of distance Mack and I were apart and the risk of either one of us cheating because we were so far away and of course we both had needs that needed to be met, with each other, as well as becoming more familiar and in touch with ourselves as a newly married couple. I often thought about the life we could have being closely together. I fantasized of going to work each day, coming home and fixing him a meal, going to sleep next to each other and having sex every day. I had plans for us to go to fun events, taking vacations and getting through college together so we could start a family afterwards. My mind was constantly clouded with these thoughts. I missed Mack's smile, his laugh, his attention to the very detail of all my attributes, the photo-shoots we used to take, and most of all I missed the amazing sex we had. Yeah we got married fast, but I felt like the spark we had even in the short amount of time we had together was the best I ever had and being in California clouded every moment of that. I tried to start working on my ship qualifications to become more familiar with the ship and it's components, the Navy history, and being out to sea and what it consists of. I had to do a lot of reading, studying, and retaining information so I could apply it to the final test I would take. Still, I couldn't focus. I just had to be near my husband. I was on a ship with nearly 5,000 people and not knowing anyone in the midst of it left me feeling very lonely. However, I made a friend that I was familiar with. Her name was Kay. Her and I were in the same boot camp retention division because we were having trouble passing the swimming portion of boot camp. We both overcame that struggle and discovered we were on the same ship. She was a nice girl, a few years younger than me but very mature for her age and her personality was as strong as mine. She was married too. We clicked almost immediately and spent most of our time keeping each other afloat mentally, counting down the days we could both be near our husbands. Sometimes she would bring me a whole box of Rice Krispies snacks to my rack and leave them there with a sweet note. I appreciated this so much. It was very thoughtful of her. There were times I would go to the library, get on the computer and talk to Mack on social media and other times we would talk on my phone. Months went by and it seemed like my efforts to get transferred were being ignored and disregarded. It got so bad to the point where I started seeing a mental health specialist on the ship and told them if they didn't get me off I was going to jump off of the ship. They took my words lightly and they didn't even do anything to withhold me from being by myself. All that was accomplished was trying to talk me out of it and assure me that I would be going home soon. Also a "Failure to Adapt" code was put into my record which meant I should've been sent home because I wasn't adapting well in under a year of service but they avoided that option as well. I really didn't plan on jumping off the ship because fear was in me, but the level of stress I was under, I didn't know what I was capable of doing in a split second. I was looking for a way out honestly. It was a cry for attention and honestly it was a form of manipulating them to get me home to my husband so my mind, body, and soul could be at peace. It was wrong to use that type of tactic but I desperately wanted to be out. I needed to be out. Not just for me but Mack's sake as well. Ship life and being far away from family and my husband was too much for me to bear. I felt like I had been stripped from reality and given a new life I wasn't completely satisfied with. The therapist gave me hope that she was going to help me get out, but she was also communicating with my chain of command which made things worse because they started antagonizing me and being super micromanaging as well as refusing to help me with anything outside of work. My main concern was not my work, especially because I had my very first deployment shortly after I got on the ship. We sailed from San Diego, California to Busan, South Korea. This was my first time going out of the country. It was cool to be there but I did not like Busan. It had a dirty appearance, the people were rude and was trying to finesse everyone out of money for goods they duplicated or not worth the cost. I enjoyed just taking pictures of the scenery and ended up buying some food and spending most of my time in the hotel I got which was pretty cheap. Kay and I got one together and we enjoyed our time off from the ship. While I was still trying to figure out how to go above all the stipulations of being collocated with my husband and maintain my sanity, Mack began to explore his options and see if he could be stationed with me in Japan. He was given a hard time on his end as well. We both in a sense started to give up on trying anymore and wait until a little later down the road. Our marriage seemed to still be holding up pretty well even in spite of the Navy's interference however, after a few months Mack started changing. He started to talk about his past and drop the names of females he's had sexual or friendship encounters with or were actively trying to pursue him while we were married. I was uncomfortable because as a man why would you proudly tell your wife about these things. I understand he wanted to be honest but why not handle it and leave it at that. I appreciated his openness but the way he was going about it in the chipper tone he used didn't sit right with me. I began to talk about when I would introduce myself to his daughter's mother prior to being around her so she would feel comfortable and know that their daughter will be in good hands when I finally have a chance to meet them. At first, he expressed that he did not care about us being cordial at all. I couldn't understand then why he would feel that way is that I was his wife and I would be around their child. One day we came to an agreement that I could write her on Facebook and introduce myself. She already had known we were in a relationship together according to him.

Prior to Mack and I's conversation regarding this and in the same month we got married, I sent a message to his daughter's mother, Bryna and I said, "Hey Bryna, as you may know I am Mack's wife and will be your daughter's stepmother. I am writing to you to establish some type of communication with you in regards to meeting you both and seeing and being around your daughter. I am in the Navy with him as well so it's going to be kind of hard to see her all the time but when I do I just wanted to make sure the timing is right and it's good with you. I will be in the states in December and it would be nice if we could get her and take her to like an amusement park, a kid-friendly restaurant, or something of that sort. I don't mind sending her things she needs you just have to let me know. I'm not trying to have any drama with you or anything like that as I do not associate myself with any and whatever issues you and Mack have is between the two of you. Hope to talk to you soon. Take care." She saw the message I wrote but did not respond to it. Instead, she blocked me. I was confused because I didn't say anything petty or try to start drama. Mack ended up telling her I had written her on Facebook but he told me there was backlash with her about it. He had told me she said that it was a hard pill for her to swallow that he was married. It bothered me a bit because I didn't understand why she felt that way and I began to question what happened with their relationship. He told me that she kept bringing up wanting to be married to him and such but he never proposed to her nor had the intent to do so. He wouldn't go into details about how their relationship ended he just said, "She knows why" he and left it at that. When she found out he was married, she blocked me, Mack, and his parents from social media. She was angry and I couldn't understand at the time why she was. I didn't take Mack from her, they weren't married, and as far as I knew he was taking care of their daughter. After this, we began to have problems with his interactions with single or attention-seeking females, money issues, and trying to figure out when we were going to see each other again. Mack started having a lot of mind control over me to the point that he incited drama and gave me the females' first and last names so I could write messages on Facebook correcting their behavior and asserting my position as his wife as he sat back and claimed to not be entertaining them. When I wrote these females on Facebook, he would turn around and scold me when doing so acting like he had nothing to do with it. I was baffled. He used to tell me stories about an ex-girlfriend, Madison and that he was very hurt by their relationship. He claimed that she cheated on him and left him for a white boy and he used to log into her Instagram page to check things out. I didn't figure it out until later that it was him that was cheating on her while with Bryna and got them both pregnant at the same time. I told him he couldn't give me the love I deserved because he was still stuck in the past and hurt by his ex. He burst out crying like a baby on the phone to me confirming what I said was true. He thought of and called Madison seeking closure from her so our marriage could get better. I did not like or agree with this at all. He sent me screenshots of him texting her asking to talk to her and that he wanted to clear the air. She thought he was referring to the abortion she had when they were together but he told her it was something else. She called him and he said he cried to her because he wanted to know why she did what she did. He told me that she said Mack was very complicated, a constant cheater, and had a lot of growing up to do. She said she felt free when they broke up. He also told me he had a letter saved on his phone that she wrote to him about how she felt within their relationship. This made me feel so weird because you shouldn't have gotten into a relationship let alone a marriage still holding on to the past. When he was done seeking the closure he wanted from her and I expressed how upset I was, he blamed me for telling him that his past is an issue and that he tried to take this as a step to help our marriage. I said to him, "Help, Mack?! Don't you think you should've done this beforehand?" This birthed a level of uncomfortability in me because he still harbored feelings for Madison, with and without the closure. As punishment for calling him out on what he did, he didn't talk to me for a few days and when we did talk this issue was swept under the rug. Another instance of problems we had is when Mack told me he was driving to get his daughter and her mother, Bryna, out of state due to the mother having family problems. I told him I didn't think a married man should be going to transport his child's mother from one side of the state to the other because of her not getting along with her parents and that his concern should be about his child and her safety only. I just knew something didn't sound right. I told him the potential threat it could serve to our marriage and how I didn't agree with it especially with me being overseas and not being able to go and meet Bryna and my stepdaughter. He later changed it and said he's not going to get his daughter and then changed again and said he going to get her without getting her mother. I tried to give him the benefit of the doubt but at the same time I had a bad feeling about it. I felt in my heart he wasn't being truthful.

Mack and Bryna had gone a couple of years without talking to each other or him seeing their child and I had a gut feeling they were still holding feelings for each other and engaged in adultery especially after what Mack said about us not getting along and how she reacted to the fact that we were married. I didn't hear anything else from him about going to get my stepdaughter and her mother. However, there were some days he would not answer my call. He started acting in an odd manner. At some point, I found out he had got his daughter and was spending time with her. During his time with his daughter, he would not Face Time me at all. I recall him telling me he wouldn't be talking to me the entire day or night and for me to not be alarmed. That made me feel uncomfortable because why would you neglect your wife for days. After all, she's overseas and you're supposed to balance your daughter and wife not abandon one or the other. That caused an argument because he saw no wrong in what he did. It became hell for me that every time I talked to him, there was some sort of conflict that went unresolved. Mack's inconsideration of everything birthed a level of anger inside of me. He did not want to take accountability for anything unless it was something that he directly benefited from. Due to us being married and both in the military, he started receiving an allowance allotted for housing for us in addition to his regular paycheck. The amount was about an extra $1500 each month or so that paid for expenses to house us as a married couple. I was overseas so obviously we weren't living together at the time. All I asked of him was after he paid the rent to send me the remainder of the money so sometimes I could get off of the ship I was living on and enjoy some time away and in a hotel. Every time he received that money, it would always be an excuse as to why he couldn't give me the remainder. His account was always in the negatives and he was also asking me for money too. It didn't get any better as time went on and it was unfair to me that only he was benefiting off of something that was jointly ours. I started to realize that I couldn't comment on any of Mack's behavior without him reacting angrily or punishing me by giving the silent treatment. This is when I realized that I may be involved with a man with a narcissistic personality disorder but I wasn't sure.

Mack and his mother begin uploading pictures of his daughter and Bryna on Facebook. I liked the photos because his daughter looked happy and she is a cute girl. I had no issue with her nor did I know exactly what was going on behind closed doors. My insecurity lied within Mack and his ability to remember our marriage and vows and not allow loneliness to draw him into something he knows he shouldn't be doing just because I am far away. After a few days of Mack ignoring me, he began to come back around. Things got a little better after and he communicated with me but it was very an odd feeling inside of my body that something was not right. He would only talk to me certain parts of the day and sometimes it was hard to reach him which was very unusual. When we did talk he would make comments about not wanting to have sex anymore and what if he didn't know how to have sex. It was very odd to me that he would say this being that we didn't see each other for months and it was around the same time as his daughter and her mother was around. A couple of weeks after I discovered his daughter and him spending time together, I got a message on Facebook from Bryna. It was random and I didn't know what it was about. I remember praying to God that she opens her eyes and understand I am not a bad person and when I first wrote her a message it was with good and mature intentions.

She said, "Hey I wanted to talk you for a second. I think it would be more reasonable if I and you could get to know each other and maybe even be friends. I don't dislike you I don't know you enough to like or dislike you but you're my daughter's stepmom and I think it's important that we hold a good relationship because I'm going to be trusting not just Mack with my child but you as well and when it comes to my child I take that very seriously. I understand that you are Mack's wife and I respect it but one thing I always go by is you respect me and I'll respect you. I'll treat you how you treat me and that's just how things goes. Before I can admit I was being a bit petty because I felt like you were trying to come at me because you thought me and Mack had something going on but I can assure you we don't. It's nothing at all I just want us to co-parent and raise our daughter to the best of our ability and that's all I ask of him."

When she wrote this message I was happy because I thought God had answered my prayers. The part I didn't understand is that she said she thought I was being petty towards her because I thought her and Mack had something going on. In no part of my initial message to her did I even imply or express the thought of something going on with them so this was confusing to me but I brushed it off, accepted what she said, and when I got a chance I had told Mack about it. I was able to decipher later on, that sentence was her throwing a hint to me that something was going on between them and that I would figure out exactly what she meant later. When I was able to take a vacation from Japan in December 2015, Mack and I split the cost of my plane ticket. My flight was 17 hours long. Things between us seemed to be getting better and around the time I went to Virginia to visit him, he decided that he wanted us to have a son and that it would be another way for me to get out of being in Japan and stationed with him as well.

During my visit with him, he took me to Philadelphia to go meet his parents. I met his mother, Tamesha, Correll, his dad, and Sherry, Mack's future stepmother. Tamesha appeared excited to meet me, at least she acted like it. This was the first time she met me in person. She gave a hug and immediately started asking questions about me. We had only been communicating on Facebook. She was very loud and appeared like the ghetto type to me.

His mother started questioning me by asking how I enjoyed being overseas and then asked if I wanted to have kids and how we were going to go about me getting pregnant. It was funny because she brought up that I was probably going to get pregnant before I get back to Japan and try to get out of sea duty. I brushed off what she was saying because I did not feel the need to run it by her for her approval but I knew then that Mack had been talking to his mother about our plans. I felt if you're my husband we shouldn't be discussing things that go on in our conversations and in our house with our parents we're supposed to be grown, married, and don't need validation from them.

She did say that we needed to enjoy our marriage and get to know each other for a while before we take it to the step of having kids. I got a chance to meet his sister, his aunt, and his cousins but they didn't converse with me much. Mack, his mother and I took pictures together with his sister and cousins. I met Mack's female cousin, Vee and her husband at their house and they cooked seafood for us. Mack went into the kitchen to talk to his male cousin, P.J. while me and his cousin Vee chatted and I played with their daughter. She told me how hard it was being away from her husband while he served in the military but she had confidence we would make it despite the distance. She seemed straight. After meeting them, we went to meet Correll and Sherry. We was staying in Correll's old house during our visit.

I wanted to stay in a hotel because the conditions of the house were not up to my standard especially not the bathroom and shower but Mack told me to stop being bougie which I wasn't, I just like to be in clean surroundings. He did end up taking me to a nearby naval base so I could shower and get myself together. When we had gone to his dad's fiancé house, I met Sherry. Correll has asked me why I had gone to the base and I had a confused look on my face because I was thinking why did he have to know that and why was he questioning me. At that point, I knew that Mack had said something and it made me feel uncomfortable but to protect his dad's feelings, I told him," I went to the base to just check things out." Mack started laughing and I knew then that he had told them something. The visit got very awkward. His dad had asked me if I planned on getting out the Navy and what I would do after I got out. I told him that I did plan on getting out of the Navy after my four-year contract was over and that I wanted to move to California and become an FBI agent. His dad then told me that Mack missed out on a football scholarship because of a girl and I had this look on my face accompanied with the thoughts, "Okay, that's not a good sign." His dad took us to a seafood restaurant there called Chickie's and Pete and paid for our meal. I felt like I belonged somewhat with Mack's family but not completely. Something just did not sit right to me with Mack's family.

We ended up leaving from the restaurant and going back to his dad's house for the day. We were supposed to go to church the next morning together, but I didn't and stayed at the house until he came back. Later, we took a train from New Jersey to explore New York. For my birthday and Christmas, Mack didn't really celebrate it much. He barely bought gifts at all and didn't make any part of my birthday romantic or thoughtful in anyway like I thought he would. We ended our time with seeing his family and exploring New York to head back to Virginia to spend New Year's at home and prepare for me to go back to Japan on the day after the New Year.

One day while he was at work, in between the time of my two week vacation with him, I happened to be using his MacBook for my personal use and saw a message between him and this girl named Shelby. I went through the messages and I saw where he was asking her if he could come over and if they can do it or not referring to sex. The girl mentioned that she had some kids at her mom's house and she didn't have the time to but they could on another day. I called the number and told her who I was and started questioning her. I also had let him know I saw the messages between him and her and he got angry. He came home from work later and gave me the silent treatment. He wouldn't answer any of my questions. He just took his computer and cleared it out. Shelby sent me the texts between him and her and he was cheating with her. They had been exchanging explicit messages since we started dating. She told me Mack told her I left for Japan and that we were no longer together. I told her we were married and she seemed defensive and mad about it. On another occasion, I also found condoms under our bathroom sink as well as a

Christmas scented Bath and Body lotion bottle. We weren't having sex with condoms because he wanted me to get pregnant so I knew he had to be cheating. When I had told him my findings, he was getting ready for work in our bedroom and when he was done, he walked right past me not saying a word, and went out to his car and as I walked outside with him trying to get answers he said in a very harsh tone for me to "Get away and that he wasn't going back and forth with me about it." He then drove away, his tires screeching, leaving marks in the parking lot. He later lied about the lotion bottle and said it was a bottle he got for me however, the lotion appeared to be used.

The next day I told him to take me to the courthouse because I wanted to file for a divorce. He gave me an ultimatum that if I didn't give him my wedding ring back, he wouldn't take me to the courthouse. I refused to give it back because he messed up and it was my gift. We continued to argue about what he had done and I was set on getting to that courthouse. It was either going to be a Lyft or him taking me. He ended up taking me to the courthouse, walked inside with me to get the paperwork and we walked out.

When I got back to the car, I told him we were going to get the papers signed and end the marriage as soon as possible. He let his knees hit the ground, said sorry, and pleaded for me to not go through with it and promised things would change. I didn't believe him at all but looking at the divorce paperwork it was going to be more complicated than I thought and I didn't have much time to take care of it before going back to Japan.

Over the next couple of days, we said our goodbyes and I caught my flight back to Japan. I dreaded going back only because he couldn't be with me and I didn't know when we would be stationed together. I wanted to see if things would change with us living together and if me being overseas really affected him but it did not. When I got back to Japan, I already knew I had to be pregnant. We were having sex like two to three times a day for two weeks straight and there was no way possible I wasn't. I decided two weeks after I arrived back in Japan, to take a pregnancy test since I had missed my period by two days. It was a digital test and it read that I was pregnant. I was happy, excited, and nervous. I tried figuring out a cute way to announce to him that the test was positive and instead I just called to share the news with him. He didn't seem too excited at first. It was like his mind and speech went blank at that moment. A weird feeling of his uncertainty went through my body. We talked for a few days after that and he began to come around to the fact that I was pregnant. We started talking about the process of pregnancy, naming the baby, and when I would finally be able to come home to him now that this was a factor.

Later on, we talked about when we would share the news with our families. I waited until after I had my first doctor's appointment and found out when I would be due before I mentioned it to my family. As the weeks went by, I began to question him further as to when he would tell his family. He didn't sound that enthusiastic any longer. His family was on my Facebook page and I didn't want to share it at least until he notified them. He wouldn't give me an answer. I let a few months go by and decided I would go ahead and share it since it's my page and because I was so excited I couldn't hold it up any longer. It also seemed to me like there was a problem with him sharing it as if it was something to hide and as if he would get scolded. He gave me the silent treatment for a few days and that's when I made up my mind I'll share it because he wasn't going to ruin a happy moment for me and what I thought would be a happy one for him too. After all he was desperate to have a baby with me since we met and now that the time came, he seemed indifferent. After my pregnancy announcement to him, his mood began to fluctuate. Some days he would be okay, other days he would not. He hinted at me having an abortion at one point but he didn't come out directly and say it. He and I weren't getting along nor was he speaking to me when I shared it. It had been a couple of days of silent treatment I believe that stemmed from a disagreement that he wasn't budging on. There was a 12 hour time difference between us so when I shared it publicly, it was daytime for me and night time for him. When he woke up and saw that I tagged him in the post, he was upset. He claimed his family was mad they found out on Facebook and questioned why he didn't tell them. Also, I didn't know it at the time but the same day I shared it, there was major negative stuff going on with Bryna and their daughter.

When Mack had transported her and their daughter from South Carolina to Pennsylvania to live in Mack's dad house due to a dispute she had with her parents, Pennsylvania didn't work out for her, and she went to live with one of her friends in Arizona a few short weeks after. She got involved with a drug dealer guy who had given her some dirty money and she put it in her bank account. Another guy came looking for the money and had her at gunpoint about to take her life. That was a sad and unfortunate case. Mack's daughter was with a baby sitter and she ended up in the state's custody for about a week or so because her mother wasn't anywhere to be found. Mack yelled at me for revealing my pregnancy because of what was going on and I had no idea until after my post was made that it was going on but my pregnancy had nothing to do with her. His family was pissed they found out from my social media because Mack wasn't mature enough to tell them and he was trying to hide it from them because they didn't want me pregnant or to be married and I didn't understand why back then. Outsiders had too much input which was definitely not a good thing for a healthy marriage. A mature and private husband wouldn't have allowed that. Mack made a happy moment an unpleasant one very fast. It wasn't fair to me I was being punished for someone else's problems. However, I will say that my making a pregnancy announcement and the issues she was experiencing had no relation to me exclaiming my happiness of my new baby. He was so angry he didn't respond to the Facebook post, his family didn't respond to it and even when people tagged his name congratulating him and us, he did not respond. I thought that was cold and rude. In the navy, I had to go to the medical clinic in Japan and take a test to confirm that it was positive so they could make arrangements for me to start transitioning off of the ship I was on. When I got my official medical paperwork and my chain of command found out, they weren't happy. They knew I was trying to be stationed with Mack but was mad they didn't find out I was pregnant before I actually got it approved by medical. I was a lot smarter than they thought. I was given a hard time as soon as I stepped aboard that ship because I was a black female, newly married, and they wanted me to finish qualifications on the ship and finish my contract before I got relocated or pregnant. My immediate supervisor who was a black male started questioning me and brought me in with a higher ranking employee and told me I could get in trouble for malingering, which means faking a sickness. I wasn't faking a pregnancy at all and they knew it. I had paperwork to prove it. They also tried to scare me by telling me that I wouldn't be able to leave Japan and I would probably have to stay out there with no help or to give up my son. My superiors was trying to pull whatever string they could to screw me up because they felt like I messed up and was getting my way of leaving that duty station. Their tactics didn't work and I was removed from the ship a few days later and sent to a temporary processing unit while I wait for my official orders to transfer. I was so relieved to be off the ship and away from the toxicity of my all male chain of command. I kept in contact with the pregnancy coordinators regarding where I was going to be assigned to. Originally they were going to send me to San Diego, California but I told them Mack was stationed in Virginia Beach, Virginia and I needed to be with him. My request was granted and he and I were both happy. I thought this meant our marriage would get better and we would be together to make it work. Little did I know this was a recipe for disaster but also a reality check for me.

A couple of months later, I took a final flight from Japan and landed in Virginia. He claimed he couldn't get off work to get me because his chain of command wouldn't allow it which I believe was a lie so I had to catch an Uber home. When I got home, there was an Edible Arrangements for me in the fridge with a welcome home card. When he came home from work the next morning, I told him that I needed to use his car to get back and forth to work until I was able to get my own car. He gave me a hard time about it at first but then gave in. I wasn't going to tolerate not being able to drive his vehicle and hear him complain so when I took him to work the next day, as tired as I was after a long flight, I went to the dealership and bought a vehicle. He was mad because I didn't let him check the car out nor did he know that I was able to get a car. He had been looking through my mail and checking my credit report and saw my original denial letter for a car I had applied for when I was still living in Japan. Pissed that I did it without him, he gave me silent treatment and attitude for a couple of days. Instead of spending time with me on his weekends off, he would go back and forth to Philadelphia claiming that he was going to visit his family. It realistically didn't sound right to me since he was doing that a lot already while I was overseas. We had already not had a lot of time together before I left for Japan and when I came back I thought he would want to spend as much time as possible with me since we were newly married and before our baby was born. It became a problem that he would leave me behind at home and an even bigger problem that he would start a problem or create an argument right before he left so he could give me silent treatment and do as he pleased while he was gone.

One of the times he did allow me to go to Philadelphia with him, that was only the second time I had met his family. His mother paraded around like she was so happy to see me but at the same time she looked unhappy when we talked about my pregnancy. After we left Philadelphia we came back home and continued with our usual routine until one day, things drastically changed for the worst. On his birthday in April 2016, after I got home from work I noticed as I was walking in our room his phone was sounding off and it was a text message from his female best friend, Patty, whom lived in Philadelphia. She had responded back to a message about them hanging out there for his birthday. Previously, I expressed to him, I felt uncomfortable about him having this friendship without introducing us to each other so I can pick up on her vibe especially because he told me he used to like her in middle school. He refused for her and I to meet up and that was a sign of a problem to me. He realized I had his phone and got upset, tussling with me to get it from me. I held it so tightly I refused to give it up because I was so pissed of being left out and him traveling so much to Philadelphia when we hadn't even spent a lot of time together and enjoyed marriage. He pinned me down to the bed and placed me in a position where I was unable to move. He was screaming at me about having and going through his phone and verbally abusing me while I screamed for him to get off of me. At this time I was five months pregnant and it was not comfortable or good for him to be doing that to me. After I screamed and pleaded for him to let me go, he said he was calling the cops. In my mind I was asking why he is calling the cops when he assaulted me. When 911 answered the phone, he said, "My wife and I got into a dispute that was verbal but turned physical" "She hit me and I need help" I immediately got on the phone with my family and said, "Mack is lying on me to the cops about a disagreement we had and he told them I put my hands on him." They told me to calm down. I did not want to hear that at all. This man has done so much stuff to me mentally, emotionally, and physically and he always played victim when I brought light to it. He was dangerous and so were his lies and actions. The fact that he could lie on his pregnant wife was absurd to me. What a little bitch he was for that! I thought to myself, " Mack, you supposed to be a man, tell the truth, and here you are crying wolf" I can't respect that. When the cops showed up, it was two of them, both were white males. I talked to one of them and he talked to another. When I was asked what happened I told the officer, "We had a verbal dispute and there is no need for y'all to be here." I didn't tell them the truth of what happened because I didn't want Mack to get arrested, however I did not know he and the police were going to formulate a lie on me. According to the police report and arrest form, he told them that I punched him three times in the upper torso which was a lie. I denied it but yet and still they handcuffed me and took me to jail. After I realized he did that, I decided to tell them the truth about what he did but they weren't buying it at all. I was shocked that it happened especially with crime scene not being called to the scene, no evidence of injuries or the EMS not being present to assess him for injuries. They allowed me to make a phone call to my military chain of command and my mom to let them know what's going on. The officer then read me my Miranda rights and placed me in the back of the patrol car. I was nervous and shocked this was happening to me. I wanted to really cut up and resist arrest because I was pissed. I had calmed myself down and started thinking positive because I knew God would take care of it. I had worked in a jail before so I understood the process of it. That assured me that I wouldn't be stuck forever. I got there and they took me through the intake process and made me change out of my clothes into a uniform. I was able to talk on the free pay phone they had in the holding area. My mother told me she contacted him to figure out what was going on and he told her the same lie he told the officers and she had the nerve to believe it at first because I was arrested. In her mind, she thought that meant I was guilty. I explained the situation to her and she said, "All that he talked about was how you didn't buy him a birthday cake and how that made him upset." Who the hell is worried about a birthday gift when this man was mistreating me throughout our marriage and my pregnancy and then had me sent to jail on a lie? Anger filled my entire body and talking to my mother and my sister didn't make it any better. She questioned me on a recorded line on if I did it or not trying to get me hemmed up. I felt like they both wanted to see me down after seeing me up so long. The point is Mack shouldn't have lied and had me sent to jail at 5 months pregnant. I found out I was able to get bonded out without paying by having my military supervisor come and get me. It was humiliating for me to even call and ask for them to get me but he did. My supervisor, his wife and family came along and they tried to console me as much as possible telling me their experiences and such but I wasn't trying to hear none of that. The conditions of me being bonded out was that I could not return home or have any contact with him for three days because they automatically place a temporary restraining order on those who have pending assault charges. My supervisor had to drive to the apartment complex and pick up my car for me while I was on a different street. My ex had placed a bag of clothes and uniforms in my trunk so I was glad I didn't have to be without some of my belongings. The arresting officer had directed him to do so. I stayed in a hotel for that night. The next day, I had to go to work in uniform and explain to them what happened. My hair was a total mess because right before I got arrested I had just took out my sew-in weave and was going to get my hair done later that day but my arrest interfered with that. It was embarrassing. Thank God my mug shot can't be found on the internet. When I walked in to work, everyone was just looking at me trying to figure out what was going on. I was taken in an office for questioning and they provided me with a barracks room to cool down in for a few days without having to be at work. I started searching for my own place because I just knew I was not going back home and being around him after what he had done. I had been under a lot of stress since he found out I was pregnant but he did not care one bit. I used to beg him to the point of crying to stop doing things to stress me out but he wouldn't.

After the restraining order expired, he had the nerve to call and ask if he just saw me at a store with a guy. He wasn't worried about the fact that he sent me to jail or how I was feeling. I ignored his remark and told him that I was going to find a mutual party to come and pick up all of my belongings from the apartment because I was moving out. He tried to question me on where I was moving to and I told him it was none of his business. In my head, I was done and about to file for divorce. I ended up arranging to meet him in front of the leasing office where the managers could see both of us in plain sight while I had Mack load my things into my car. He refused to come to the office at first to give me my belongings and gave me an ultimatum that I need to first give him my previous tax statement so he could use it to get his financial aid from school before I could get my belongings. I didn't give a crap about that I just wanted my stuff and to get out to my new place. His dad, Correll contacted me and said,

"Correll said, "Hello baby girl how you doing? I heard what happen I just wanted to stay strong & keep your faith. I know Mack can be very difficult to deal with & I know he's probably putting you through a lot. You guys just need to sit down and talk maybe, go to counseling just to try to work things out. I think you guys make a beautiful couple and I really want to see you guys make it. Y'all have baby on the way & you really shouldn't be stressing over anything to make sure Mir comes out a healthy little football player. Just want to say I love you and I got your back. I had a long talk with Mack & told him he needs to be more sensitive to your needs & understand more! So please don't stress I got you I'm going to kick his ass when he gets home. If you need anything you can call me anytime you want." I replied, "I'm not sure what side of the story he told you but I went to jail on a lie he told the officers when it should've been him that went to jail but I tried looking out for both him and I and our careers and fear of retaliation and I ended up going because they spoke to him after they spoke to me. I am truly hurt over it all. I was going through so much with him since I had been in Japan and it got worse when we start living together. I can't take it anymore. I have tried and tried and tried. I did not put my hands on him at all that night but he did something to me after he got angry during our argument." Correll said, "I know you're hurt & upset I just hope you guys can work it out & fix whatever you guys are going through. Maybe y'all can go to counseling & fix your family. Like I said if you need to talk you can call me if you need to."

I replied by saying, "Okay."

I didn't feel like anything they said to me or Mack was going to change anything nor did I feel like their apology was sincere at all and little did I know this feeling would later come to the light and be true.

Their primary concern, I thought, was to butter me up and make me feel like he's on my side, so I didn't run off with the baby and cut them all out of having contact like Bryna did when Mack had cheated on and mistreated her and caused her to move to South Carolina with their new baby. They knew Mack's history of impregnating females, giving them a hard time throughout and stressing the female out enough to run off from him.

I ended up finding an apartment to stay at not too far from where he was living at, but I did not tell him my address. I didn't want him watching or bothering me. I didn't talk to him for a couple of months but every now and then he would find a reason to text me. A couple of weeks after my arrest, I got a call from Bryna. She was calling me because she couldn't get in touch with him for a while and was trying to arrange for her daughter to come to him over the summer to spend time with us. I revealed to her that we were no longer living together and that I hadn't talked to him either. I explained to her what happened with the arrest and of course she was shocked. She said that she doesn't want her daughter, who was 3 years old at the time, in the midst of his crap nor should my newborn baby be in it either. After telling her how to go about the situation with Mack, I then asked her to clear the air on what occurred when he got his daughter while I was in Japan. I figured this would be the perfect time to ask her because she was pissed at Mack and she would be compliant and tell me all I needed to know.

In one of our short conversations while I was in Japan, she had told me my husband wasn't as honest as I thought he was and she had something to tell me. I didn't listen because I figured it was coming from a bitter and insincere place and Mack used to tell me everything, at least I thought he did. She told me he brought her and his daughter from their home to our home and allowed them to stay there for like a week before taking her to their hometown to live with her family members. She told me she slept with him multiple times in our house. When she went to Philadelphia to live with Mack's dad, Mack came and stayed the night and Mack's mother, Tamesha invited her to spend Thanksgiving with her at her house and wanted them to get back together while I was overseas. I recall when I tried to talk to Mack's mother Tamesha about the situation initially she wasn't trying to have anything to do with it at all although she was backstabbing and finding out information about Mack and I and he would tell me. I asked her was I supposed to agree with Mack allowing Bryna to come to our house and our apartment because it seemed to me that when she found out he was married she was trying to come along. She started to take up for Mack and say she feels that Mack is very honest with me in her opinion, sometimes too honest. "He feels nothing should be kept from his wife. I respect that but he doesn't know how we think." So basically, she does know what Mack and I had going on and I questioned in my mind why she was trying to make me feel comfortable about him when he wasn't making me feel comfortable. Of course, as naive as I was, I believed her when she said he was honest. She then told me, "I know that he will bend over backwards to try to see his daughter and Bryna never followed through. I know that he does not want her! I also know that he has no intentions on ever cheating on his wife. As bad as I would offer for them to stay here just for me to get a chance to finally meet my granddaughter I respect your marriage enough to say oh hell no you go stay with your grand mom and I'll keep the baby. If the baby doesn't want to stay that's fine but I will not let her here knowing Mack might stay over. I trust my boy but I don't want you feeling uncomfortable or disrespected I'll talk to him."

The part where she said, "I know he will bend over backwards" which I took very literal ended up happening so she was right about that because he bent over to sleep with Bryna. Second of all, why would it even be a thought in your mind to offer for them to stay with her, when one, he is married, and two, the mother has her own family? Mack and Bryna staying in her house isn't a guarantee he wouldn't attempt to sleep with her there either. The baby is who is important here. Lastly, she said she respected my marriage "enough". The key word enough was a red flag to me as well. Basically. she respected it somewhat, but not completely. After she told me this, she said, "The car is one thing, they need transportation. The apartment is another thing depending on the situation. I say no. I'll hear what he has to say and why I feel like I've already butted in it too much but you gave me some info I didn't know about." Hold up now, she said the car is one thing, meaning it was okay for Bryna to be in the car, our car with their daughter and then the apartment is another thing. I thought, "What the hell!"

Why would she think that Bryna should stay in a married woman's house or in her car that belongs to her and husband? It would not be happening if I was there, it shouldn't even be happening while I'm not. We were married! I started expressing my feelings about how he would be upset about me reaching out to his mom but she told me before if I wanted to talk to her I could and showed no empathy or even thought of it, if it was her in my shoes, or straight up just seeing it from a woman to woman perspective. Only other stuff she would say is, "Lord help me and y'all are too young" and then she dismissed me by saying goodnight. What did it have anything to with us being young? We were married! A few days later, I was having a hard time reaching him. I reached out to his mom and was like I didn't know that I couldn't talk to my husband all day because he was spending time with his daughter. This hurts so bad I wouldn't do that to him if I was in his shoes I would never do anything like that. She disregarded what I said and asked have you talked this over with your mother? "What did my mom have anything to do with what I was telling her about what her son was doing to me?"

It seems like she was trying to cut out the conversation and reach out to my mom as if something was wrong with my feelings. I told her, "Yes I talk to my mom I'm just not understanding all this." Tamesha then said, " I think I may connect with her for thoughts even though it has absolutely nothing to do with us." I told her, Please don't. I don't want to involve her anymore in this and I really shouldn't be doing this either. She replied, "Whoahhh wait, What?" I said, "Neither of you should be involved in it. I just vent because it bothers me a lot. This is all new." She said, "Vent in prayer especially at 3:30 a.m." I was in Japan and I kept forgetting the 12 hour time difference but she was obviously up and responding to my messages. After what I said I told her "If you talk to my mom about it, it's going to make things a lot worse than it is for me and Mack right now. I can't deal with this the rest of my life this is too much.

That's when his mom said, "Mack just left here not too long ago he came to my job and spent time there until I got off he went to get a cheesesteak and met me and my niece and my sister here where we were able to spend time with her for the very first time. We have been waiting for this moment for years; you're stealing my joy with your insecurities and lack of empathy. We talked and I tried to support you but you're continuing to think selfishly. It was absolutely normal to have some of these feelings and emotions but you're stuck. Mack left here tired and stressed and cannot enjoy this moment either because you're stressing him. He's rushing to get them out of here regardless of how exhausted he is just to please you. He's going to sleep on the side of the road if need be. I am beyond pissed my daughter just called and she just missed her only niece. She's upset I can't do this with you."

I started to feel really weird about his mother because it was like how was she being so emotionally unconnected to a young woman who is married to her son going through a troubling time and brushing me off although my marriage was none of her business. I know she had to have known everything was going on and after all her and Mack both would drop information to me they shared with each other but anytime I came to her about what her son was doing she backed off. I would be blamed for how I felt. She was deviating from the real issue at hand and very standoffish. I wasn't thinking selfishly. I had no problem with my husband being around his daughter but it just did not make any sense to me on why he would abandon me and spend the whole day with his daughter not contacting me. I'm all the way in Japan. She tried to blame me for Mack being stressed and tired. For me it was all about respect and obviously his mother nor him or the baby mom Bryna had any respect at all. At this point I started to see the real her I didn't even respond back to her.

A few hours later she sent me thumbs up. I asked her what the hand symbol was supposed to mean. I also said, "I'm not trying to steal your joy cause drama or anything I'm trying to have peace myself here as well." She then tried to cover up by saying the hand symbol is a thumbs up but I hit it by accident.

A few days later I decided to apologize to her. I shouldn't have because my feelings were valid she was being very inconsiderate and standoffish but because I was naïve and trying to be accepted by her I did it anyway.

"I just want to apologize about everything that happened recently. I wasn't trying to steal your joy or anything or make the experience unpleasant for you I know I shouldn't have involved you and I was wrong on my part and you're right 3:30 in the morning wasn't too good. Sometimes I honestly forget about the time difference. I apologize to you if I came off as selfish. That was definitely not the image I want to put out there. I hope you're doing well."

She replied, "It's Okay, my son hasn't been completely honest with me. He told you more which is why

I probably couldn't understand some of your anger. I still haven't to spoken to Mack about everything but I will."

I didn't write her anymore after this but now I knew by the time I received that message from her, she already saw Bryna's baby. She definitely did know what was going on she was just trying to pretend she didn't. Mack had slept with Bryna at this point. I also recall Tamesha uploading pictures of Mack and Bryna laughing and portraying them getting along on her Facebook page where they were sitting very closely together; almost on top of each other on a one person loveseat, with Mack's ring visible. Tamesha used to upload pictures of Mack and females all of the time and it made me feel really uncomfortable but he claimed they were all his female friends from high school. You might as well call Tamesha Mack's Messy Mammy because that's exactly what she is to me. She did everything she could to make me feel uncomfortable and show me she had no respect for my marriage and didn't want Mack marrying or having a kid with me.

Tamesha is a "pick me" type of person, she'll go along with or do anything for a situation to be beneficial whether it's ethical or just messy, she wants to be accepted and also whatever keeps her son is happy and in contact with her. An example is, If Mack doesn't want her being civil with or understanding of me, she's going to listen to him because the cost of her son cutting her off like he's done before when she displays she doesn't agree with his actions or follow his lead is not worth her having conversation or a relationship with me and my son. Mack doesn't like the idea of his family being cool or even civil with me especially when he's mad at me so he wants his family to share in that dislike or hate by discarding me and anything I think or feel." He needed them to make her feel warm without me interfering. Mack wants his family to be cool with the mothers of his kids when it's beneficial for him. For instance, for a while when Bryna was mad about our marriage, something he valued for the benefit of him, when she started talking about child support and the fact he wasn't being there for their daughter even after he slept with her and her threats to reach out to me, he didn't want his entire family being nice to her especially if she was trying to get to me which would've messed up his agenda. So instead they named her bitter and jealous of our marriage and ignored any of her claims against him which ultimately she did end up reaching out to me because they was ignoring her while they was trying to groom me and make me feel warm and welcome without her interfering. I know this because he used me as a pedestal into his games for a bit until I figured out he wasn't the victim and was using me to spite her for what he did to her. Bryna told me when she was living in my house when I would call or Facetime Mack, she said she would be right there listening and a few times her daughter almost made a loud noise that would've ruined everything.

Bryna has also told me Mack and his mother had arranged for her to write that message to me on Facebook pretending to be civil so it didn't genuinely come from her, she was manipulated into doing it to make it look good to me and to hide my suspicion for anything going on which is just sick and wrong. She said Mack had told her all of our marriage business. They were both in my bank account and he was giving her money. They had pictures of him and her which were stored in hidden files of his phone. Bryna said they claimed each other as best friends and both went through each other's cell phone while lying down together and how Mack told her the story of how he and I got together and how I never wanted her in our house or the car which was true. He's a married man. What logical sense would it make for a married man to be in close and private contact with his baby mama while his wife is overseas? The fact he has to sneak, lie, and cover up says he knew exactly what he was doing was wrong. It's not a matter of having trust issues; it's a matter of respect. He did not respect me or our marriage by doing all Bryna said he did.

To make sure she wasn't lying about any of it, I asked her to describe the inside of our house. That's when she told me that he had got a brand new bed in the house, he had no furniture in the living room, no groceries, and my clothes were in the closet. She said her and their daughter watched Netflix on the bed on his MacBook and his daughter had marked the coffee table up with crayon. She told me how he wiped it up so I wouldn't notice it when I came home. All of which she said was true. She also confirmed that the concern I had with a charge on his bank account at a pharmacy was also a Plan B pill. When I asked her why she participated in all of this, she admitted to me later that she still had a soft spot for him. Like what the hell? I'm sorry but I don't care how I feel I don't crave or have a soft spot for a married man period. She claimed she didn't want to be back with Mack and didn't like him, so why would you sleep with him and later claim you were using him for money, rides, and a place to stay. That sounds a lot like prostitution to me. She said she wouldn't be telling me this information if he would've just done right by their daughter which to me is morally wrong. How could you go to sleep every night knowing you did that to someone's marriage and a woman you don't even know? That let me know she was out for revenge using me being his wife. When I first discovered that charge on his bank account app, I was in Japan and had a feeling that's what it was, yet he denied it and told her about how creepy it felt that I knew. What's even more crazy is while I was on my flight from Japan to Virginia, he sent me a screenshot of a text message from her that said "I might be pregnant" and he responded asking her how but I didn't catch on to the fact that she was implying a possible pregnancy by him. Mack had slept with her and manipulated her into writing a fake apology to me that said about her not wanting to cooperate or add me on Facebook so we could get along for their daughters sake. She acted as if I was just trying to be her friend because she was some highly adored person of mine. Her and her twin sister used to make fun of me on social media saying I was the ugly wife and when Mack got mad at her he sent it so she could know that he saw it. Ugly isn't anywhere within me until you rub me the wrong way but it takes a lot for me to get to that, at least it used to. I asked her if she was willing to provide a statement that I could use to send to his command in the military to help get him convicted of adultery since it is a chargeable offense and because he was using our basic allowance for housing to sleep with someone else in our house. She acted like she was going to do it. I would put my investigation skills to use and ask her questions in a text and she would respond. She told me the date she left home to be with him, she told me how she saw when I used to call his phones a lot and how I didn't want her in my house or the car. She told me the password to his email and Netflix account. She mentioned that he has hidden apps in his phone full of old pictures and letters from his exes and the ultrasound of one who aborted his child. She said they lay together in bed and he referred to them as being best friends and went through each other's phones. When we got off the phone, I texted him and I told him I now know the truth about what happened when his daughter came and that I wanted nothing to do with him outside of our unborn son. The same day Bryna revealed these things to me about her and Mack's relations, he was calling her trying to stop her from telling me saying that she was crazy and trying to cause problems and then that's when she told me she think it would be best for him and her to deal with matters of their child in court.

After my arrest and finding this out, I decided not to have anything to do with Mack until it came down to our son when he was born. He would text me a few times a week trying to make conversation and not taking accountability for cheating and what he did and I wasn't budging at all.

It's crazy because he used to talk very hateful of Bryna. He said he couldn't stand her guts and that he was going to get primary custody of their daughter and make her pay him child support. He didn't hate her that much to sleep with her. I've learned that anytime a man bad mouths their baby mama it's because he's hurt, he tried to get over on her by trying to have his cake and eat it too and didn't work, or because she got fed up with his crap not taking care of the child. So they place labels such as the bitter baby mama and sometimes without taking accountability of where they went wrong. That's mainly a lot of the reasons these type of men spew hate for the mother in my opinion. In my mind, I had it made up that I was done and getting a divorce so I could be free of him and his catastrophic mess. He texted me an apology for cheating. I didn't realize then that this was part of his manipulation tactic to reel me in so he can do me in even worse. I got text messages of him saying, "I'm trying to put my pride aside. I've been thinking about you and Mir so often and this not talking thing between us is driving me crazy inside."

I told him, "Well I don't know what to tell you that I haven't already told you." Little did I know and ended up finding out later that him and his female cousin Vee were reviewing my messages back and forth because he was sending screenshots to her and she was formulating what to say next to me and how to butter things up about what happened between him and Bryna. I saw that she was telling him to tell me they stopped in Virginia to get rest and to remain safe and some other crap. I wasn't buying it because it was all foul.

Additional texts from him was when he started reminiscing on the time he flew to see me in Florida before our marriage and how was trying to put his pride aside. He also said if anything happened with me and our son, he would be crushed and how he would always care about me. He claimed to have wanted to start over. I didn't believe any of it.

In reality, all it was to me was more manipulation into staying with him and putting up with his crap. He even sent another text message about it sometimes takes almost losing a person to realize how lucky we are to have it. He admitted to maybe having the wrong mindset and telling me that he didn't intend for me to go to jail but wanted us to be separated for the night. He was trying to blame the state for coming in our house and arresting me instead of acknowledging the fact that he said, "How do you honestly feel about everything? I always wonder where your head is at when I think about you, I wish I had said something sooner about how I've been feeling but I knew you weren't talking to me."

"How do I feel? Hmm, a lot of damage has been done to me, a lot of dishonesty, betrayal, lies, and deceit. I don't want to be on that rollercoaster anymore. We are not compatible at all. It's too late to try to mend things. They are completely broken. I don't want to be in any type of relationship or intimate relationship with you." I said.

"Do you remember when you were home in Florida after I left Tampa from seeing you after a school and the very next day we didn't know what to do with ourselves? Since we've stopped talking it's been the same way. I know we have had our disagreements and fights but at the end of the day, I know if anything were to ever happen to you or Mir it would crush me and I can only hope you feel the same way. I may shut down in situations but I will always care about you. I want to go back to those days of just kicking it, and having fun even if it means starting over, let's go out somewhere and just talk or any excuse just to see you again."

I ignored his message and went to bed. I said what I had said so there was no need for him to try to convince me otherwise. The next day he texted me on July 4th wishing me a happy holiday. I responded back to his previous message telling him there was no need to reflect back to the past.

He responded, "Sometimes it takes almost losing what we have to realize how lucky we are to have it. I may have done a lot of wrongs and my mindset may have been somewhere else, but after all that's going on and not seeing or talking to you for so long, not being able to rub Mir throughout your pregnancy, reality sets in. This is not what I want, we were both excited to bring our own child to the world with so many plans, it hurts that as he's growing and you're frowning that I'm not there, that hurts the most. Everything aside you're a great woman, there is more I could say but this text would be huge. I did not ask them to send you to jail or take you to court, but since I didn't the state or city decided to take action, I only asked that we be separated for a night and after then was when they told me that you had to go to jail. Why would I want to put the mother of my son in prison? I'm not out to ruin your life you should know me better than that."

"I only knew Mack for less than two months before we got married so, no, I only knew what he presented to me at the time. It was silly of me to even get married to him like that but I was young and naive.

"You once told me that you had both of your parents there as you grew up and I know your parents' marriage and relationship wasn't smooth sailing all the way through, I want Mir to have both his parents there in the same way, he deserves that, man I love this boy to pieces." He said. "I'm eagerly awaiting this parenting class; I wish he was here already."

Mack was so full of it. He said anything and everything he could because he knew he really messed up and I was coming for him in court. Of course being pregnant and hormonal I withdrew away from him, while at the same time buying into his bullshit. I again declined to even engage in anything further with him and was just really tired of going back and forth.

While these words sounded very genuine, heartfelt, and convincing, Mack didn't mean not a bit of it, not for long anyway. Like I said he had his family members talking to him, trying to maneuver how to get back into my life even for a little bit, just so he could continue to use me and wreak havoc yet again. Getting back with me was just a temporary fix to help him figure out what I may do next if he messed up again or because he was financially struggling and wanted help. With a narcissist, they will do everything possible to punish you or coerce you into staying – including love-bombing you again to make you remember the good times. During the same time they're throwing in crumbs of affection, they're also plotting on how to best covet what resources of yours they can get before the relationship is over. I believe the bigger picture was he was afraid of how the child support was going to be because he knew he wasn't doing right by his daughter and I realized that after talking to Bryna so I'm sure he had a feeling I wasn't going to play with him when it came to helping out with our son. When it came to the assault charge placed against me, I hired a top notch attorney, and when I went to court my attorney tried talking to Mack to get him to voluntarily drop the charges. He wouldn't say one word while sitting next to the victim advocate. In fact, he played the victim. My attorney kept trying to talk to him and he would not answer. She came back to me and told me he was weird. I agreed. She said to me, "If he presses those charges on you and they go through we're going to press charges on him too." She waited about an hour before she attempted to go talk to him again and that time he said that he would think about dropping the charges. At that point my attorney was confused, why would you want your six months pregnant wife charged and sent to jail especially for something you know did not happen? She talked to the prosecutors and they said they were going to give me twelve month probation and as long as I didn't violate it, my charges would be dropped. I explained to her that I have a career I'm pursuing in Criminal Justice and having anything on my record like that would significantly impact it. She told me I may have to go into the court room and tell them exactly what happened on the day of my arrest. I was nervous because I didn't want them to charge me with something I was innocent of and it affects my future.

When I walked in the courtroom, my attorney and I sat down at the stand. I didn't even have to say a word and the next thing I knew the judge announced that the prosecutor decided to motion for a *nolle prosequi* and they dropped the charges on my case. I thanked them and walked out of the courtroom and as I walked out, I looked at Mack's face and he was very pissed off at the outcome. You could tell he wanted me to be charged and locked up. After court was over and I got back to my car to check my phone, Mack's cousin Vee, reached out to me via text asking me to call her when I get a chance offering that she could help things amongst our marriage and that we need to start over and go on dates. This is the point where Mack must have known I was about to be finished with him so he started having his family members reach out to me to reel me in and portray Mack as a different person than what he was displaying. This was honestly just too much for me. I knew it wasn't first year blues. Mack had a problem and his family was all trying to help cover up and keep us together to keep him out of their hair and they recognized I was a good woman. I told her there was nothing she could do Mack's true colors came out on several occasions as it is. There's no repainting a person to appear new when they've already shown their colors, that's a set up for heartbreak right there. I did end up talking to her but I was dead set on preparing to divorce Mack. He had done so much foul stuff already and I knew it would never change. Mack wasn't ready for commitment and marriage at all. When Sherry and I talked, she said he told them he didn't want me locked up but when it came to my attorney and me he was acting the opposite. She then said, "When you talk about him and when she hears what he's saying it's like we are speaking of two different people. That's the narcissist in him." He shows a victim and innocent side of him in front of others and to those he's involved in a relationship with he shows an abusive demeaning villain side behind closed doors which is an attempt to make the real victim seem crazy and delusional outside of the household when she attempts to speak out.

On one of his attempts to reel me back in I thoroughly broke everything down to where he could understand why I wanted nothing else to do with him outside of Mir. I said, "Mack, we just can't be together anymore and that is something you are going to have to accept if you haven't already. I love/loved you so much more, than I have ever loved any guy in my life, than I even loved myself and that is/was a problem. I was tolerating any type of treatment or time you would give me knowing you barely if at all loved me but I have no more love to give to you. Only to the handsome baby boy we will soon have in our world. We have been through so much in the short (almost year) we have been married and a lot of the things endured are just not normal for a marriage. I tried to look out for the best interest of our marriage several times and I have you several chances to get it together even while I was in Japan and it's just really apparent that you were not ready for marriage at all whatsoever. You are still young (which is no excuse for your doings), immature, and have a lot of growing up to do (which I'm sure you already know and have heard a lot). You still want your freedom to do whatever it is you want to do without someone telling you that you can't. It doesn't happen overnight and the months we have been apart it surely hasn't happened either. There are A LOT of things you have did some things I am not even probably aware of that are totally unacceptable in a marriage. I tried to honor you as my husband and put you first before anyone except God and respect you about things you didn't even respect me for. Honestly, you have a lot of baggage and old things you are holding on too. You give me the silent treatment for days when we would have disagreements, telling me the door is always open for me to leave, that there are other people waiting for me to slip up or other crabs kicking the bucket, hurt from Madison, calling her for closure and crying to me about it, old flings you still mess/associate with, Bryna, telling her all of our marriage business and sleeping with her almost getting her pregnant because you had to get her a plan B pill which she was more than delighted to brag about. (Nothing cute about bragging about sleeping with a married man regardless of past dealings), neglecting me while I was on deployment blowing your phone up because you were around her, you cheated on me with Shelby, still hanging with Patty even after everything had happened on your birthday, just blatant disrespect with no regard to how I feel being that I am the woman you chose to marry not any of them. I don't know what your idea of marriage is or was but it's not in sync with the reality of how it is. We are very unequally yoked, I don't want to make things work anymore and I made that clear a few times already. I don't want to constantly relive the unpleasant memories you've given to me. You gave these females the opportunity to laugh at me knowing you weren't and still aren't doing right by the marriage. I'm not gonna be a fool to believe you got your act together because it's going to take time, a lot of time and pain on your end as well to realize things. I just hope when times get rough financially (especially with 2 kids, if there aren't any more I'm unaware of) emotionally, physically, all of those females are able to help you out and I highly doubt it. Please be mindful of the things you keep doing to each female you get involved with because not everyone is tolerant of things other are and the grass isn't always greener on the other side. I really wish you would've put more effort into our marriage for us and Mir to grow up with both parents together not living apart, living separate lives and having the potential to become like a lot of black boys that come from broken or split homes but it's okay I'm going to make sure he doesn't exhibit any of the behaviors of one of those black boys and it would be ideal for you to contribute to being a great father to him (and not with materialistic things either) but giving him your time, love, and affection and correct guidance as well as discipline when necessary."

He responded,

"I cannot accept that Faith. I want you so bad that it hurts. I have had time to really think about things, and having my daughter for the time that I've had her has changed my perspective and mindset on so much. Being a father is so challenging, but I've learned things I don't think I would have if I weren't one. Sacrifices, priorities, responsibilities, not being selfish has to be the biggest I've learned, I make sure before anything else that my daughter is set and has everything she needs before I get or do anything for myself and I know it'll only be worse with Mir. Honestly it's been tough at times trying to find a balance to everything, but I love being a dad so much, it's feels so rewarding to see your child genuinely happy, I'm so anxious to raise Mir through the years and watch him flourish. I have learned to say to myself "I have caused this" to situations that I know that I was at fault for, as low as things are at this point I am only looking to grow as both a man and a father, do the best that I can for my children, and make a positive impact in the world even if a little. You know you are always welcome to talk to me whenever, I will always be here, and that I will always care about you and Mir. I will respect your decision."

I thought about everything Mack said before we went to court and called bullshit on everything he said. It took me about a month to think about everything and he kept reaching out sending memes and paragraphs professing his undying love and trying to reel me in such as agreeing to going to marriage counseling and trying to fix things which I mentioned before but he was stubborn until he came to terms with it. As frustrated, filled with anger and completely turned off by Mack, I decided to use this counseling opportunity as a last resort and see if it was worth a second chance and recovery to avoid a divorce.

Looking back, this was a form of trauma bonding that I had with Mack and can occur when you are involved with a narcissist. I didn't realize it but I was a codependent to him which started in my child hood and spilled over into my relationships and marriage to Mack. A codependent is characterized by a person belonging to a dysfunctional, one-sided relationship where one person relies on the other for meeting nearly all of their emotional and self-esteem needs. It also describes a relationship that enables another person to maintain their irresponsible, addictive, or underachieving behavior. It can create low self-esteem, people pleasing, poor boundaries, dependency, and painful emotions. The list goes on. Trauma bonding is the type of toxic bond that occurs when the abuser alternates between creating highs and lows within the relationship and offer reward or punishment as they deem fit. They will train the victim that happiness is solely dependent on how well they can serve and plead. The bond can long outlive the relationship, leaving the victim craving comfort from the very person who hurt them. It's also when making it work involves betraying yourself, when sexual chemistry is the glue, and when your nervous system is on high alert from consistent uncertainty.

Traumatic bonding occurs as the result of ongoing cycles of abuse in which the intermittent reinforcement of reward and punishment creates powerful emotional bonds that are resistant to change. The longer you are involved with a narcissist, the stronger the trauma bond is and the harder it is to break away without them simply going back to doing things that occurred in the courtship phase to win the victim back yet again. People that have trauma or unhealed wounds from childhood are perfect for developing trauma bonds and getting into these types of intense relationships that feel like love but they're really not. The bond it creates also makes it very difficult to get out of them, even when they are highly dysfunctional for everyone because you have developed an addiction to this person. You are bonded, glued, stuck to them. Do you ever see insanely unhealthy people that can't seem to get out of a very toxic relationship? That's trauma bonding. The more the codependent reaches out to the narcissist for love, recognition, and approval, the more the trauma bond is strengthened.

This also means the codependent will stay in the relationship when the abuse escalates, creating a destructive cycle. Anyways, after rekindling with Mack, I started being around my stepdaughter and spending time with her. It was the first time I met her since we got married. We went to the beach, out to eat, and did other family oriented things. My stepdaughter went home a few short weeks after Mack and I reunited. Before she went back to Bryna, I bought her favorite character bath towel and bracelet set as well as made her a photo album full of pictures of myself and her, Mack and her, and all of us together so she could look back at the pictures when she went home and missed us. I should've known that soon after things were going to go back to how they were before maybe even worse. He needed help and a break from her before she went back home so he was trying to get me acclimated to her as quick as possible. What I thought was him trying to make things work and for us to be living together again, it turned out to be him also trying to con and use me for a place to stay because his lease was ending at the same time. I didn't realize it at the time but looking back everything is an ulterior motive with him. Even Bryna told me it was always the same with her. When he would give her money when she was sleeping with him, it was to help out with their daughter and her while she was staying in the house and also to keep her from revealing that she slept with him and so he wouldn't go on child support. When he went to return my stepdaughter to her mother, I wanted to go with him, as I had never met the mother before, and wanted to introduce myself to her. He didn't allow me to go, making up some lie as to why he couldn't let me. He made me feel as if I was in a box shut out from his daughter and her mother even though I was his wife.

We continued to visit each other's houses while I made up my mind about whether I wanted him to live with me again or not. In between time, Mack started buying things for our baby after we had gone to a place to find out the gender early. We both sat in the room as the technician rubbed my belly with the device to figure out what I was having. When I looked at him, he appeared to be happy and speechless. The technician exclaimed, "You're having a boy. Here I was preparing in a few months to give birth to his first boy. I immediately started buying stuff even before I knew the gender, I bought neutral items. He didn't and I complained about it.

Before Mack and I got back together, and before my stepdaughter went home to her mother, he started buying things for Mir. He only did this because previously I was complaining about how I was the only one preparing for the baby and he wasn't buying anything for him but had packages from eBay, Amazon, and other stores getting car parts, tires, camera and camera accessories, and other stuff for him shipped to the house. I was doing all the planning and preparation for our newborn to come. He didn't mention a baby shower, helping me pick out stuff or being the lead of the house setting the tone for things. His mind seemed to be focused elsewhere until we got back together. I hated being the more dominant one than him. It's like I made the decisions on everything and when I asked for his input he wouldn't budge if it wasn't centered on him. He wanted to do whatever he could at the time to impress me so he had a place to stay. Of course, I didn't know it was a plot, I thought he was starting to come around to his senses. He returned to his apartment and packed up his belongings and began to end his lease to come and live with me. I told him since he allowed my stepdaughter's mother to live in our apartment while I was overseas; I was not giving him a key. I needed to build up the trust that was lost and I did not want anything happening again while I wasn't home.

When I would talk to his dad's fiancé, Sherry she would tell me if we're going to start over we need to not do things half way and completely start over which meant to give him a key and allow him to pay half of all of our bills. I didn't agree on the key part at all. It's not that easy after he brought his Bryna into our house and God knows who else. He should've been grateful I allowed him to move in after what he did. I was 8 months pregnant when he moved in and I was hoping he would help me out with things in and around the house when I needed his help, but he barely did that unless I complained repeatedly.

We went to a few counseling sessions and saw couples dealing with what appeared to be the same as us. He looked shocked when he heard one woman sobbing in class because her man seemed oblivious to the hurt he caused her. This counseling session was a way of trying to fix the broken pieces within our marriage. He appeared to be compliant to all I asked of him and incorporated methods along with me that our counselor recommended. Things began to look a bit brighter. He was cleaning when I asked him to, taking accountability for his actions and he made our one year marriage anniversary special by taking me out to my favorite seafood restaurant.

It only took about a month for the normal him to resurface but I was enjoying the facade he portrayed. I noticed when he would meet me home after work; he would take a shower and claim to go to the gym. I wouldn't be invited to watch him workout. Then I started to notice he was spending a lot more time outside of the house and not helping me out. His phone started being on silent and he wouldn't make any phone calls or texts around me. One day I approached the living area and saw him lying on the couch and when I turned the corner, he quickly hid his phone. I asked why did he do that and he said he didn't want me seeing what he was doing. This then drew a suspicion that he had something to hide but I wasn't sure what.

A few days later, in the morning I asked him to be honest about what's going on because something isn't feeling right and I did not want him in my apartment giving me silent treatment, not cooking or cleaning willingly, and not helping with the bills, regardless if he had a key or not. This is when he told me, "I do not like or love you." I wasn't too shocked because he never displayed it to me except in the beginning of our relationship which was the love bombing phase those narcissists usually show a good side to reel and charm their victim in.

I told him he did not need to be living in my house by telling me that and I asked when he could move out. He told me within two weeks. I brushed it off but really took time to think about and evaluate everything and what he said to me. I was nine months pregnant and on top of being ready to have the baby, I was frustrated because he didn't understand marriage, monogamy, or anything associated with it and for him to utter those words at a time I needed him most it sent me into tears and then rage. I began to meditate about the overall status of our marriage and all of the pain I endured in just under a year.

I remembered the times when I would cry to Mack about things he was doing to me by the way he was acting, twisting words around, and playing victim and he would continue about his day as if nothing was wrong. He disregarded the fact I cried after having to explain something to him that was bothering me repeatedly, just for him to disregard and not change it. It was things about finances, and females he made me feel insecure about as well as him leaving me to go to Philadelphia all the time when we didn't have time to enjoy my return from being overseas or our marriage in general. Every time Mack was nearing the weekend for him to go to Philadelphia to see family, at least that's what he would tell me he was going to do, he would purposely create an argument out of something and then ban me from going with him. When I pointed this out to him, he would get in an angry rage and get upset at me for pointing out what he was doing and would punish me by being silent and not acknowledge any of my text or calls. He would sneak and be around the female best friend and other females he used to have a crush on and hang out with them knowing I felt insecure about it.

I recall him saying, "I want to do 22 year old things and you can do 24 year old things and I can't because of this marriage and you've ruined my idea of a marriage"

I guess he meant he wanted to continue living life like a single man and sleeping with any female he wanted to and because I didn't tolerate it, he felt I was putting limitations on him. I remembered when I was in Japan and I talked about ending things because he was acting shady with the female issues we were having and his inability to balance his wife with his daughter making me feel like I was left out. I remember when he had me so mind controlled that Bryna was crazy, bitter, and wouldn't let him see his daughter and how he was claiming he was going to get full custody of her. Of course, as a new wife, I believed my husband was telling the truth but in reality he was brainwashing me to believe the worst about her, so I too could be an enabler; a flying monkey for him when he unleashed his realm of lies and chaos onto her. In popular psychology, a flying monkey is someone who does the narcissist's bidding to inflict additional torment to the narcissist's victim. It might consist of spying on the victim, spreading gossip, threatening, painting the narcissist as the victim and their target as the perpetrator.

He had me so convinced he was going to get custody, we started talking about the planning of my stepdaughter being with us and how I was coming back to the states after confirming my pregnancy and how I was going to make sure she had her own decorated room, I started looking at hair salons, and trying to prepare for her. Of course when Bryna and I talked I got the truth of everything and that's when I stopped entertaining what he said about her and he claimed I was against him and that he got stuck with two kids. Like what are you talking about, you lay down and made these kids and now both relationships are down the drain, you claiming you got screwed over, how immature.

I didn't think he had any good qualities of a husband that I wanted to continue living the moments I had already lived. I knew something was wrong when he watched me cry uncontrollably out of stress and anxiety over something he had done and he didn't even flinch or try to comfort me. He didn't attempt to apologize nor was he remorseful. Instead, he carefully twisted it around to be my fault or go about his day as if I didn't exist. I knew then I was dealing with a heartless monster, not a person. He's not a soul mate. He's a soul taker. He will love bomb, discard, devalue, grow bored, lie, cheat, gas light, manipulate, and inflict silent treatment as punishment. Once he's discovered and corrected about his inhumane behavior, he'll move on to a new and less informed victim and immediately he'll begin to make her feel special, and that she's the one for him and nobody else is. I remember this phase all too well. He'll then convince the new victim to feel like his exes are crazy, delusional, obsessed, etc. When in fact, he is the perpetrator and has mistreated and cheated on them to make the new victim feel secure and as if she won the grand prize especially if the old victim left him first. The new victim will feel like she won a grand prize alright, the grand prize for the most unpleasant rollercoaster ride of life because that's what it felt like for me and from what I've been told all of those who came before me felt the same way as well. After reflecting on literally everything that happened in less than a year of marriage, I woke up that next morning fed up and told him, "Pack your stuff and get out."

A little advice I can give to anyone dealing with a narcissist and trying to sever ties with them, if you're married to or have kids with one is as you prepare your exit as quietly as possible (preferably with the help of a good lawyer and a safety plan) you have a better chance of departing safely with your sanity and your finances still intact. Sure, they may think you're a fool for the time being, but once they realize you secretly had the upper hand all along, they'll be outraged for completely different reasons – namely, due to the loss of control.

Mack exclaimed, "You're giving Bryna what she wants and that's to not see us together."

I said, "No you gave her what she wanted when y'all slept together in our house. That gave her a lot of ammo and insight."

This also let me know he was in it with me to keep up a façade using me to spite her because she was hurt by what he did to her in their relationship which was the same he did to me except that they weren't married. He whined saying, "I don't have anywhere to go." I said, "I don't care, why you don't ask all the females and your female friend you made plans behind my back with to help you move out and get a place." Again he said, "I don't have anywhere to go." I started sending him hotel information and other apartments. I wrote his dad's fiancée, Sherry on Facebook and told her what he said and she said," That's verbal abuse and you shouldn't tolerate that."

I then texted his dad and told him to tell his son to pack his stuff and get out of my house. Of course, his phone was on silent so I couldn't hear when he did, but Correll told him what I said and then I noticed him getting garbage bags and packing all his things. It took him about two hours but he took it right to the storage unit he had bought down the road. He said nothing to me while on his way out the door. In fact, he acted as if I wronged him and I no longer existed. When he left I didn't hear anything else from him. I never said the marriage was done nor did we agree on seeing on other people. Nothing was said, I just wanted him out of my house because he wasn't helping and the negativity and my hormones were just too unbearable for me especially being that he had already taken me through enough hell. I didn't feel like we needed to live together any longer. I had a lot of peace when I was living alone.

A few days later as it was getting closer to my due date, my water broke on the night of my son was due. I was going to drive myself to the hospital but it was too far away and I was afraid I would not make it. I called Mack twice to tell him so he could come and take me to the hospital but he didn't answer. I ended up texting his dad's fiancé and calling his mother, Tamesha telling her to get in contact with him. Tamesha was able to get in contact with him after only one phone call. She called me back and told me he was on his way and he arrived in fifteen minutes. By the time he made it, EMS was pulling up. I could barely walk so they had to come and get me to assist me downstairs since I lived on the second floor.

      While we were waiting for Mack came in and stood near the door just watching. After EMS got me down the stairs, he locked the door with my keys and followed behind us. I arrived at the nearest hospital to my house and they said I was in active labor. They started hooking me up to monitors and watching my progress. They told me I would be having the baby the next day. Mack had been telling me that after the baby is born he's going on vacation for five days. I told him he should not do that and that he should spend time helping me out with the baby. This caused an argument because he refused to listen and be understanding. The contractions I was having started to get worst so the doctors gave me some narcotics and pain medicine to ease the pressure. They came in and checked on me periodically. He left and said he was going to the store. I couldn't think of any reason why he would need to leave the room when I was getting ready to give birth. While he was out, he called me and asked if I wanted something. I told him no. With Mack, everything he does have an ulterior motive and I mean everything. The little things and the big things he's done for me all came with a price for his benefit and it usually was revealed shortly after. He called me back after I declined his offer and said that he left his debit card in my house when EMS came to get me. I knew it was a lie because we weren't in the house for long and he never brought his wallet in or reached in his pockets. Before I left home, I did a check to make sure I didn't leave anything behind and there was nothing in sight. Plus, I was monitoring his debit card account on the mobile app. This is how I was able to figure out where he was and what money was being spent on. I didn't trust him at all and this was an accountability thing for me as well since he always cried broke and was going in my bank account to get money when he made more than me at the time. He was very adamant that he left it in the house and that he wanted my key to go check. I refused to give him my key because it didn't sound right and I felt there was more to it. I told him to come and check both the hospital rooms I was in. He then said what if I don't find it there. This is when I knew he was planning on not finding it. He could've easily gone to the bank that next day to get a card on-site or use the other debit card he had. He came in and checked the room and didn't find it. I still didn't budge with my house key. He came and spent a little more time in the room and fell asleep. One of his female Chiefs from the Navy came into the room and sat and talked to me. I had never seen her before but she said she saw him out in the lobby area and told him she would stop by. After chatting with me and waiting to see what was going to happen with me, she told me to tell him when he wakes up to give his Chief a call and keep them posted. They wanted to know the name and when the baby was born.

When Mack woke up I told him this and he said he wasn't going to tell them anything. When I asked him why he said, it was his business. They did end up telling him congratulations in front of everyone anyway and he told me how off guard and embarrassed he felt. I was perplexed because how could something that is supposed to be a happy event be so private that you don't want anybody at your job to know so they can congratulate you or give gifts? He told me hours later he was going to leave and come back the next day. I asked him why and he told me he had something to do. What could he possibly have that's so important to do that he couldn't be in the hospital with his wife to watch his first son being born? This pissed me off. The next day the nurses came in ready to get me started to give birth. He was at work and I had told him to tell his job that I was in the hospital having a baby so they could give him time off. He refused to and I couldn't understand why. He ended up asking them to leave for the day and he made it in time to watch the whole birthing process take place. He took a few pictures and sent them to the family but didn't ask to take any of him and the baby. Mir was born on September 21. He was born at 1:15pm and weighed 6lb 15oz. He was so handsome with a head full of hair and big bright eyes. I cried in disbelief that I went through labor and came out with a healthy baby successfully. It was such a breathtaking moment.

I took the initiative to take pictures of Mack and Mir but he didn't seem too thrilled to do so. I didn't understand why he was acting the way he was acting. After our son, Mir made his grand entrance; Mack told me he was ready to go and became very impatient and did not partake in the joy of having a new baby. He didn't even want to stay the night in the hospital to help me out with the baby so I could get some sleep. At this point, all the signs were there that I had a baby by the wrong man. Mack is very immature, inconsiderate, and a pain in the butt and both of his parents has told me that before. You would think him having two kids in two different states would grow him up, but it didn't. When it came time for me to be discharged from the hospital, I had to wait a few hours for him to bring my car to me that already had the car seat installed. I was expecting my parents to be there to come out of state to help me out a bit which they were going to, but my dad got in a bad car accident from a seizure nearly losing his life so they couldn't make it to me for months.

Prior to Mir being born, my sister had exclaimed her happiness for my son's arrival and had planned to come from Florida to Virginia and visit with him. Mack and I were still going through our rollercoaster of marriage and he wasn't kicked out as of yet. I was having a conversation with my mother about hotel rooms for my parents to stay when they came. I'm very particular about being uncomfortable or questioned in my own house about anything period. I had enough of that while living with my parents and being under constant surveillance. After delivering a baby, I wanted to have my space. I informed my mom the name and price of hotels and if they needed me to do so I could get them a military discount. I asked my mom what my sister had planned on doing or if she had talked to my sister about her coming to Virginia to see the birth of my son. My mother claimed she didn't know her exact plans. All my sister had told her was that she was going to come as well. In the back of my mind, I'm thinking well where my sister is going to stay. She has always been notorious for trying to bunk up in somebody else's house or get freebies and discounts on everything even when traveling and I wasn't going to let her use me nor get even a glance or chance to be in my marital business or business period at my house especially after delivering a baby.

I sent my sister a text message and I told her that she's more than welcome to come and watch the arrival of my son and if she needed information regarding hotels and discounts I didn't mind providing that to her. A few hours later I got a phone call from her and she was going off so much about me not letting her stay at my house. What was such a big deal about getting a hotel? Anytime I travel I always get a hotel. I cannot stand staying in someone else's space even if it is for a short time. Another thing I was wondering was when I was going to get the memo of her plans or was she going to just come up to Virginia and tell me last minute and put me in a position to where I have no choice but to say yeah because we're face-to-face just to avoid the confrontation that she would start if I said no.

She started to get emotional and was saying, "Here I am thinking that you were so excited for me to see the arrival of my nephew but in reality, you're telling me I got to get my own hotel room so I'm not coming anymore I'll just send a gift up there." My sister was always a moocher, I'm the complete opposite. She would go to restaurants expecting discounts or free food to get out of paying because she had a large family and her financial situation wasn't where it needed to be. My parents used to praise me for not asking them for anything because my sister would always be the one asking for help for her and her kids and I never would.

Honestly, when I had hard times, I would go to a stranger at the bank or loan companies before I went to the family just to avoid being talked about or reminded about when they helped. Her deciding not to come let me know right then and there that she did not have a genuine interest in coming to see me give birth and see my son. She just wanted to use me in my house because I'm telling you if it was genuine wanting to partake in a special moment, she would have no problem getting a hotel and still being able to visit. She wouldn't have gotten angry and decided not to come all because I didn't want her in my space. She acted as if that was owed to her a spot in my place so she could save money.

My philosophy is if you don't have the money to go, don't go especially not with expectations that somebody else is supposed to pay your way. I recall a time when I had visited home, my sister and her husband tried to bribe me into promising them that when I do come home at any time that I won't spend money on hotels and that I could stay at their home with them. I wasn't agreeing to that at all because I already knew it was going to be a situation where if I stayed at their place, when it was time for them to come and visit my place, if I had an issue with them staying there and recommending a hotel, they would quickly throw it in my face that they allowed me to stay at their place. So nope I wasn't playing into that game. I don't know why they were so concerned with all the money that I was spending out on hotels, I was in the military and I could afford it. If I want to visit and spend money on a hotel I'm going to do it. I don't go anywhere if I don't have any money for all of my expenses. This made things worse for me by having an unsupportive husband, a family unable to make it and having to do things alone.

When Mack did reach the hospital and took me home with Mir, he told me I had a few hours to get some rest and then he was going to be gone for five days. I questioned why he would do that to me and leave me behind to care for the baby alone. The Navy gave him ten days of paternity leave which was supposed to be spent with me and Mir. Why would he not want to bond with our child and give me a break? I had a terrible pregnancy because of all he put me through and he wasn't making it any better. I wasn't able to get any sleep at home tending to the baby and just being extremely stressed out and confused about Mack. When he got home I couldn't even sleep. I felt like I needed to sleep and tend to Mir because Mack wasn't going to do anything but be on his phone or sleep. I ended up doing homework, making bottles, and making sure my parents were okay.

Mack left that night and went to Philadelphia. He only called one time on Face Time while he was there. I had no idea what he was doing but trust me when I say I started putting things together. While he was in Philadelphia, a couple of days after I gave birth he was back to his usual nonsense. He told me when he got back; we needed to talk about the separation. He was in such a rush to get the paperwork going. I told him that I was going to get the divorce initiated and there was no need for him to worry, I had it all covered. He started complaining and saying that I was too demanding, bossy, and overbearing and that he was ready to get everything over with. I wasn't any of those things; I just had expectations of not dealing with a cheater and staying with one which is what he expected me to do so instead of taking accountability for him messing up the marriage and me trying to fix it he chose to be critical. I told him, " I know I'm a good woman" and he said, " I know what a good woman is trust me." This implied to me that there was someone else in the picture that he was sure was a good woman. I told him his definition of a good woman is someone who will tolerate all of his crap and stay. I wasn't that woman and he didn't like that.

When he got back from Philly and came to see our son, he didn't say anything to me. He had brought me gifts from his family and a gift that had Mir's name on it but it didn't say who it was from. When I asked him, he claimed it was from a friend. I didn't discover until later, the friend he said gave me that for Mir was a girl he was dealing with, whom I would soon find out who she was and what her name was. One day he came to my house and took a shower and washed his clothes without asking me, saw Mir for a bit and then left. He never spent more than an hour at my house. I let him know shortly after he left,

"So we're on the same page, when you are here in my apartment, you are only here to see Mir, You are not authorized to do your hygiene or go into my kitchen and help yourself or use any of my stuff. Where you're staying at should have a shower and there are laundromats you can wash your clothes at. You are not allowed to spend the night here or be in my bed. You must call me in a reasonable amount of time before you come to my house. If you pop up without telling me, I will not open the door for you. If you don't follow these guidelines, you won't be allowed to come inside of my house and we can conduct your visits across the street in the fitness center or somewhere we both can agree upon. We are separated until we're able to get divorced, therefore my things is just that, mine. You won't be coming into my house disrespecting or using me. Respect me and my stuff or get out. If you don't leave when I tell you to, I will contact the police and have you removed and possibly trespassed from here. Point blank. We can make this easy or complicated. If you think I'm being a bitch, re-evaluate everything you have said and done to me and realize that your actions and words are the cause for why things are the way they are and have to be. Let's not complicate anything further than what it already is and has been. Take care, God bless, and I hope you enjoy your day." He ignored my message because he did not agree with the boundaries I was setting in place.

Mack is notorious for breaking boundaries and taking advantage of females. He's a user and if you don't stop him in his tracks he will continue to do so with no remorse. I was keeping in contact with my attorneys and they told me to get an address for him to be served at. When I texted him and asked for one, he said, "I don't have one."

I told him that his base address will be used to serve him. He insisted it get sent to his new address when he got one but I didn't have time to wait. On that same day, I sent him a list of things to get from the store for our son and he didn't comply with that. He wasn't able to get one of the items I needed and said that he had no money. How did he not have money? I'm unsure. He was making about $3,000+ each month so he definitely was lying. A few days later, Patty, in Philadelphia responded to a message I had sent her a year ago about respecting the fact that I am his wife and she shouldn't feel comfortable being around a married man without respect to meeting his wife. I'm not sure why she waited so long to respond but I believe it's because when he went to Philadelphia, he told her everything going on so she felt the need to respond and be very hostile and demeaning to me by calling me out of my name, bringing up my past that he had told her and telling me to go find my sons real father. I sent the messages to Mack that she sent to me and he ignored me. He did not correct the female nor take up for me which further confirmed he had a part in it. This further confirmed this marriage needed to be over. He never was at my defense for anything that didn't benefit him but for females he saw a benefit in, he would be.

One day while Mir was sleeping and when I got bored and curious one day since I knew his username and password from him giving it to me previously, I logged into his Google mail account from my phone and inside there I could see his emails. One of the emails was a confirmation of an Edible Arrangements order. I knew we weren't on good terms and that he didn't buy them for me. The pickup location for the order was about five minutes away from my house and I started to go wait in the parking lot and see what happened but I decided not to. Mir was two weeks old and I didn't think I should do that with him but the thought crossed my mind. Sherry and I were chatting on Facebook and I told her what I saw. I told her it must be someone in Philadelphia. She said it's definitely not and I don't know why he would even do this so close to home. I was baffled as well. When I went into the Notes section of his iCloud account, I saw a list of females' names and birthdays. One of them was Bryna's information and the other was another ex-girlfriend of his named Madison. The last one was a name I had never heard of before, her name was Moesha. I thought to myself who is Moesha? Little did I know, what I was about to find out.

CHAPTER SIX: Arrest and Adultery

My first instinct to figuring out who Moesha was is to go on Facebook and search her name. There she appeared with three different profiles. I checked all of the profiles out. Two of them were old accounts from when she was younger and the third one was the most recent and active account. I saw that she was also in the military like Mack and I. I told Sherry the name but she didn't confirm or deny anything except she said again, "I don't know why he would do something close to home like that." She knew something. I decided to send Moesha a friend request and a message with pictures of him and I to just give her a warning that Mack is married with a newborn and if she is involved with him she needs to be careful because he is bad news. That day she accepted my friend request and wrote back on the message implying that she's not worried about me or him. That's when I realized that she does know him. She told me to call and ask him since I blow his phone up any other time. This girl must've forgot the fact I said I just had a baby by him and that I was his wife calling his phone repeatedly to figure out what was going on with the way he was acting and his disappearances was a completely normal reaction to someone figuring out that they are being deceived and not having help with their child. The conversation ended and I sent screenshots to Mack letting him know I was on to what he was doing and why he was mistreating me. Later that day I noticed I had two missed video chat calls from Moesha. I wrote her a message and asked her what she was calling about and told her to enjoy Mack because if he cheated on his wife to be with her, he would do the same thing to her and to take care. She responded saying, "Cause I wanted to wish you nothing but happiness my dear, you don't have to see screenshots though. He already knows what it is and so should you. I'm not the type to talk my darling. But if you never want to run one, let me know. That should be the only time you up in this inbox. But anyway take care of my baby boy, can't wait to meet him. Bye pumpkin"

It was concerning the fact that she claimed my baby as hers after only dating Mack for less than two weeks. This was scary for me because all I could think about was how desperate she wanted a baby by Mack and the fact that she may try to kidnap Mir or do something to him. I wanted to keep my baby away even more because what she said was very foul and made me feel very uncomfortable. Of course, Mack was in the background hiding his hand by not participating in it by defending me, but rather egging her on to continue to bother me. I told her how much she sounded like a fool and blocked her from there. Before I blocked her, I saw posts from around the same time I gave birth about her going to Philly with Mack spending time and making references about him being worrisome.

I had planned to take Mir to Philadelphia to meet Mack's family when he was a couple of months old but after this encounter, I refused and told them all they are going to have to come to Virginia to see Mir. Besides, that's what they should've done anyways instead of expecting me to travel to them after just having a baby. Sherry told me that she was going to tell me there was no point in me coming up there because Moesha's been coming up there with Mack and she wanted to look out for me. Sherry told me Correll didn't care at all he just wanted to see the baby. So at the cost of my feelings, just delivering a baby and suffering postpartum depression as well as regular depression he was going to be inconsiderate about my feelings if I ran into Mack and Moesha? That was so insensitive and if anything they should've come to me. I shouldn't be driving hours to go see them but I guess that was them taking advantage of me instead of protecting my feelings and my baby from being in that drama with Mack and Moesha.

Before I removed Moesha off of social media, she had made a status saying, "When she gets mad, she has her doubts but when she's happy nothing can come between them." The last two statuses I saw was that she was making a master plan and that she was most definitely planning on going back to school while carrying her little one. This sounded a lot to me like she was already pregnant or planning to be pregnant by Mack while he was still married to me. This girl was obsessed with pregnancy from what I could see. I texted Mack's phone and told him our son was more important than him being out with a female. He didn't respond. When I would call his phone wondering where he was at, he wouldn't answer. The time he did answer I emphasized what he was doing was wrong and that I knew about the Edible Arrangements. He became very hostile and told me he wasn't coming to my house that day. He knew he was caught and didn't want to face me. I'll admit the more I discovered what Mack was doing behind my back, the more I did not want Mack to be around me either and I became extremely bitter but that's normal, what else was I supposed to be at the time, happy and filled with joy?

I was already going through a lot and it had me in a very dark state of mind. Some days, I can't remember how I made it through while taking care of Mir but I did. It got to the point where I stopped letting him see our son for a few days because I needed to process what was going on and get myself together. I wanted to begin healing so I wouldn't lose my mind at the mere thought of everything and it was impossible with him being around me for a short time barely helping. He showed up to my house unannounced one day after I had told him not to come over. I was home but I didn't want to be around him at all. I could not face him and the last thing I wanted to do was act out of emotion and it turn violent because of the pain I was feeling inside. Yeah, you could say it was selfish and me being bitter. I have no problem admitting to that but how could he think I would be mentally and emotionally okay being around him playing up under my nose with someone else while I'm still his wife and having a newborn son?

I was livid. I told him that day that I was going to let his command know about the suspected affair as well as him getting served the divorce papers on base. I texted one of his superiors and was telling them how I don't know where he is living at and what he's doing but when I first had the baby, he left me to go out of state and I believe that he is involved with someone else but I wasn't 100% sure, it was only speculation with a high accuracy of being correct. I also wanted to find out if they had information on where his address is so I could get the divorce papers served to him. The woman that I had met in the hospital which was a female chief of his texted me back and said she would get with his superiors in the morning and have a talk with them. I remember this day like it was yesterday, I had called to talk to my grandma on the phone who I confided in and I was literally crying so much on the phone uncontrollably to her about how Mack has been to me and how I didn't deserve it and how unfazed he is by his actions and how it affected me. My grandma assured me that God was going to take care of everything and that there was no need for me to worry. While it was true, it's so hard to believe it when you're in a situation that looked like it had no end or sunshine coming.

Literally, the next day is when my grandma's words and God's work definitely showed itself to be true. Mack texted me the next morning and said that he was on his way to my house. I told him that he was no longer allowed to be at my house and that we could meet at a public place. I wasn't sure he had made it yet but I had sent him a warning message before his expected arrival that said, "This is your warning. If you do not get away from my door and leave my house I am calling the police and having you removed immediately so it's best you go on like now. I do not want you, your drama, or that girl at or in my house. You don't even really care about Mir truthfully. For the little few minutes you come, it doesn't even help. You know just as well as I do you just come to cause problems and I'm not tolerating it. Your whole paternity leave has been spent away and in Philadelphia with your girlfriend neglecting your newborn son and wife, so like I said, leave now or police will be arriving shortly. I am not playing with you."

He never showed up nor did he respond and I thought it was because of my message but it wasn't. I called his command again to see what information they had for me and that's when his direct supervisor told me he was getting ready to give me a call. Instead of providing me with an address for him, they didn't have one and when I asked him about the update I gave them on him misusing his paternity leave he didn't speak on that either. He proceeded to tell me that Mack had been arrested.

"ARRESTED, ARRESTED FOR WHAT?"

My heart sank and started beating really fast. The supervisor said, "He was caught in the female barracks room with a girl."

That was considered an unauthorized area for males to be and they knew he was married to me. I wasn't shocked that it had anything to do with a female; Mack's life seems to be based around females. It was the fact that he had actually got caught and arrested for it. I listened to this man tell me some of the details of what happened and he told me an investigator would be coming to my house to talk to me.

"I have tried on several occasions to redirect Mack because I could tell he was lost with no direction but it didn't work." He said, "I really have no hope for your husband and we are recommending he get kicked out through an administrative separation."

Mack had a lot of behavioral issues in the Navy and being caught in this girl's room while I had just given birth to his son put the icing on the cake that it was time for him to go. When we hung up the phone, I shouted and cried because God got him. God knew what was going on while I stressed and worried so much trying to put together my own investigation. He really got him back for everything he lied to me about and I didn't even have a part in it. I thought when I had informed them about me suspecting him cheating that it was a follow up from that but the man told me that they told him and the girl to stay away from each other before I had delivered my baby but neither of them listened. Apparently, they saw that they were having interactions more than they should have and tried to intervene on my behalf.

Thinking back to when I was in the hospital, Mack told me his chain of command wanted to speak to him about something but when I questioned him on what it was about he ignored it and told me he would be getting moved to another shift and workspace. A few days later, I heard from the investigator and he set up a time to come to my house and talk to me about everything that was going on. Mir was a few weeks old at the time so he figured it would be more convenient to come to my residence and discuss things. He discussed what happened and how my ex got caught, confirmed that it was in fact Moesha he got caught with, and asked if I would like to provide a written statement. I agreed to do the statement and I also let him know that there were more adultery that were committed as well and I confirmed it with two other females. He told me

I would be able to get a full report of what occurred and what was reported by witnesses on the base.

In between caring for my son, Mir, I would let my mind roam freely and compose what I was going to write in the statement.

In the letter I wrote," I am making a free and voluntary statement to the Chief who was known to be a Command Public Information Officer."

I stated the date I kicked him out of my house due to current and ongoing marital issues we were having as well as verbal and emotional abuse. I expressed the knowledge of him purchasing an Edible Arrangements for someone with the caption on the arrangements as, "It don't take a whole day to recognize sunshine." I knew that due to us having marital issues the arrangements weren't being delivered to me. I also had a suspicion that he was fraudulently staying in the barracks where he wasn't supposed to be, since we were married and both received money to be used for housing us as a couple. I included information about the notes section in his phone and the female name I found and what had happened after that. I revealed the text messages from Bryna about living in my house and him making remarks that he shouldn't have married me and should've married her and she had at one point mentioned him letting her and their daughter move in.

Finally, I included the messages between the Shelby girl in Philadelphia who admitted and sent screenshots about them being intimate together before and during our relationship and marriage. I included all screenshots as proof to back up everything I said. A few days after I submitted my statement, I received a report of the arrest of Mack and Moesha from the base security precinct. The first page was the incident report with the subject of unauthorized guest, meaning Mack was unauthorized in Moesha's barracks rooms and the Uniform Code of

Military Justice Article number. The complainant was Moesha's roommate who was a military police. The offense Mack committed was Failing to Obey General Order; Standards of conduct.

The other witnesses were included as well. The report stated that the police precinct received a call from the barracks petty officer that a male individual was staying in the roommate's room. The witness and the barracks officer found Mack hiding in the closet. He was instructed to pack up his things and follow them downstairs to wait for his chain of command to arrive. The reporting personnel asked Mack for his identification which he refused to provide. The roommate who is a military police officer (MPO) gave account that on a few days she would hear her roommate Moesha talking to a male and they went into her room. In the morning time when it was time for Moesha to leave again, the MPO stated Mack stayed behind. At one point he got up to use the restroom and went back into Moesha's room. When the MPO left and got back to her room, she saw Mack lifting up a planter outside the door and placing something underneath it. He entered the common area and she asked him who he was. He told her that he was Moesha's boyfriend. When Moesha returned and went into her room they could be heard talking. The following morning they exchanged I love you and the MPO heard Mack go back into the room. She left the room and Mack still stayed behind.

The time of both Mack and Moesha's arrest and escort was notated and they were at the police precinct together. After all information was processed, both of their chains of command retrieved them from the precinct. On the next few pages were voluntary statements made by the MPO, who happened to recently arrived from boot camp and training school. In her statement, she stated on occasions she would hear the bed squeaking, Mack grunting, and Moesha moaning. She also heard them both in the shower and talking to each other. The next couple of witness statements were from male enlisted military staff. They noted in the report that the bed was not made and a suitcase was on the floor. The closet door was unlocked and when they opened it they found Mack standing there. When they asked him if he was in the military, he told them yes and that he works there. They asked him if he attended the barracks policy training and he said yes. They asked that question because he made a statement of not wanting any trouble and that he was about to go so there would be no problem. The males asked him to pack his things so they could go downstairs to wait. Mack told them with an attitude that he was going to leave. They reiterated that he needed to pack his belongings and exit the building. He then walked to his car and the staff said he had and I don't care type of attitude as he walked to his car. He was instructed to just wait and he told them he's not walking around with his laundry so he's going to put it in his car and get his I.D. When asked for his I.D, he refused to give it to them. By that time his chain of command showed up and security was called to take over the scene. The other witness gave the same and included that there was no need for them to call his command and when they asked for his I.D. again he refused and said he's good.

Following all of this was Mack and Moesha's front and side view mug shot. Although the mug shot was in black and white, his facial expression displayed that he was disgruntled. Moesha's face looked clueless and innocent as if she was unsure why she was placed in front of the camera holding up a board with her name and case number.

The next day he showed up at my apartment unannounced after I already told him to not come to my house. He never stayed longer than thirty minutes to an hour and realistically he wasn't much of a help. He would bring some diapers, some wipes, and formula here and there but every time he did that he looked completely unhappy doing so when he brought it to me. I knew his family was directing him to do it in fear of him being on child support but it didn't last long. He wanted to come around a lot more after I found out about his adultery and it was more so to aggravate me with seeing his smirking face, a face a lot of victims of narcissists are familiar with after a backstabbing or heinous act has been committed.

At this point, I'll admit, my heart was so full of anger and bitterness; I could not stand for him to even be in my presence especially not in my home. In my mind, I just wanted to hurt him so bad in every way possible because he didn't have a problem hurting me at all before, during, and after my pregnancy. I was already depressed and going through postpartum depression. I couldn't separate the act he committed and abandoning our son from having a two parent household like he previously promised to give after our first separation. I was heavily in my feelings and I know his parents was well aware of everything going on, I reached out to them. Normally, I don't like reaching out to families and would rather resolve it between myself and the other person; however, they always used to tell me that if I needed to talk that they were there. It wasn't until all this went down, that they started acting funny and didn't want to hear anything about my feelings of the situation.

His mother and father were pretty cold and unsupportive of what their son put me through. However, the only person who was supportive and attentive was Sherry. It raised my brow a bit at times, but what she was saying seemed to be genuine and heartfelt. I didn't discover until later though that it was not all the way genuine and it was a way to be friendly to me just to be involved with my baby. That's a part of the story I'll explain later in the book. The first message I got from her was, "Happy Mother's

Day to you! I've been hearing about everything that's going on and I've been trying to stay out of it being as though I'm the newbie to the clan. But just know, I sympathize with you and I know what you're going through 100%. In fact, I was you when I was pregnant with my daughter and her father and I broke up when I was two months pregnant. It was heart breaking. I know you probably don't want to hear this but trust me there's definitely light at the end of the tunnel. Mothers have a way of pulling through and being strong through the toughest situations. Our natural reaction is never to run or give up. That's what makes us so great. You'll see. Right now just focus on you and your son. Believe it or not, he feels every emotion you are feeling right now. So try to pick yourself up and please stop crying. I promise you, this situation is going to turn around in ways you'll never believe. As a woman I'm telling you to let Mack learn his own way; they always do. Let him see that you'll be just fine with or without him. I know it's hard but you're going to have to "act" hard for a little while. Once he sees no more tears and sees you moving on with your happy life, I guarantee you'll see a change. I know you don't know me and we've only met once but please believe me. I didn't tell Correll I was reaching out to you but just now I got your back 100%. We've gotten into our own heated discussions over all of this because I have strong feelings about what Mack should and should not be doing. I just want to shake some sense into him. So hang in there Hun, try to enjoy this day and know I'm fighting for you behind the scenes."

I responded, "Hi Mrs. Sherry, I am just now seeing this message. Had I not went through my message requests, I wouldn't have seen this at all. Thank you for writing me and Happy Mother's Day to you as well. As far as Mack goes, it has been extremely hard dealing with him since I was in Japan. Everything unfolded after I found out about him going to get his child's mother and not knowing anything about it until after the fact. Since then it's been quite a roller coaster ride. A lot of stuff he's done he's attempted to hide from me and justify to the point he's been making me feel crazy for my thinking when I know for a fact what's right and not right in a marriage. I've been shown so many red flags about him and even more so now that I am here locally. It has hurt me so much to my core that I have tried to love and care about him so much, tried to honor him as a husband and support him and lost my contract in Japan after getting pregnant for him all so I could be here with him and I got nothing in return but a lot of heartache, regret, and pain. I'm trying my hardest to cope with it knowing I'm going to be okay and things are going to get better. I'm thankful for the values my parents instilled in me and past experiences I have dealt with before that gave me knowledge and strength on how to deal with certain things. I've realized a while ago that Mack is still young and we were both raised two different ways and in different environments. I just thought things might be slightly difference once I got back but I was surely wrong. The stuff I've tried to tell him myself to help him and help our marriage, he isn't receptive to because he doesn't have full understanding of what he truly got into. Communication and selfishness are two things he struggles with a lot both of which causes huge issues in a marriage. I'm going to take what you said into consideration and back off and just focus on myself and my son. God knows I don't want anything to happen to him."

"Yes, that's exactly what you should do. Focus on you and your baby. And yes it will be hard at first, but you can do it. Find something to do in your spare time for your own sanity so the situation isn't always on your mind. Try to stay positive and happy so the baby can feed off your positive vibes. I'm not sure how your relationship is with your family but knows you have me here for you now and after the baby is born." She said.

"No problem." I said, "I just don't understand why I can't be respected and valued by him. I'm not sure if you know about the friend he has but he hung with her anyway after I've told him I didn't feel comfortable with him doing that and I don't even know her. It's total disrespect to me and people keep trying to convince me to work it out with him and it's like how. I'm constantly being put last when I put him first. It hurts to be on the receiving end of the pain knowing he's just down the street from me enjoying himself not knowing or checking up on me for days to see how I'm doing. This isn't love. It's like a slap in the face to me to know I come last. Some of his people trying to make me feel like I'm wrong for my feelings of how marriage should be in my opinion and that I haven't known him well enough to say I tried but I know I did even while I was gone. There's no going back to dating days or trying to make it work after I was sent to jail and uncared for. All he cared about while I was in jail was his birthday. And most recently he told me he wanted an apology and I didn't do anything to him that night Everyone keeps saying they don't want to be biased but I feel it's only because they know some or all of the stuff I'm saying about him and things is true but they don't want me to know that or make him feel like they agreeing with me."

She said, "Unbelievable. I really don't know what to say about his actions. We both know he's wrong. He doesn't think he's wrong though. Like you said, he wants to do what he wants to do. When right now he should be stepping up being a man and taking care of his responsibilities. I'm in no way telling you to try to work things out with him. Because no one can make him do anything he doesn't want to do. And right now he doesn't seem like he wants to be married or responsible. That's why I was telling you to focus on you and your son. I mean, think about it. Do you really want to be arguing with him and the nonsense he's doing? Do you really want to be worried about what he's doing when you're not around? I'm pretty sure you don't. Trust me, I know all of this is heart breaking and frustrating but count your blessings honey. That the truth has come out. Yes I know it's late because you're already married and pregnant but I believe every situation has the potential to be worse. And it could've been worse. He has lots of growing up to do. I think both of you had different ideas of what marriage was supposed to be like. Not saying anyone's idea was wrong or right buy they're just not in sync. Y'all aren't on the same page or level. But what I do think y'all should do is go to family counseling not necessarily marriage counseling or couple counseling. But family counseling to talk about and learn how to co-parent in a functional way. It's unfortunate things are this way but you cannot save or change him. The dysfunctional cycle needs to stop and the only way that's going to happen is if y'all get counseling so your son grows up with parents who work together for the sake of him."

"Exactly." I said. "Everyone has tried to talked to him and tell him things but he has his own way of thinking of what's right. No I don't want to keep hurting, arguing and stressing or having to check behind him constantly. A man does not do these things or make his wife feel inferior or last to anyone, put their wife in jail, etc. I feel like I've put in enough effort to realize it's not working now or anytime soon regardless of what anyone tells him. The fact that we are living in two different places right now makes me wonder what he's doing when I'm not around meanwhile I'm continuing to hear that separation may cause things to work out later when in reality it is contributing to him doing more and more of what he wants and thinking less of me. I feel like it pretty much hit rock bottom and it can only get much worse from here. I don't want the baby to be involved in this and be out of my hands either because he isn't responsible enough and I don't trust him taking care of the baby properly. It's just saddening and sickening to have to think about it every day. I wanted this marriage to work because I'm a firm believer in it not so much divorce but as he grows up and realizes things I can't wait and continue to get hurt in the process and my mind is pretty much made up to let him go completely. You are right I agree. There are effective co parenting classes offered by the military and I am going to look into it."

"That's a good idea. And I'm sure you know what you need to do once your baby is born too. This is so sad. I told Correll I am so disappointed in Mack. I believe he can also use some type of therapy to find out why he does the things he do. Something ain't right. And for the record, I agree and have said most of the things you've said. But the reality of the matter is no one can change him. So as far as you, "How is your living situation? Are you ok?"

I replied, "I believe he does too. Honestly, based on the psychology class I took, he shows very strong narcissistic personality traits to me. It's scary. I'm living okay. I have all of my furniture except my living room but I'm working on it. My command has been helping me get on my feet and recover."

She said, "I dated a guy before like that. Nothing I ever did was good enough and I always doubted myself. He also had a lot of female friends. I couldn't take it anymore. I just got tired of the drama. I was literally exhausted. When we broke up, I was up hurt but eventually it was like a weight lifted off my shoulders. Girl, you just don't know. That's good that they're helping you. So are you going to get your own place there in Virginia Beach?"

I replied, "I feel the same way. Everything thing I do and still isn't enough. I have my own place now in Virginia Beach. About five minutes from him. It's in a centrally located area. He travels this road near my apartment often and I wouldn't be surprised if he figured out where I live because we looked at these apartments' together weeks before."

She said, "Yeah. Usually guys like that need weaker minded women. Strong women and those types don't mix well. Look at it as a blessing. I'm not saying y'all will never work but he has a lot of growing to do first and foremost. Well I'm glad you have your own place. Faith, despite how things look right now, you'll be just fine. If he finds out where you live, that's cool. I doubt he'll give you any problems. Meanwhile, look for that family therapist. You're almost five months right? Getting near that time to start baby shopping. You have enough on your plate you don't need any unnecessary drama or worrying."

I replied, "I agree 100%. My personality and my views are probably too strong for him to handle that it scares him honestly because he's used to dealing with girls. I am looking into doing some counseling to help me cope with everything and to get back on track so I can be mentally and spiritually strong for my sake and more importantly Mir. I am 21 weeks today. I have bought him a lot of outfits so far and I have a mattress for his crib. I am getting the crib in a couple weeks, car seat and all of the basic necessities using a list I got from ToysRus and a close friend. Yea, definitely a lot on my plate right now, so I'm seeking out peaceful methods for the coming months and the future.

She said, "Ok cool. And like I said before, please don't hesitate to reach out to us for anything. And please don't use any unnecessary energy and time arguing with Mack. It's not getting you anywhere. You've tried; you've given all you can. It is time to be selfish and be all about yourself and Mir, of course."

I replied, "Okay I won't and I don't plan on contacting him. He's going to have to contact me. I am just glad to finally see his real colors and I'm not going to even try to repaint them. It's clear he does not love or care about me at all regardless of what his words may say and what he may portray in front of his family. I don't know why they feel I should go back to the dating stage to get to know him better because they don't feel as if I've been in long enough to say I tried. I know well enough that he's not for me, he needs to grow up and there's no more me and him relationship wise. And that's exactly the mindset; I am about my son and myself now. He may wake up from the dream he's in one day but it be too late as far as him and I go. Hopefully he will wake up for his children's sake."

"Yup!" She said.

"I'm going to go fix myself some food and take it in for the night. Have a good night and I'll keep in touch!"

"I think his family keeps saying that more for his sake because they know he has messed up and he's about to lose a good thing. Have a good night's sleep. I'll be talking to you."

I took her words at face value wholeheartedly believing she was being genuine about it. Sherry and I would talk just about a couple of times a week on Facebook messenger so every conversation she and I have is still in my messages. She would give me information on what was going on with Mack since I wasn't talking to him much and that he was coming back and forth to Philadelphia. She also mentioned that after my arrest occurred, he kept reaching out and I ignored him, which I did but there were a couple times I responded back to him but he had me blocked while I was pregnant and I wasn't even bothering or wanting to speak to him since my arrest so it didn't make sense.

She said, "I don't think he understand he messed up big time and your attitude is his fault. As usual (because most men think like this) they think they can say sorry or just wait for time to pass by and everything resets. But women don't work like that."

At one point, I brought up the fact that I was just fed up after my arrest and finding out Bryna was in my house, I said, "I don't believe in divorce but I cannot and will not stay around while he does what he wants. I will continue to be hurt."

Sherry said, "Neither do we. That's why Correll keeps on him about calling you and fixing things."

"You have to remember, Mack grew up in dysfunction. That's why all of what he's doing makes sense to him." I said, "Mack has to grow first and I can't wait on that. It will be a while. Divorce is definitely the route I'm going. I tried everything. I talked about counseling he didn't want to do it. He won't let other females go. He does not want to be married. He has a lot of baggage and we are so unequally yoked. He is the cause, I tried and his family will have to accept it when it's final. He having two baby moms, one a girlfriend and one ex-wife is his issue. You're right though. He grew up in a dysfunctional household that I understand. I didn't though. My parents are still together 25 years later and I have looked up to their marriage so much. It breaks my heart to divorce but it's in my best interest and for my son too. On top of that I'm trying to continue in criminal justice and having a record will prevent that if another episode with Mack occurs so to eliminate that, I choose to look out for me the same way he is doing. Mack doesn't want to fix his marriage and his dad can't make him. He will revert back to old ways quickly if he's forced to change."

She said, "He had a crazy mother." Sherry said. "The mother and father lived together for years but weren't together for the sake of the kids. But meanwhile lived separate lives. They argued badly all the time. And he made up for the dysfunction by buying them anything and everything which made the kids materialistic."

I said, "Yup, you're right. Which explains why Mack is constantly buying materialistic things to fill the void he has? I'm talking five or six items for his car interior being shipped every few days."

She said, "EVERYBODY needs therapy. Mom, dad, kids, you and me! All of your feelings are natural. I totally understand how you feel. You're not wrong at all. His family is going to have his side because that's his family. Not saying that's right but that's how some families are. At this point whatever happens is a result of his actions. I don't know what happened on his birthday or in December between y'all but I think y'all could have started some counseling and tried to work things out. Instead it just seems like things just spiraled out of control. You can't base a marriage off of living with each other for two months. Marriage is hard and yes you have to fight through some things. It's give and take with a lot of compromising. But he just gave up and didn't want to try. So everything else from this point forward, oh well. I just think somehow he needs to be held responsible for his actions. He didn't get corrected enough in the past. That's the problem. When you're not used to getting chastised and corrected when you're young, then you become an adult and someone corrects you. You have a hard time receiving it."

I told her, "I had an issue with Mack putting another woman and his female best friend before me."

She said, "No woman wants to share her boyfriend/husband with another woman or "best friend."

I told her at this point I was focusing on and looking out for myself and my son and she said, "I understand that. You got to do what's best for you and your son. You can't keep putting yourself through the emotional ups and downs."

She and I had so much conversation for just meeting each other one time in person; you would've thought we were the best of friends for years. She was so open to telling me things, without judging and being me, at least she appeared that way for a while. After Mack got caught with Moesha, Sherry told me Mack called his dad and blamed everything on me about him getting caught with Moesha and that I framed him when in reality I was on bed rest after having Mir not knowing where he was even at. Mack's constant blaming has a name for it. It's called scapegoating which is a hostile social-psychological discrediting routine by which people move blame and responsibility away from themselves and towards a target person. He was always notorious for the reactions and feelings of mines to his abuse by blaming me.

She said, "Well, either way, I don't care. Even if it were you, he still was somewhere where he shouldn't have been. Bottom line."

Sherry also warned me to let my command know everything going on because Mack's mother, Tamesha was pretty much out for revenge and was going to call my superiors to say I was harassing her with information about what her son did to me and my son and she didn't care to hear it. Sherry would always give me words of affirmation such as don't worry about Mack and Moesha their karma is coming for him, she was a downgrade, ghetto, sugar mama that paid his cell phone bill. She would tell me how none of his family but Mack's grandmother would respond to the Facebook posts of Mack and Moesha about their relationship and send me screenshots to prove it. She helped a lot when it came to the evidence I needed in court. She told me when Mack tried to bring her to Philadelphia no one wanted her around and said to me that Mack stopped talking to his family for several months because they weren't accepting of his girlfriend and that "bringing the dippy chick to their house is out of the question." She had also said they shouldn't be even thinking about a third or fourth child at this point. Mack's command already knew about the affair going on before I knew. I had suspicions but no proof. Mack and Moesha were under investigation for what they did and were warned to stay away from each other, but they did not listen. He didn't tell me where he lived at nor did he ask about our son.

When I somewhat got out of my feelings about the stuff, I started researching information about attorneys that way this process could get started. I went and met a few of them and decided on whom to go with. When I hired my attorneys, who happened to be a top law firm in Virginia, they would always give me pointers on how to handle Mack and matters of our case. At first, I was headed in the wrong direction by allowing my bitterness and anger of all the toxic behavior going on, stop him from being around our son but they quickly informed me that it would not look good for my case because things could turn around to where he gets custody and I get visitation because of my unwillingness to provide visitation. I had to get my act together really quick because there was no way in hell, I was going to allow it to even go that far. I texted him that day after speaking with my attorneys and told him a few things so we would be on the same page. I let him know about medical issues Mir was having as well as appointments with dates and times for him to attend. My attorneys had drafted up divorce papers so I told him in advance when the court date would be. I gave him information on the best place to meet that would be most convenient for me considering I was the one bringing the baby and still healing from giving birth. I also told him that he was not allowed to bring any additional persons that we had not mutually agreed on while the visitation is conducted. I told him this because in speaking with Bryna, she told me while she was pregnant with their child and after she gave birth Mack tried to schedule visitation and bring his girlfriend, Madison, at the time along to show in Bryna's face that he no longer is with her. She also added that Mack was trying to start a fight between the two of them and that Madison was pregnant at the same time she was as well which caused a bunch of drama which is also why I banned him from coming to my house. I didn't want that to happen to me and with Mack, he does things regardless of your feelings as another way to hurt you after the relationship is done. He didn't respond to my text message outlining everything. He blocked me. I know this because we are both iPhone users and when your texts are successfully delivered they will appear in blue. When the other person has blocked you, the message will appear in green. He didn't show up at Mir's appointment later that day either.

After that appointment was over, I sent him a text with the results of what the doctor said regarding Mir's medical issue. That text was green as well and he still didn't respond. I would send him daily pictures of Mir and continue to keep him informed of what was going on with him and still, he would not respond. I didn't hear from him for months.

November 2016, I decided to share my story with Facebook and break my silence. I didn't want to hold up a façade anymore and after Mack and my entire marriage bliss was posted online, I figured I would address the public by telling my story and how to avoid what I went through. I got a lot of feedback from people, some of which were in toxic situations and could relate to me. I got more support than I imagined and I knew later that I was going to turn everything into a book, Around the time of my birthday in December 2016, after coming back home from being away for the holidays, when I checked my mail I noticed an envelope addressed to me from Mack. I open the envelope to find a card that said this "This is your story unfolding day by day" with a picture of a typewriter. On the inside, it said, "It's your story. Fill it up with what you love and know that some of the best chapters are to come." Handwritten in the card was a message that said, "Great things await you, and the best has yet to come, Happy Birthday Faith."

This card did not sit right with me. It was not cheerful, but it was a dull card and symbolized to me Mack's subliminal message to me that he read my story on Facebook which I ironically got this card a month after I released my story so I knew he had to have seen it. I knew because we weren't talking or getting along that he didn't mean well so this card meant the complete opposite and that an ulterior motive for this was yet to come.

After he got served court documents, he filed a petition for custody. I don't know why he did that considering I already had something initiated, but I guess he did it because he wanted to say he filed something too even though he wasn't seeing Mir at the time and wasn't responding to my messages. When we went to court on the papers he had filed, my attorney was able to get it dismissed and have everything taken care of on the court date we already set. We were a few days into the new year of January 2017, and I received a text message from an unknown number. The person asked if Mack was over at my house. I asked who it was texting me and the response I got back was, "Just answer the question." I then figured out that it had to be Moesha, Mack's little newfound mistress. I responded and told her that I don't know how she got my number and to not text me, asking questions and that she should know where her boyfriend is at. She responded to the text telling me she just wanted to make sure that he didn't want me back. I told her to not push me into calling her command and telling them what was going on and that she was harassing me.

She said, "Girl goodnight."

I told her I would call her command for sure the next morning and that is when she informed me that she is out and that they aren't going to do anything. I told her I don't have time for games and she should not be calling or texting my phone about a man that doesn't even belong to her because he's legally married and that in due time she will see that she has no prize at all. She said, "I was most definitely right and thanks again for the warning."

I sent Mack screenshots of what went on and she texted me from his phone saying, "Girl he doesn't care, he's busy and goodnight." She just wanted to be relevant. Sherry said, "She's in your shoes now."

I told her that I felt like I wanted to fight Moesha at that point and Sherry said, "Please don't stoop to her ghetto level. She's not that bright. She's ghetto and dippy, which equals fun and no seriousness. I am sure why he likes her. She's ghetto, like his momma." I asked if Sherry had seen her come up there with Mack and she said, "I saw her briefly when he came here for money a couple of months ago. The mom has never met her and refuses to meet her. Dad is gullible."

CHAPTER SEVEN: Divorce and Drama

Here we were at this point after they both were no longer in the Navy; the divorce process began to start. Sherry told me Mack and Moesha ended up getting an apartment together and was trying to figure out how to maneuver the expenses of it after them both not being in the military anymore. Sherry said about Moesha, "She faked being suicidal to get discharged and it worked. But you didn't hear that from me. I don't think either one of them thought this dumb plan through."

I was thinking this girl was serious about this being with a married man that she gave up her career completely for him. Sherry also inquired about how the court process was going and when we went next and I had told her that the witnesses would be there to testify on what he did in the Adultery case and she said, "Oh wow. I would love to be a fly on the wall because I know he won't tell everything."

The first court date we had was a few days after Mack got kicked out in January 2017. When we went before the judge, I had an attorney representing me and he didn't. The judge advised him with the type of case there was, that it would be best for him to get an attorney and if he didn't, he would still be treated in the same manner being pro-se. He gave Mack about a month to figure out if he was going to self-represent in this matter or get an attorney. Court was adjourned. Mack hit me up after that court date to start seeing our son before any order was in place. He had gone months without seeing him and when I sent him pictures of Mir he would never acknowledge or ask how he's doing. He would ignore it. When I invited him to Mir's appointments he would never show up nor follow up about any of them. One time when Mir was sick, I asked him to buy a humidifier since the doctor said it would help. I had been taking care of Mir and footing the $190 a week daycare bill without Mack's help while he was buying and providing for his mistress. Periodically, he would buy a box of diapers here or there and the formula but every time he brought it he had an attitude and he never helped me with daycare.

Instead of buying the humidifier and nose drops, he gave me $20. My money was low and I told him I didn't want him to do just half, I wanted him to buy it since he hadn't helped me out with the major expenses. He wouldn't go and buy it and bring it to my house to make it more convenient for me either. As far as his visitation goes, I had reminded him that we would meet in public places. I told him I didn't feel comfortable with it being in my house so I suggested public places for him to interact with our son. I also told him that he is not to bring his girlfriend to our visitations at any time. He tried to argue with me about the locations I picked because they weren't convenient for him but the locations he was picking were further than the ones I was picking and in a different area then what he claimed was convenient. I told him it would be best for us to continue meeting at the same spots as before and he got mad and argued with me about that. He wasn't being considerate of the fact I was still recovering and did not need to drive a long distance with Mir.

At one of the visits, we met at a bookstore in the Virginia Beach mall. He saw Mir for a little bit and before he left, he told me to keep his girlfriend's name out of my mouth. I said, "I don't care about her, you're still married and I don't want any drama." About fifteen minutes after we both left the area Mack called me on the phone and asked what I wanted. He said, "If you don't keep my girlfriend's name out your mouth I'm going to have her beat your ass." At this point, he was inciting a fight between us and I was not tolerating it. Mir was still a new baby and I wasn't taking any chances with him getting me in trouble with the Navy, the law, and losing my baby. I texted him and told him visitation was cancelled due to his threats. He didn't respond. I went to the magistrate's office and filed a petition for his threats. They gave him a disturbance of the peace charges. He didn't ask to see Mir after that nor was he able to until the charges were clear in court because there was also a restraining order on him.

On Valentine's Day, Moesha texted me early in the morning from his phone saying, "We would like to wish Mir a happy Valentine's Day. I love you." I could tell it was her because of the spacing in her messages and her punctuation. Also, Mack didn't refer to Mir as his nickname; he would say his full name. When I responded to the message and told her to stop pretending to be him and leave me alone, I noticed the message went through green which meant I was blocked. When I told my attorney about Mack's charges, she said unless we have actual proof of what he said, it wouldn't hold up much in court. She suggested I drop the charges because we had a lot bigger fish to fry with the divorce. We went to court like a month later and I took her advice. I was updating Mack on Mir's health and he would not respond. I guessed he was still angry I pressed charges on him. My friends were sending me screenshots of him and Moesha openly professing their love for each other on social media. This girl was tagging him in statuses referring to him as her husband. On one post she said, "I'm going to dinner with my husband." Another said, "I'm going to church with my husband." He came to court on several occasions wearing a wedding band and not the one I bought him. He would flash it where I could see it. I was saving all the screenshots and printing them all in court. Everything they were doing was allowed to be used in court especially because they were admitting their relationship together. They continued to do it thinking it was harmless fun and to piss me off as well.

Sherry and I would talk on Facebook and she said that Mack was looking for a job and didn't have income coming in. She said that he and Moesha didn't properly plan to get out. She told me Moesha was working at Olive Garden.

Sherry said, "Mack was supposed to better himself self and he ended up married/divorced, with another child, kicked out the military, arrested, and now with no job." I laughed.

This girl had got out the military just to go be a server and live in low-income housing chasing after Mack. I knew Mack had to have some sort of job because he was living in an apartment after the Navy and I discovered the apartment address from a bank account we both had access to. As soon as he knew I figured out the address; he called the bank so fast and had his information removed. For some reason, he was trying to hide his address as if I was going to come and cause trouble and in reality, it was both of our responsibility to provide our addresses of where our child will be and to send court correspondence as well. Sherry also said that Mack wasn't talking to any of his family because of Moesha and that he was being isolated by her and for that reason and the fact that Sherry and Correll were about to get married in a few months, no one had money to give him to get an attorney. She told me to keep it on the hush that he was coming back with no attorney.

She said, "It seems like he sees a lot coming his way and so he's trying to dodge it for now. But there's no way to. So the next best thing to do is stretch it out as much as possible until he comes up with a plan B. I've put myself in your shoes. I've been you. In and out of court with my daughter's father for years, so trust me I know. That's why I told you, in the beginning, I was here for you. Mack's mom and dad are doing what any parent would do and that protects their son. Although that's not doing him any good because he doesn't see the error in his ways if they pacify him."

The next month we had court, the judge asked him if he had an attorney and he told him no so we proceeded. The judge informed him that the court hearing was for an adultery divorce and to handle child support matters. Mack told the judge that he did not have a job. The judge asked how was he able to keep up with his daily life if he doesn't have a job. Mack told the judge his tax money. When the judge asked him how much tax money he got he said about $1000 or so dollars. The judge said well how much is your rent and that's when Mack told him it was in the $900 and the judge was like well your tax money is only a month of rent so how else are you making it. My attorney told the judge that Mack was also an Uber driver and she had a picture of the sticker on his car. He told the judge that "Uber isn't a job; it's for income purposes only."

The judge looked at him with a side-eye and at that point is when I believe he knew Mack didn't have it all together. I tried to hold my laughs in at that point but it was so hard. The judge told him he did not care that he did not have a job and imputed an amount of income on him based on what he could be earning and calculated my income into the factor. The judge told him he had to pay $750 in support due by the 1st of each month and that he was going to continue the court case to another date for the attorney to get everything together with the witnesses of the adultery and for him to find a job. My attorney told the judge that Mack refused to give his address.

Mack tried to use the situation from my prior arrest to say he didn't feel comfortable giving me his address. Knowing that the situation was old and dismissed out of the courts, he still was holding on tightly to it to use it against me in court. The judge gave him a verbal order to provide his real address to him. He questioned the judge if he could give me a friend's address instead. The judge said, "No give her your address." He ended up giving his address which was in Norfolk, Va. The judge gave him temporary visitation which was on Mondays and Tuesdays from 5 pm to 8 pm. The judge set it that way because Mir was four months old, Mack wasn't involved, and the judge didn't find it feasible to have our son bouncing from house to house for long periods at such a young age. The judge told him that our son was not to be around any new lovers until the divorce is over. I knew that Mack had Moesha living with him especially after they both got out the military and needed each other and that was another reason why he didn't want me to have his address either because he knew if she was caught it would be trouble.

This particular day we had court was the day I was moving to Norfolk in my new apartment in close vicinity to the military base I was working at. I wanted to be prepared for Mack's visitation with Mir that Monday so I could be on time. After court was over and before I had to go back out to where I was living in Virginia Beach and start moving my things, I went to the address I was provided in court to check it out and make sure it was a safe area and become familiar with the neighborhood. I drove by and then left out; I was only there for about thirty seconds. I didn't get even get out of the car. As I was approaching the stop sign to leave the area, I saw a silver car turning in on the opposite side of me. The girl in the car was Moesha and she was looking directly at me. She sped up to where Mack's car was and before I turned at the stop sign, I noticed she got into his car and he did a U-turn. Mack followed my car, every turn I made, he made. I saw Moesha recording my every move. After about 10 minutes he stopped following me. Not thinking too much of it, nor did I reach out to him and ask why he followed me like that, I went back to my apartment in Norfolk and started gathering my things up to move. I spent that whole weekend moving everything by myself. That Monday, I got a knock on my door at night by a group of police. When I opened the door they told me I was being served with a stalking protective order. I was confused as to what they were talking about. When I looked at the order, I realized Mack told the magistrate that I had been stalking his house that whole weekend which was a complete lie. I had only gone once; I didn't cause trouble or anything. The address was given to me in court; I didn't obtain it through other means. The order was for me to not have any contact with Mack outside of Mir. I already was not doing so it didn't make a difference. I started to drop Mir off each week for his visitation. I never got out the car once, I let Mack come and get Mir from the backseat and put him back in. I would record every interaction I had with him to protect him from lying against me and trying to get me sent to jail. I saw his girlfriend peering out the window a few times and I knew that she wasn't supposed to be around our child.

On the first day, Mir went to his house, I texted Mack a list of things he needed to know about Mir. I don't know if he read it or not but he did not acknowledge it. I even told him about how to operate the safety bar of Mir's car seat but he told me not to tell him what to do. I ended up having to fix the safety bar myself so in the event, something happened Mir would not be harmed but he did not care about that at all. He couldn't stand me enough to even be concerned about the safety issues I was bringing up. One of the days, I had got off work late and accidentally left Mir's formula at the babysitter house trying to be on time for the visitation. Mack texted me about it and tried to argue about why it wasn't in the bag. I told him that its $20 and for him to go and buy it at the grocery store. In my opinion, as a father, you should always have extra of everything when your child comes over but that was not the case with him. I told him to be a dad and go and buy it and that it is his responsibility to contribute as well. I happened to be out taking care of business and a bit far away. He had the nerve to say isn't this child support is for and told me to bring the baby food and stop being childish. I wasn't being childish at all, it was his visitation and he could've gone to the store right by his house to get it. The crazy thing is when he brought up child support, he wasn't even paying it at that point so I had to remind him that yes that's what it's for and he hadn't paid out any money towards it. I decided to go ahead and stop what I was doing and buy it because I didn't want our child to starve in his care. Since Moesha was in the house, she could've easily went and got it. After all, she was claiming my son was hers right after I had him which was very creepy to me. I wanted to protect my baby from her. There are so many crazy stories of kidnapping and she gave me that vibe when she said that trying to be funny.

When I would take my son for visitation with Mack and Moesha was around, they would sometimes leave my son in the same diaper as the one I sent him in and it would be full of piss from all the formula Mir drank. I have had to text Mack a few times and tell him to make sure Mir comes back clean and that he should change him right before I picked him up. He would not acknowledge the text at all. Mir would always come back to me crying every time I got him back, and when I would send him, he would be calm and collective.

One of those times during visitation, the same day Mack and I had court or a couple days after, I received the diaper bag back and a can of formula was completely overturned. This had never occurred and it was obvious they purposely did it. They never replaced the can either. A month went by before we had to go to court again and the judge was giving Mack time to get a job as well. Literally four days after the judge put in the child support order, Mack filed for a modification. I don't know how he thought he was going to get away with decreasing the amount in that short amount of time after it was decided and before he even put any money towards the account. I got served the modification papers and by the next Friday we were in court. The judge denied it and told him he's going to have to make the payments. Mack was alleging that the judge used his income from when he was in the military which was not true. The judge dismissed the case.

The 1st of April rolled around and I did not see a payment of child support. I told my attorney that he had his girlfriend in the house with him when I would drop my son off for visitation. My attorney gave it a few days before she filed a Motion to Show Cause as to why he didn't make the payment and a contempt order for violating the fact that he had a female around our son during our divorce trial.

In between that time, Mack texted me demanding he get a copy of our son's birth certificate and social security card. I didn't have a copy to give to him and he should've got that the information on how to obtain both that day I got released from the hospital but he wasn't there. I ended up telling him the instructions on how to obtain those documents and that it would cost a fee and he still insisted I bring the documents. I didn't know why he was so anxious for it but I figured out later it was because he was trying to add our son to his military disability claim so he could get more money. We went to court that next month later for that hearing he start getting very disrespectful with the judge. The judge questioned why he would file to decrease his child support behind his back.

The judge said, "You haven't even given your wife a nickel." Mack continued to be disrespectful and he told the judge, "I got to make sure I'm good before my child is good," He was implying that he's taking care of himself before he takes care of our child. The judge told him he is going to serve 90 days in jail for contempt of court by not paying his child support.

Mack began to blurt out and cut the judge off and the judge said in a stern tone to the bailiff's, "Take him out." Mack started screaming, "Y'all don't care about the fathers' rights" and he continued to carry on loudly even more. The officers walked over to him and instructed him to put his hands behind his back. For a minute he was giving them a hard time and then he complied. They escorted him out of the court room into another room. One stayed in the room with Mack and the other came back out to monitor the court room. The judge told my attorney and me to go have a seat back on the benches. My attorney and I looked at each other not knowing what was going to happen from there. The judge went over all the other cases until he cleared the room out so we had to sit there for hours and wait. My adrenaline had kicked in because I had never seen Mack carry himself the way he did and especially to someone in a higher authority but he did it and it changed my complete outlook on him more than before. After the judge cleared his docket, he told the bailiffs to bring Mack back into the courtroom which they did. They sat him down in his chair still handcuffed. The judge said, "You aren't going to disrespect me or your wife. Now, I am sentencing you to 90 days in jail, but I am suspending the sentence and giving you 60 days to come up with the money from the past few months. If you don't, you will be serving time in jail." My attorney told the judge how Mack had a girl around our son and presented to the judge a screenshot I had got off of her page of her claiming our son as her stepson and parading him in a video. My attorney told the judge our intent is for him to not go to jail; we just want him to comply with the order and the child support. They didn't send him to jail for either that day. The court was adjourned and we were dismissed.

A few hours later I got a text message from an unknown number. This was the second time I got a message but this time I was able to identify exactly who it was. It was Moesha again. She sent me a picture of her and him together and said "Girl as bad as I want to beat your ass I'm not going to but please stop trying me. Stop looking at my pages, stop being a dumb old ass hoe. You can't be a mad ass for the rest of your life. "Grow up and have a good ass day, he isn't going nowhere girl and don't worry about blocking me I got it covered."

Little did she know although she said she wasn't going to touch me, she still made a desirable threat and it was valid in the police and court's position. I wasn't the one taking information from her page because I had her and Mack blocked on Facebook. However, during our divorce proceedings anything they posted in regards to their relationship during our marriage could be used against them so my friends were helping me out. Apparently Mack was going back and reporting how court went to her and she wanted to be involved and take up for him. Mir was supposed to go to his house that day for visitation. I brought a male with me to serve as an extra eye just in case something went down. Mack approached the car not paying attention to the fact that there was someone in the front seat. It wasn't until he opened the door to the car that he noticed I had a back up male in the car while he was trying to get Mir out of the car seat. Instead of getting Mir out of the car and taking him inside of his house, he placed the car seat back down, Mir cried in confusion, and Mack went to the front door of his house to get Moesha to stand at the door and watch. Moesha appeared out the door laughing and smiling. At this point there was a restraining order against me by Mack for lying that I was stalking him continuously at his house when I had only went to confirm the location once when I first moved to the area.

The day I picked him up and brought this male with me again, Moesha decided it would be funny for her to bring out the baby bag and for Mack to bring out the car seat with the baby in it. She approached my car door and went to open it and that's when I kept telling her to back away. She was laughing saying, "I got the bag." He never had her come outside with him before, usually she stayed in the house because she knew she wasn't supposed to be around my son and make it obvious in front of me. She refused to listen and opened my door without my permission. I was recording everything on video. It took everything in me not to get out the car and beat her ass. I really wanted to beat her until she was black and blue gasping for air for all her disrespect towards me not the fact that she got Mack, the problem guy, away from me but because of her interfering with our son. Mack put Mir in the backseat of my car and told him to say bye to her and told her to give him a kiss. Moesha kissed my baby on his face and laughed. I again told her to stay away from me and she laughed as her and Mack walked away holding hands and said, "Bye girl, have a good one," while still laughing loudly. After I picked Mir up, I went and got a restraining order against Moesha. I rescheduled the visitation that Mack had the next day with Mir because I wanted her to get served and not be anywhere near to retaliate against my child. After she got served, she turned around and filed one on me. I didn't get out the car one time, so there was no reason for her to file one on me. I wasn't threatening or anything. This was my first time with an in person encounter with her.

She had approached my car and it didn't make sense that she went to file an order when I never had threatened, continuously harassed her, or anything like she did to me but I believe Mack was hyping her up to do it. He has a lot of mind control over females and has no problem getting in their head and having them all against each other especially over his lies. That girl is crazy over Mack and didn't like me and all I wanted was for her to not be involved with Mack and my matters and to protect my child from the animosity.

When I attempted to take Mir to Mack's house on the rescheduled day, he came out the house at the time he was supposed to get him and walked in the other direction as if we were not there. I texted him and reminded him that this was a makeup day and he texted me back saying to get away from his house before he called the police. I told him okay we are leaving the area now. He was angry I took out a restraining order against this girl for continuously harassing me and he decided to stop seeing our son for good. My attorney said even though I had an order against Moesha, Mack still had visitation and I still had to obey the court order and take Mir for visitation. Each Monday and Tuesday I was still showing up and texting him when I arrived to come outside and get Mir. His and her car was home. He would not respond. It got to the point where I would say your visitation has started, give him five minutes and then leave the area.

A couple of weeks went by of this and I kept my attorney updated. I had got a letter a week later in the mail from Mack and it had no address underneath his name. It was addressed to me. When I opened the letter, it said "Do not come anywhere near me, Moesha or my apartment or I will call the police. You want to mess with people's lives. Jobs and futures with your mental and emotional instability, bitterness, and false accusations of harassment and I don't have time for it. Do not contact me in any way shape or form."

How could he sit here and say all of these things as if I'm just being a villain for no reason and that he's innocent? Mack caused so much drama and I had proof of every alleged harassment action in texts so there was no reason for me to lie.

I forwarded this evidence to my attorney and she told me we will show it to the judge and to no longer go to his house, just send him a text every Monday and Tuesday about when he wants to see Mir. She said it would further proof his disinterest in our son and more interest in causing drama between Moesha and me. I told her I didn't want him to say I was harassing him via text about visitation and she assured me that doing this would cover me in court just in case he lied and it's going to make him look bad. I took her advice and sent those texts every Monday and Tuesday asking if he would like his visitation yes or no. All of my messages were going through green from my iPhone to his which meant he had me blocked. Around the same time I got the restraining order on Moesha, one day I attempted to leave my house but noticed that my tire had been slashed and my car had been keyed which was also retaliation by them or one of their friends. When I had someone come check my tire out at the tire shop, a switch blade was found implanted in my tire. It's ridiculous the amount of revenge they had out for me, for taking all matters to court instead of physically beating them the way I really wanted too. The texts to him continued for months, eight months to be exact. I didn't hear from him at all about our son and I started to believe he wasn't living in the area anymore.

However, a few weeks later, after the restraining order on Moesha and with Mack not paying any support to me, he filed yet another motion to get child support decreased. This time he filed it with the child support division but they denied it being that it was entirely up to the judge and our divorce proceedings were not finalized. At the next court session, he ended up bringing job information that he had and they took it into account and redid the figures of our support. They reduced the amount about $300 less than what he was paying before but it was only going to go into effect for the next couple of months. He still owed arrears for the previous amount before the decrease. I had friends who were friends with Mack still on Facebook so they were sending me screenshots of what he posted. One of the posts was him bragging about buying a brand new Dodge Charger. At this point he was about $1200 in arrears. He made sure he made the post public so everyone could see it, even I because at the time I didn't have him blocked on my Facebook. His family was congratulating him on his new purchase and making elaborate comments and I was reading every one of them thinking how could you all be happy he bought a brand new car but is in arrears for child support and facing jail and wasn't seeing our son. I continued to receive screenshots because everything him and that girl posted on Facebook was going to build an even stronger case for me to get a divorce based on terms of adultery. He had also changed his location on Facebook to living in Philadelphia.

By the court session we had in June, the attorney told the judge he wasn't seeing our son and wasn't responding and that he left out of state with Moesha. Mack told the judge that he wanted me to drive halfway from Virginia to Philadelphia to meet him so he could take our son to Philadelphia. The judge told him no he could not do that because he had went several months not seeing our son and he moved for a female with no regard to our marriage matters and our son. The judge told him he's going to have to come to Virginia when he wants to see him. My thinking is why did Mack think that was going to work to his advantage to be an inconvenience to me when he left my son and me for a female, basically abandoning us in the marriage, doing the same during the divorce matters and continuing to do so knowing the judge had knowledge. I had all the proof to back everything that was brought up in court too. He didn't care. Regardless of all the evidence being brought up, he continued to do his daily postings with this girl carelessly not realizing he was doing a lot more damage.

By the time he and I went to court for this and he gave me all of the arrears he was supposed to, Moesha and I had went to court for the restraining order she placed against me and she dropped it. My attorney and I were ready to show the judge she lied and that I was no threat to her and she was causing the problems. I presented all the paper trail of evidence from her harassing me about Mack and the court entered a two year protective order against her which also included my son from being around her as well. It was due to expire in May 2019. She looked so pissed. Her dreams of playing house with my son and harassing me was over.

Moesha has a history of harassing Mack's kids' mom. Bryna texted me a few months prior to this court date and had said, "Hey Faith, it's Bryna, I wanted to ask you how you were able to file a complaint with Mack dealing with his girlfriend. I've been having issues with him and this girl, I currently have had him on the block list for over a month and he still has his girl leaving messages on my phone and everything else and I'm over it.

I spoke to Mack's mom and she said you filed and I was thinking of doing the same thing." This was when she and I were not talking a few months before I had hit her up. I started to text her back and tell her to sleep with him to find your answer but I figured I wouldn't do it at all and just ignored it. Besides I wasn't sure if she was working with Mack and his mom to try to figure out something for me to say in a text message I didn't trust any of them.

A few weeks later after Moesha and I had court, Mack and I had court in June 2017. At our court session, he told the female judge to her face, on the day that his child support arrears were due in person, that he would hold off on seeing our son until the next court date we had in October. Court was adjourned. I still continued to text him under my attorney's direction asking when he wanted his visitation. I then stopped after a few weeks and just started printing out all of those messages to give to my attorney to prove in court that his interest really wasn't in seeing our son.

During Mack's absence, his mother Tamesha texted me and said, "Hi would you allow me to get Mir for an extended period of time in August? A week? Two weeks? A month?"

She lives in Philadelphia and not one time did she come down after Mir was born to help me out and visit her grandson while her son abandoned us for Moesha as soon as Mir was born but she thought I was really going to let her take my nine month old baby out of state that she had never met, while Mack and I were going through divorce proceedings with nothing finalized. She must've thought I was a joke. Had I given her my son, Mack would've most likely kept him from me until court or tried to file some type of custody in Philadelphia. I was already on to the potential mess it could turn into.

I told her "Hello I do not agree with this because Mir has not seen or been with y'all an extended amount of time. I have offered several times since Mir has been born for y'all to come down and see him and that did not happen. First, you should come see him frequently for a few hours before asking me to just give my child away to blood strangers he does not have a bond formed with. Also,

I am following the court order and don't feel comfortable just giving my child away like that until the permanent order is in place and when Mack actually wants to be around his son. Until then on Mondays and Tuesdays from 5pm to 8pm Mack is supposed to text me 24 hours in advance to get Mir for those times but he hasn't. This is the best interest of Mir."

She responded back, "I don't agree but that's fine. I don't know what you and Mack have in place. That order is for you, Mack, and Mir."

In my head I was thinking you're included in it too, Mack is your son, and he's responsible for coordinating his family being around our son on his time, I can choose whether or not I want to coordinate.

I then told her, " You're entitled to disagree however it's not in the best interest of Mir and you're asking me to do something out of the blue almost ten months later. I'm sure you wouldn't just drop your child off to someone they've never met or been around and feel comfortable. We're talking about an infant that has only been around his mother consistently. You should read up online on the effects this could have on a child. Hope all is well."

I also knew that Mack was taking Moesha up there to be around his family and sending Mir up there his mother would have no respect or regard for the judge's orders, my feelings, and the situation as a whole. I didn't want nothing to happen to my baby. Mack's entire family had already proved how untrustworthy they were during my marriage. She never responded to my last message but three days later I got a call from her but then she hung up. When I texted her and told her I saw that she had called and hung up she said, I was getting ready to respond to your text and hit call by accident." I have told her that text was from three days ago and I inserted laughing emojis.

After that call I told her," Look if you aren't trying to make arrangements to see Mir on a serious note then please don't call or text playing on my phone. I don't have time for it. I unblocked you to give you an opportunity to reach out to me to see Mir but I see it's not a priority and honestly it's not my responsibility to ensure that either."

She texted back hours later after midnight starting up a conversation again saying, "Hi I would like to see Mir again. (Mind you she's never met him before) I tried calling you after your text but no answer because obviously we have miscommunication via text messaging. Being as though I'm out of state, and I'm trying to have my own relationship with you and Mir, I need to know what I'm allowed to do. I simply asked you a question, you gave me an answer. What will you allow me to do outside of what you, Mack, and Mir have going on? In parentheses she put, "I know you probably can't answer right now, I texted you when I could. Respond, if you will, at your convenience. I understand."

I thought to myself, "That's cute you show somewhat consideration for knowing you texted me after 1am and knowing I won't answer." Cool. I could tell by the language of her text, being professionally written that she was either trying to prove a point to someone or print this message out for it to be presented in court, the same way her son does.

I ended up telling her, "I'm only willing to do visits at my apartment clubhouse during the day on days that I have off. He is not used to anybody but me and my family and I don't want him to suffer being in an unfamiliar place away from his primary attachment figure, me. That's something that has to be worked up to not just done immediately and full force, that's what the judge was trying to do with your son. At this age, Mir is not ready to go overnights. He won't understand what's going on and I'm sure he will act out because of it. I have no problem with you or any of his family in Philly seeing him, but it has to be under my terms as I have been the only one raising him and I just do not feel comfortable just sending my baby off just anywhere. I'm not that type of mom. I know you are out of state that's why arrangements can be made in advance to accommodate that."

She called me again and I told her, " I don't want to talk on the phone, that's why I did not answer." She then texted me, "What is the address for this clubhouse and what are the days and times I can see him. Being as though I am out of state, I would have to make arrangements in advance as well. That's why I asked about next month. In the future, just to save time, you can just give me the facts that I ask for. We could have been done this convo in maybe three limited texts. I know you like texting. Please understand that things can get taken out of context or lost in translation when doing so. I don't mind if you record my conversations if that's your concern about phone calls. For now, I'll do it your way."

So first of all I laid everything out on the table crystal clear for this lady when she texted me. Her little attitude she was catching about the messages being done in three limited text was not my problem and further more if you want me to be cordial with you especially when it comes to time with my child you're not about to be nasty to his mother. After all, who would want to send their child to someone they don't get along with? Furthermore, I only met this lady twice in my life since I had married Mack. Once was around the time I got pregnant and the other was right when I moved from Japan to Virginia. I really didn't know her nor did she respect me or my marriage so how could I trust her with my child. So I responded back to her text and said "The address for the clubhouse is this. Just text me dates and times and I will tell you if it's a yes or no.

My schedule tends to change. I always give facts just so you know. I don't beat around the bush I'm pretty straight forward and yes you're right it can be but it is what it is though. I've made myself pretty clear with this and a lot of things prior so I don't think there ever should be any confusion from my part. You texted me Thursday, I texted you back clear with this and to the point so as far as this three limited texts and texting me back three days later that's your doing, I have no control over that. If there's ever something you need to get off your mind that related to me please let me know. One thing I'm not going to do is go back and forth with someone 47 years old over my child that I pushed out and have taken care of on my own with little to the bare minimum financial support but it's all good. God got this and I ain't worried not one bit. Now let's be civil."

She texted me back saying "Only relevant info I read that could've been given in response to my first text. We could have been done in two messages actually. Thanks. I'll contact you my dates and times for your approval."

I texted her back and told her, "You can scratch out the truth of the message but it's the truth and apparently the apple don't fall too far from the tree." After I sent that message she said "You obviously want to argue for no reason. I just want to see my grandson that's all. Everything else is pointless, irrelevant, and not working towards modeling positive relationships for Mir. This is very important. I do go and did go to school for all of this. No internet for me. If the judge gave you all of this false information, maybe you should advise him to check the internet. I know you like the last word."

It was obvious we had animosity amongst each other. I don't like her because she basically disregarded everything that was going on and just wanted her way with my child but not even respecting me at all. She's the last one who should talk about modeling positive relationships for Mir. Correll's fiancée, Sherry told me how she punched Mack's sister and gave a black eye to her and she went to live with her dad for a few months. She also had told me Correll and Tamesha were in court back and forth trying to get his child support reduced and convince his daughter to tell the courts she wants to live her father so the child support can go away completely but his daughter turned her back on her dad. This sure sounds like the positive model of relationships for my son to be around a grandma who did that to her own daughter because of an argument about her likeness for being around Sherry. The last message I sent to Tamesha before I blocked her was for her to leave me alone because I was starting to feel harassed. I told her "Go through your son to see Mir. You are not allowed at my apartment. No more being nice to you nasty old miserable 47 year old acting child. I don't have an obligation to talk to you so don't ever text me again. Grow up and goodbye." At this point I was sick of Mack's family. Their inability as well as his to take account for his actions and instead they chose to treat me nasty as if I was the perpetrator and he was the victim. After this text, I blocked her. The only person who was apologetic about the situation was Mack's cousin Vee. She apologized to me for what happened with everything and said she wish she would've talked to me before I got married and pregnant she would've told me not to do it because she is a woman first and she knows Mack is a jackass. I didn't believe her because she was the first to congratulate me when we got married and was in my Facebook inbox vouching for Mack. She knew then he wasn't worth a thing, she just wanted to sound good.

In regards to my divorce matters, my attorney had me get in touch with the military police that caught Mack and Moesha together so we could hear her testify on that case. I talked to the girl and she told me everything exactly how she said it in that report. She said she used to hear them having sex and getting in the shower together and how he said he was her boyfriend. One piece of information I did not know was that Moesha was possibly pregnant around the time they caught her in the room with Mack. On the day of court in October 2017, the military police said a positive pregnancy test was in the bathroom and it did not belong to anybody but Moesha. Before the court we had where the military police would testify, she and I had breakfast.

One of my shipmates from my command also came to give account that Mack and I had indeed been separated for a year just in case the adultery case did not hold up in the legal standard or the judge's eyes. This court date came around and it took an unexpected twist. We spent eight hours in court that day. My attorney presented all of the evidence from Facebook about Mack and Moesha's relationship. The posts she shared were a sticky note that had their initial relationship start date which was a couple of days after my son's born day. There were posts that include Moesha referencing that Mack was her husband and that her and him were going out to eat, another one was when she said I'm going to church with her husband. There were a couple of photos of Mack kissing her on her forehead and cheek. She made some posts about pregnancy and how she couldn't wait to have babies with him. There was a picture of her wedding ring he bought her. On her and Mack's one year relationship anniversary which was the same time my son turned 1, she posted a picture and the caption "My baby and I finally made it to a year, a very successful and stressful year. Thank you so much for choosing me to be your life partner. I pray in this next year we continue to live a happy life, start our careers, and family. Thank you for becoming my all. With love in every letter, your wife."

Mack shared the photo and posts on his page which was basically an acceptance and admittance of the relationship, we had the screenshot of the post of her and my child which she had captioned, "My step baby boy and I looking just like his daddy," the posts where she was planning to get pregnant by Mack and hinting at a possible pregnancy and once someone questioned her about the gender of the baby she told them she couldn't reveal it. There were posts she made talking about asking Mack's daughter to be her flower girl and that she's got to ask Mir, referring to my son. She had also made mention of them having five kids together and Mack commented back about them getting started and her replying that they already have. There were a few posts where she mentioned her family getting ready to plan her and Mack's wedding and included a date in there that was a few months down the road even though Mack and I at this point hadn't got a divorce or a date on when it would happen. She made a petty status that said, "I just want to thank all the females that did my husband wrong. Thank you for sending him my way; he's everything and then some so special shout out to y'all." Moesha also wrote and tagged him in statuses that said they both moved to Philadelphia together. They had taken beach pictures as well and a few on his car where he was proclaiming her as his girl. She even had the nerve one Father's Day when he posted Bryna and my kids, to say up under the picture, "Our daughter picture better be up here next year." Mack's mother, Tamesha responded back to her comment telling her to "Chill." When Bryna and I talked about it, she said how jealous and childish this girl sounded asserting a comment about a baby that didn't exist because it was a post not about her and she's jealous of his kids because she didn't have any with him.

When the judge questioned him about the pictures, he was in denial. He stated, "They look like me but they aren't me." When the judge asked if he moved to

Philadelphia, he answered that he did and he was also questioned about Moesha living there too and Mack said, "She did but she lived somewhere else." The judge knew it was a lie and a few days prior he has posted them being together. Bryna had confirmed to me later that Mack's dad was allowing Mack and Moesha to live in his house while he lived in his fiancée's house. Mack's mother had revealed that to Bryna, that's how she knew. When it came to the witness, the military police girl who was Moesha's roommate got on the stand. Mack appeared very nervous. My attorney began to question her asking if she recognized Mack and asked what his full name was. She answered with his entire name. She asked what was her association with Mack and also questions about Moesha. The girl gave her account of how she would see Mack in the dorm room and hear him and Moesha before she laid in bed to go to sleep. She stated she would hear them having sex, Mack grunting and Moesha moaning which was the same thing she said in her witness report from the Navy report that outlined his arrest from the adultery and misconduct. Mack denied knowing who the military police girl was and claimed that he never saw her a day in his life. Mack denied that him and Moesha had a relationship going and referred to her as just a friend. The judge looked at him because he knew he was lying about everything. The judge had to rule out the witnesses' hearsay because it did not come with video evidence nor did she say she walked in on them having sex which is what he was looking for to lay the burden of proof to solidify the grounds of an adultery divorce. When it came to Facebook posts my attorney presented, Mack said that the Facebook posts were not from his page because the profile picture was different and he looked darker in the picture. He claimed that someone made a new Facebook page of him which we all knew was not true. My attorney told the judge that it is Mack's profile and that he had recently changed his profile picture from the time the screenshot of all the posts was made. One last screenshot she had to show to see if he would confess to it being his Facebook page was a post he had made on our son's first birthday. He never called me to acknowledge our sons birthday nor was he in town because he moved to Philadelphia after I got a restraining order against his girlfriend and took it out on seeing our son but he made a post on Facebook that said, "My fat man turns 1 today, and I can't even spend this day with him. This boy means so much to me and I continuously pray that a fair solution to having time with him comes in the very near future. I love you Mir, always have and always will." It's amusing how he could cause and egg on all the drama between myself, him, and Moesha yet get on social media and play victim (also a narcissistic trait) as if there was not court ordered visitation to see him. There was visitation in place for him to see our son for a few hours at his house after my working hours on Mondays and Tuesdays due to his age and unfamiliarity with our son, and although our son's birthday was on a Thursday, if he was in town or still living near us he could've very well seen him and celebrated it with us. He's one of those social media dads so when it comes to the kids birthday, he will post for attention for himself but when it comes to posting the child on regular days, unless him and the mother are on good terms and/or together and if his parents aren't posting and tagging him in pictures then the kids won't get posted unless it's a special occasion.

Bryna told me before that Mack doesn't claim kids until it has a benefit to him like recognition from others or for monetary purposes and she referenced before how when he was living in Philadelphia and he was working at a store, one of her family members asked about their daughter and he acted embarrassed and the people around him that heard about it started saying they didn't know he had a daughter. She said he denied ever having a child.

Getting back to the post of our son, He acknowledged that the post was our son and when questioned about the date that it was posted, he did say that it was our son's birthday, however he said did not make that post and someone made up a fake page. So everyone in the court room is looking at him crazy at this point. He legit denied everything and anything. The judge was so shocked he denied everything that he became speechless. He ended up stopping in the middle of court and had my attorney and Mack go to the back in his judge's chambers. He talked to him and let him know exactly what's going on and brought him back out with hopes he would get in tune. So the grounds for an adultery divorce were tossed out only because he denied it even with all of the proof. We moved along to the portion of income to figure out how much child support he would be paying based off of our incomes. I was still in the military so I gave my attorney my military earnings statement and she allowed Mack to see it and give the judge the papers to be kept in evidence. Next, when it came to Mack's employment my attorney had questioned him on where he works, how much he makes, and how many hours he works each week. Mack was still on the stand from being questioned about him and Moesha's relations. He told my attorney that he worked for U-Haul making $13 an hour.

I knew he was lying and I whispered to my attorney that the child support enforcement division who garnishes money from his check and disburses it to me had told me a couple weeks prior that they verified he was no longer working for U-Haul. I told my attorney that Mack had walked in the courtroom with a government identification card similar to the one we were issued in the military. It was inside of a clear lanyard on a keychain around his neck. My attorney told the judge that I saw him walk in with it and we requested he come off of the stand and retrieve those items for my attorney to review. Mack gets off the stand and grabs the lanyard, gives it to my attorney and at first she sees his driver's license and behind it was the government issued card. She asked him what it was and he said, "It's an ID." She asked, "Where did you get this from?"

He shrugged his shoulders and said, "I don't know." My attorney said, "You do know that being in possession of a government ID card and using it in an unlawful manner is a federal offense." The ID was a representation of the company he was working for on the military base as a contractor. My attorney exclaimed to the judge her frustration and said, "Your honor he is committing perjury about everything." She gave him that look of seriousness and alerted the judge of her findings and the judge asked that she bring it forth to him. Mack took a seat and the judge examined the card. He made a copy of it front and back and wrote some notes down. The judge then looked at Mack and said, "Where did you get this?" Mack again said, "I don't know." The judge started getting facetious and asked him, "Did some aliens put it in there somehow?"

Boy was it hard to contain the laughter built up inside of me. I was so stunned at his act. The fact that he wouldn't confess to it was embarrassing and hilarious at the same time. The judge asked him what company is he working for and Mack told him. The judge also asked how much he makes and he said $20 an hour and works 40 hours a week. The judge asked, "Why did you lie?" Mack said, "I was scared." The judge said, "What were you scared of?" Mack remained silent. The judge asked Mack again. Mack continued his silence. The judge started getting annoyed because Mack wouldn't give him an answer. He started calling him, "Mr. B", "Hello Mr.B" and repeatedly asked the question hoping he would confess. Mack didn't budge. He just looked at the judge like a deer in headlights, star struck that his true place of employment and income was discovered. The judge then asked, "Mr. B do you have anything that you want to say at this time." Mack was saying, "Uhhhh Ummm." The judge asked him again and he uttered the words, "Sorry" in a soft tone. The judge then told him, "The attorney and I have asked you several questions regarding the adultery and your income. You denied everything. You have aggravated everyone in the court room at this point and wasted so much time. You are being charged with civil contempt of court for perjury and you will serve 10 days in jail. We are continuing this court date out a couple of months and will see you next time." My heart sank. I really could not believe that Mack allowed it to go this far with all of his lies and now this was going to delay our divorce, child support, and him being around our son. The bailiff's went over to Mack, told him to stand up and put his hands behind his back as they handcuffed him and took him out of the courtroom.

I was also relieved because Mack had made my life a living hell and I was tired of it. It was about time he served consequences for his actions. He had been getting away with stuff for a long time not only with me but with other females as well and Bryna. He did her dirty and disappeared, barely paid child support, and abandoned their daughter for three years with no repercussions when they went to court. In my mind, this was his karma for mistreating all females especially Bryna and I.

The day he went to jail I decided to reach out to Correll and Sherry to tell them to help Mack to stop lying about the girl only being a friend, lying about his income, and cutting up in court. Instead of talking like adults, Correll started blaming me for getting him sent to jail and how their son is locked up and they can't talk to him. I told him they can stop blaming me for literally everything Mack does himself and to me. They asked me what I wanted and

I told them that they need to get a handle on him. He was prolonging our divorce matters by lying about everything even with all of the hardcore proof. If he was so unhappy with me only because he couldn't cheat on me and continuously use and manipulate me and I told him the truth about his erratic actions in our marriage and how he acted with his Bryna, why would he lie about everything? Tell the truth so everything can be dissolved and you can continue your fake happy life and bogus marriage you started with Moesha during ours. I ended up hanging up the phone on them because all Correll and Sherry was doing was cussing me out. I sent Sherry a text and told her "Don't worry about calling me back. I didn't appreciate being cussed out and blame placed on me for something I did not do. I'll continue to keep my distance as I've been doing, the truth is coming out. Have a nice one."

She texted back saying, "Have a nice life I hope you're satisfied." She sent me a double text and then said, "In the long run you're only hurting Mir."

I texted her back saying, "I'm not hurting Mir because I didn't allow a restraining order against my girlfriend to interfere with me seeing my son. Mack hasn't seen Mir since April 16 when she (Moesha) got served for the threat she made to me. The court isn't allowing a child to be around someone there is a restraining order against that protects me and my son from being around her who they are aware of they are still and living together. I texted him multiple times on visitation days to obey the order asking if he wanted to see Mir and he also sent me a nasty letter in the mail telling me to not contact him period which the only time I did was regarding his court ordered visitation. Everything was good until that restraining order against her and all hell broke loose. He chose to move to Philadelphia and not see Mir anymore. He chose to cause all of this hell. The location of visitation was moved and he was going to get more visitations but the judge wanted him to start off small first since he has been much uninvolved physically and financially and because Mir is a baby. No one's going to come and take a baby away that is not familiar and has not spent a large amount of time that affects the child and that's what I'm looking out for. Like I have said before Mack and his family can be around Mir but since I am the mother taking care of Mir I am not tolerating anyone taking him for a week, two weeks, or a month until constant visitation has been met? If he hadn't lied to the judge about his employment because he's afraid of the amount going up and he's been trying to dodge it he would've went home that day. He blatantly lied and disrespected all the judges at each court hearing and at the last one in June said I can hold off on him seeing Mir until October. It is what it is. There are always two sides to the story and with his history of lying, no one except you and his family believe him. I understand you're upset he's in jail but he put his own self in there for lying and if he doesn't come up with the $2000 in arrears it will be the same come December. All I want is to be legally divorced and because he lied saying she's just a friend and that isn't his Facebook posts the judge had to take into account his word of mouth despite very good evidence and he also lied about us being separated since September. Believe me when I say I do not want to be a part of the family by any means and trust me I have no feelings wise for Mack at all, we are both on two different levels mentally and trust me I have moved on, he's saw with his own eyes. Like I said before, "I'm keeping my distance as I've had before but like you have said before he's definitely getting all he's done to me and some back and guess what looks like it happened in an unpleasant way."

She texted back and said "The fact that you just said he's definitely getting all he's done to you back and some says you're a bitter, conniving, scorned, low life bored bitch! Find a new hobby! Then you call his parents asking them to help you which also make you crazy and delusional too!"

I concluded the conversation to Sherry by saying, "Okay, you're entitled to your opinion. The conversation is over now. I can't deal with dysfunctional stuff. I have Mir school and work to take care of. I didn't ask for any of his parents help. I was doing this on my own since Mir was born without help from a single soul up there. All I asked is y'all to tell him to stop lying so much so I can get my divorce. I don't want to be married to him and finally support me because this is his child too. I'm not crazy or delusional. I never asked for monetary or physical help with Mir, Mack just needs to stop lying and face his responsibilities. I'm actually trying to keep in contact with y'all and keep a relationship so Mir can be around because Mack obviously doesn't want to be involved or take care in either of his kid's life but wanted to continue making more. I got tired of all the drama and victim playing and shift blaming. I didn't cause this and you said it yourself Sherry! He wouldn't be in this predicament if he didn't marry me, if he didn't lie and manipulate and didn't run off his responsibilities. He's being forced to be a man by the courts and take care of his child and he doesn't want to. Y'all can drag my name through the dirt but the truth is the truth. This convo is dead to me. You're acting just like you said his mom and dad act and I'm not dealing with it."

She double texted me back saying "You've taken this situation way too far so be done with it and stop responding. You wanted revenge and you got it. Go party!"

The crazy thing is Mack and his entire family played an active role in pacifying and enabling Mack's actions and they acted like I was supposed to be okay and keep being nice, letting them trample over me and kissing their ass; basically being manipulated or duped. The consequences of Mack's actions sent them in an uproar. I guess they thought I was supposed to continue to take the heat from them and Mack and not have any type of backbone within me and they were mad that all of their attempts to destroy and make me lose my mind as well as lie to the courts didn't go through and everything was revealed crystal clear.

Mack got out of jail and was pissed that he sent me a message telling me not to contact his family. What's crazy to me is that Correll, Tamesha, and Sherry have all given me their contact information and have been in my Facebook inbox talking to me, opening the door allowing me to talk to them and as soon as problems arise that Mack is responsible for they don't want to hear it. They were extremely inconsistent on when they wanted to talk to me and when they did not. Something just seriously started to go off in my mind that this family is fake and dysfunctional. We had court about a couple of months later after he got out of jail. The day of court in December 2017, he texted me early in the morning talking about he would like to talk to me after court was over. In my mind he must've known what the outcome already was going to be and was going to try to apologize but I was not buying it at all.

When I showed up at court I had my binder full of screenshots, messages, all of our court documents and everything that had to do with Mack and Moesha. You name it I had it. When I came through the doors of the court getting ready to go through the security scanner, the guards had asked me if I was an attorney and I told them No I am not. The way I had looked, it appeared that I was one to them. I got on the elevator to go to the floor where our divorce court would be held. In my mind I was thinking I hope this would be the last court session that we would have and that the judge would grant the divorce.

Mack and Correll were waiting outside the court doors and I heard his dad ask. "Is that her?" and he told his dad, "Yeah." I went into the courtroom and shortly after they followed. My landlord had also came to court that day as well and she was going to be the one to testify that Mack was no longer living at my house and she knew this to be true because of the occasional maintenance she would have to do and his items were no longer there, therefore we have been separated at least a year to her knowledge. This was going to solidify the grounds of divorce not under adultery of course because he denied everything and his denial had to be taken into account even though the judge knew for a fact that he had committed adultery and the evidence was pretty solid.

My attorney showed up and we both agreed that we were ready to move forward. When the judge called all parties to the stand he allowed the landlord to go first to speak her piece about us no longer living together. After that the judge reviewed all of the adultery evidence. He went over a brief synopsis of all of the court hearings that we had had at this point which was probably about five or six if not more times that we had been in court. The judge spent about a 30 to 45 minutes talking to Mack about his actions between the lying, the adultery, his employment, his arrest, his character, and everything as a whole and his dad had to sit there and listen to every last bit of it. The judge started going down the line of the best interest of the child factors to determine who would get custody of Mir. Every last one of them I've matched up with and Mack only matched up with about one. The judge then determined that I have primary physical custody of Mir. The judge then asked for all of our employment information to be brought up. My attorney already had copies of both of our income and had already done a calculation to figure out how much child-support that Mack would be paying to me. The judge came up to an amount which was not too shy of $800. My attorney then asked the judge that he also assess Mack to pay the attorney's fees. The remaining bill I had was about $4500. The judge made him responsible to pay that back to me within 12 months of our divorce, which he actually did on the very last day it was due before I could go and file contempt of court and he would've serve jail time because of that being in our divorce decree. After all, he had prolonged the divorce court more than it had needed to be but I still was responsible for paying my attorney. Her rate was between $250 and $300 an hour with a $1500 retainer fee that I paid her in the beginning when I first hired her. Every time we went to court she was right by my side I was responsible for paying her. $500 of my check each month was going directly to my attorney. I wasn't receiving child support until Mir was about six months old. That's when Mack was ordered to start paying child support, However I didn't start receiving child support until Mir was about eight months old.

After that the judge allowed closing arguments from both sides of the parties Mack didn't have too much to say because he knew he had been found out. I only said that I was glad everything was over and I felt like I got what I deserved and I thanked the judge for overseeing the case. I also mentioned how hard it was financially but I'm glad that it was over. After court was over, Mack didn't talk to me like he said he would. I ended up texting him back saying "Now that we are out of court, what did you want to talk to me about and did you and your dad want to see Mir? Correll had never met Mir so this was an opportunity for him to do so. Mack's focus didn't appear to be on his family meeting our son at all, he was focused on the outcome of everything in court but I chose to be the bigger person. He agreed to meet at my apartment complex inside of the club house. I don't trust Mack or any of his family because of all that went on and I was not about to risk my life or career behind lies so I choose to allow visitation to occur in a public place that has cameras so any false allegations cannot be told.

When we walked in the club house, I told Mir exactly who each of them was and he hesitated to even go to them. I brought some toys so he could play with them. After a few minutes, Correll said, "I'm going outside." Mack then asked if we could go to another part of the club house and talk. I already knew it was a staged talk by his family so I didn't believe any word he said especially because none of his words ever matched up with his actions. He had a smirk on his face while saying," I'm sorry for everything. I made a lot of big mistakes." I looked at him with the most stern face while he was chuckling and smirking. I did not believe anything at all and then he asked, "Why are you looking at me like I'm wasting your time?" I told him, "You are." To me, the best apology is changed behavior and I knew that he hadn't changed, he just knew he was caught. He said his goodbyes to Mir and raced out the parking lot in his car.

I didn't hear from him anymore about seeing our son. He was headed back to his dad's house in Philadelphia where he and Moesha were hiding out and living.

The next day Correll texted me and said, "Hello this is Mack dad; I just want say sorry for everything. I was out of line talking to you like I did. I was very upset about Mack going to jail but that is not a reason to act the way I did. I really do understand what you're going through and seeing my grandson really made me realize that. You have done a wonderful job with him I commend you for it. You're a wonderful young lady that really doesn't deserve what you went through and I'm sorry on behalf of my son. I just decided to reach out to you to let you know if you need anything please do not hesitate to ask and please keep sending me pictures of him if you can and please take care of yourself, God bless. Also can you send me your address so we can send him his Christmas presents if you don't mind?"

I knew the apology was bull crap. This had to be like the 4th apology from Correll after he showed his true colors. He only wanted to try to butter things up so he can have access to my son because he knows everything they did was foul so he thought I would fall for the apology. I didn't. I gave the address but the Christmas presents he spoke of never did arrive.

A few days before Christmas I decided to reach out to Bryna. I said to her, "Hey, this is Faith, and I want to wish you and your daughter a Merry Christmas. It's been a while since we were civil and had a conversation and I know last year we made plans to get the kids together and that didn't work out so well. I really needed time to myself to get through my situation and sort out all of the emotions that I was feeling being that I was a new mom and single parent. How I personally felt about the situation between you and Mack in my house greatly impeded me from doing so before. To be honest, I never disliked you; I actually took up for you more times than you know when it came to you and Mack's issues involving your daughter. The only thing is he kept telling me things about you to view you in a negative light to keep animosity between us and at the time I believed the things he was saying. I genuinely loved and wanted to be a part of your daughter's life and not on a petty note because I was with her Dad. I see resemblances of her in Mir too. I'm sure our situations we been through with him are very similar and probably a little worse on my end because I was married to him but it doesn't matter anymore, it's old and dissolved. I'm only texting you because I want us to put the past behind us and communicate for the fact that we have kids related by blood and they DO need to know each other. You're only six hours away from me and I was thinking maybe a weekend or two out of each month we could meet halfway and get the kids together to play and take them out and take pictures of them together. Mir can't go to PA for a few years because of the restraining order against Mack's girlfriend so the kids chance of meeting each other there are very slim and by the time they can I will have already moved further to another state. I understand if you feel differently but being that I am the older of us two and trying to continue is the bigger woman that is why I decided to say something."

She replied back and said, "Hey, there is no need for you to explain yourself to me, the feelings you felt towards me were reasonable. I never got a chance to apologize to you for the role I played in everything that happened and I do apologize I should have never done what I did and I'm sorry for that. I don't have any hard feelings towards you or Mack for that matter, I am civil with him I see no reason I can't be civil with you as well. We are grown women and I don't see why we can't come together for the kids they do deserve to know they have each other."

After this message, our conversation started to get greater each time. Bryna revealed things such as, "When you wrote that long story on Facebook and I was in it some of it wasn't all the way true because Mack lied of course, but stuff still happened and I was embarrassed by it. People that knew Mack knew that you were talking about me not that anybody said anything to me." She also said in reference to my story I had wrote, "The part about me trying to be your friend and liking your pictures Mack set that up. I never wanted to follow you on social media. Mack told me to because he said you'd be suspicious if I was only friends with him and he was telling me to play nice and be friendly and all this stuff whenever I'd text or message you. He'd help me write the messages, he knew everything and he even wanted you to believe I was jealous of y'all marriage when he knew I wasn't. I didn't sleep with Mack because I wanted to be married to him or because I was jealous it was for an entirely different reason. I was using Mack. Yeah I still had feelings for him but I didn't want to be with him. If I did I would of said yes before you got together but I told him no and he lied and said I was upset when he first told me he was married. I wasn't I just told him okay like what else was I supposed to say and he asked me why I wasn't upset. He made this huge deal so I thought he was calling me about my daughter and he said "I'm a married man." and I said oh okay I thought you were calling me about our daughter and he got silent."

"He wanted it to look like I was so obsessed over him when I wasn't, who else was going to drive me from South Carolina to Philadelphia, him. I knew he would because I knew he still liked me so I used him. It wasn't right at all but that's who I was at that time. Where else was I going to stay? When I got there he sent me money more freely when I liked him so why not play the role but I didn't want to be with him, I liked him but not enough to be in a relationship with him. I did cry after we had sex that part was true. I didn't run around all over the house shouting and praying that was a lie. We both cried that's what happened and after that we were really more like best friends. He used me and I used him. I went through his phone and he was telling lies to his mom about me when I was there but telling me something different. He's a liar. Always has been."

Do y'all know how I felt to hear all the things this girl was saying and to know my husband was plotting against me with his baby mama like an enemy against me? That's literally sick behavior to plot again your own wife and have the very person you bad mouthed help you do that. My thing is her and Mack would not have done that if I was living in the states in the same roof as Mack under the military so the fact that you both had to sneak to do it and lie about it in the beginning says a lot. There's no justification she could've said that made the situation better or okay because you just don't do this type of crap.

On another occasion she mentioned, "Mack did not want us to talk at all! He still seems to not like that we talk to this day. He can't lie if we talking." She was assuring with the court's ruling in my favor with everything custody wise for me by saying, "The courts would definitely rule in your favor I can't even lie like especially since they (referring to Correll and Tamesha) aren't even really attempting their basically not using their rights as grandparents. Mack did you dirty and that's just facts! I think they hate you so much because you won honestly. Mack probably didn't see that coming at all. He's used to just doing girls dirty and moving on, like me I only fought when it came to custody I was not playing with that but as far as anything I didn't really fight so he never really got real consequences until you and that's the part they don't like because they feel you were trying to destroy him when he reality he basically destroyed you."

When I asked Bryna about us not meeting up previously in 2016, when she randomly blocked me on social media the last time we had talked she said, "I honestly wasn't ready, to be honest it's hard for me to understand why you would want to talk to me let alone meet up because I mean I did overstep my boundaries when you and Mack were together and no human being just poof forgets about something like that I mean if it were me I'd forgive but I would still feel some type of way about it and I wasn't sure if you had some motive behind it with Mack, I'm not judging you because I feel like you have every right to dislike him and you have every right to want revenge that's natural but I just wasn't sure if you were coming from a place of sincerity."

When she said she wasn't sure if I had a motive behind it with Mack that was her projecting what she did to me onto me. She had a motive with things in our marriage so she figured I had to have one at this point which she was wrong.

I told Bryna, "I sensed it both times while trying to arrange a meet up especially when you brought up telling your best friend, you were going to meet with his dad which was really a meeting between us two. While I understand completely what you are saying, there are people in this world who can overcome and adapt to things especially if there are kids involved. If I did something like you did, without a doubt I would think that the same way, naturally and be afraid. That's the conviction process. Trust me I got too much to lose to have an ulterior motive and especially driving a hundred or so miles with my child, who I care about over any soul. I'm sure you know a lot of women honestly would've tried to take it into physical matters forever and a day but not me which I'm sure is hard to believe by everyone that we all know that have knowledge about everything that I got through only because they know it was all wrong and I should've could've would've but I didn't. I'm sure it's hard to believe for everyone involved that I'm sane and still in my right mind but God. I got a present and a future and it ain't worth losing and doing time over no man or woman. I chose to use my mind over emotions because I've never been the fighting type. That's why I handle things through the legal system in prayer in God because both have a way of dealing cards that have been played and can do more justice then words or hands ever could. I've learned being kind to others who have done me wrong is the best pay off. Trust me it was and always has been sincere but that's perfectly fine, we can leave it in Mack hands. I've been told several times I am intimidating because of my strong no BS personality despite the way I look and the ability to move past a situation and I understand that too."

Bryna replied, "It definitely is conviction that I feel because I Just feel bad for how I treated you and I have to live with that and I know you didn't deserve it. I mean I'm glad you are strong and have overcome everything that you've overcome not everyone can say that they can handled what you've handled. I'm not trying to be rude but I actually thank my lucky stars that I didn't marry him because that would of been the worst mistake of my life and I honestly wish I never had a kid with him at all (not saying I don't want my child) but it's nothing that Mack can offer that I would want or envy past or present. I can't speak for his girlfriend because I mean she's obviously delusional but I feel like God covered me when it came to Mack because I dodged a huge bullet and that wasn't in God's will for me to endure what you endured maybe I wouldn't of been able to overcome it and that wasn't a trail God had for my life. You went through it and it's helped you become the woman you are today and I've gone through my own trials that have helped me become the women I am today so I'm grateful for that."

I told her, "Yeah, I can understand why you feel that way about him because you're stuck dealing with him indirectly and directly with his child. His girlfriend will continue to be delusional until she gets tired of the facade and abuse if ever but I don't think so because no one has treated her like he has probably. If not, my only thing is as long as my child is not mistreated and I don't got to go to jail for it I'm good"

She said, "I feel the way I feel about him because of the way he treats my child like she's an option, and not a priority I can't respect him for that."

Christmas 2017 rolled around and he didn't call to check on Mir, nor did he send any gifts at all. When the New Year rolled around, I informed him that our divorce papers would be in soon and that he could pay the attorney's fees he owes me directly to me. He then told me that he would pay it to my attorney but I knew it wouldn't go to them. I had a contract and hired my attorneys and I was expected to still provide them payment regardless if he reimbursed me or not. I calculated the amount he would send me and how frequent to do so to satisfy the order by the date we were told. He said he would send them to my attorney and that he would come down in March and sees him. So from April 2017 when I filed the restraining order against his girlfriend until December 2017 when our divorce was finalized he hadn't seen Mir until I asked if he wanted to. I shouldn't have to ask nor remind him he has a child but I know his girlfriend had a lot to do with why he didn't see Mir.

Since she couldn't be around him, she didn't want Mack around me and Mir at all. I emailed my attorney and confirmed with her that he would in fact pay the attorney's fees to me and passed the message along to him. Literally, the next day he texted me saying "Next year I would like to file Mir on my taxes, I feel we should alternate each year."

In my head I'm thinking he's lost his damn mind. He barely wants to pay his child support without us going to court every few months and he talking about getting money for a child I take care of by myself, so he can blow money on his other kids and females. He doesn't even buy our son any gifts at all period nor has he ever. All I get is child support and sporadically at that. Why would he not want to go outside of the financial support and bask in the excitement of buying gifts, clothes, and such for your child? He has abandoned our son, doesn't check on him, allowed a girl to completely have a say during our marriage and with our son and he really thought I was about to give him some of the tax money when every time I turned around we were in court several times for him trying to decrease the amount of child support he was paying.

I knew it wasn't a joke, so I told him, "According to the IRS, the default parent, in terms of claiming the dependent exemption for a child in a divorce situation, is the one with whom the child lives for greater than 50% of the time during that tax year. There is a credit you can get with the IRS for paying child support. I do not agree and I will be filing him on my taxes every year."

Anytime money is involved, he'll respond if he's being given money or he will respond with rage if it's about expenses he needs to take care of dealing with our son, or money he owes me but it depends on how he's feeling or the status of his girlfriend relationship with him as to how his reaction would be. When they're on bad terms, he's civil and will coparent. When they are on good terms, he gets hostile, personally attacks my character with words, or flat out ignores me. He didn't even respond to my last message because it's not what he wanted to hear. Bryna and I were texting about it and she told me Mack has asked her the same thing before and she said had he done it, he would've got in trouble because she has a family member that works for the IRS.

A couple days later, Mir had climbed out of his crib and landed on the floor on his feet. I decided it was time to buy him a toddler bed. I sent Mack a picture of what I was planning to get and told him what happened. My messages went through as green which meant I was blocked. He didn't respond. Bryna and I were texting and she was mentioning how pathetic he was and also had sent me a message the next day saying she knows how it feels not being able to share happy moments of your child with their father and also stated if I ever needed someone to talk to it could be her. I never fully trusted her and I only talked to her about matters to do with Mack. There was no telling what her motive was and she did not need to go spread my business especially because she had laid up with him before and listened to mine in bed with him when we were married. I couldn't put anything past her. We got on the subject of her moving out of her mom's house and being on her own and I congratulated her because there's no better feeling than having your own and I know from what Mack told me she didn't have a good relationship with her mom and some reasons why and I could completely relate.

February 2018 rolled around and I got ahold of the divorce decree and sent him a copy of it and told him, "I know I said it should be here a couple weeks ago, I went and got mine the day it posted but here it is until my attorney gets a chance to send you the official one just in case you need it for work or something."

My message went through blue which meant I was unblocked but still no response. Two weeks later, I got a text message from his phone asking if I was going to be home for him to see Mir. I gave him the date and time and he asked for my address. He already knew my address, he got it in court the date we were divorced and when he came to see Mir that day but since he wanted to play stupid, I went ahead and gave it to him. He came and saw Mir; he was hesitant to go to him but warmed up.

A couple days later I had sent him a picture of our son wearing the shirt, "Best son ever." My son was so handsome it, I couldn't resist sharing. He didn't respond. A couple days later he had asked me to send the pictures I took of him and Mir when he had come to see him. I sent them. When Mir's new bed and accessories arrived I sent him pictures and videos of him entering his room. He didn't respond. At this point I was really pissed. It was obvious he was very bitter still. I sent him a text a couple hours later and said, "You know it's really sad that at the very least you don't even call or Face Time to check on see Mir the most innocent person of the situation. He's the most lovable handsome and happiest little boy ever, you're really missing out on a lot even if you can't be here in person, financially taking care of him, that's cool me sending pictures of him you don't even say anything or ask for when I don't send is just ridiculous. You have to put aside your personal feelings of how "dead" I am to you, and are there for him because as he gets older he's going to understand things more without me even saying a word to him."

He responded and said, "Thanks for the comment, but it's not needed."

I had mentioned the dead part because Bryna had told me, he discussed everything that happened with her and told her I am dead to him. She was so proud to tell me that and to warn me to stay away from him because he doesn't like me. A few weeks later, he asked what size clothes Mir wears and I told him. A couple of weeks after that, He then asked which days I was free. I told him on weekends only because of my work schedule being hectic and since his visitation was supervised due to the restraining order against Moesha, the visitation had to be conducted by me in a public or mutually agreed upon place and I had to be there. I decided to change up from meeting at the clubhouse to a place where Mir could play and interact with him. We met at an indoor play center. He met with him and spent about an hour and then left. He saw him again a few days later and this time we met at a place called the Nauticus which was an actual tour of a realistic ship similar to those in the Navy. Before we stepped aboard, a camera lady asked to take our picture and he agreed. I was reluctant and you could tell in the picture that I was. I didn't want to feel anything close to being a family with him again but we took the picture. I was surprised he wanted to because I know his girlfriend would be livid if she found out. After we took the picture, he told me he would make a copy of mine and pay me half of the cost of it. Again, I was surprised but I was like okay. I didn't hear from him at all for another few weeks. Bryna and I was texting and she was saying how Tamesha loves all her grandkids when as far as I knew she only had two, my son and Bryna's daughter. She was so eager to tell me Mack had a third child on the way and sent me the ultrasound of his new baby and told me if I ever needed it in court just in case he ever lies, there it was. It was weird of her to send it, I believe she was trying to be funny.

A few weeks before the official divorce occurred on paper; Moesha revealed her pregnancy and posted an ultrasound tagging Mack in it. She was about three months pregnant. She thought that she was in the clear to post but little did she know if we lived in a state that honored marital interference laws, she could've been sued for it. In a small minority of states, a spouse may sue a third party for willfully and maliciously interfering with the marital relationship. This interference results in winning away the love of a husband or wife from his/her spouse. This suit is usually brought against the adulterous spouse's lover. I also would've sued Bryna because she admitted as well but I figured I wouldn't go through the hassle and let God handle it because nobody can get vengeance better than him. If I wanted to, I could've gone back to the courthouse and had the divorce reversed to be tried again for adultery since he lied to the judge about her being pregnant and they would have held off until the baby was born to take a paternity test so it could be factored into my divorce and to clear Mack out financially for all the pain and suffering. December 2017 we had court, the day the judge said he would grant a divorce although on paper it was not official until late January 2018.

I didn't receive this ultrasound until a few months later. After the ultrasound was sent, Bryna said, "Tamesha told me to put him on child support because she said it wasn't fair that her child was the only one not getting child support (basically because I was getting it) and she was unhappy with Moesha being pregnant and apparently Mack and Tamesha weren't speaking at the time. Bryna was like, "His mom said I'm an angel because I waited so long without child support."

I was thinking, "No girl you're dumb. You slept with him while he was not taking care of y'all child on a continuous basis so what sense did that make." Bryna told me Tamesha tried to put Bryna and Mack back together while Moesha was pregnant with Mack's third child because none of his relationships with any female will work out because he didn't do right by Bryna. Mack also reached out to Bryna before and asked what she thought about them getting back together with his three kids. She claimed she wasn't budging because she was in a relationship with someone.

I thought to myself, "Sis, you were in a relationship when Mack was married and that didn't stop you from sleeping with him then. You finally got some morals now?" The fact that Mack and his mother knows she is in a relationship and Mack is in a relationship with Moesha and them trying to convince her to get back with Mack shows they don't have respect for her or his relationship the same way they had no respect for my marriage. It's just messy. That is a reason why I personally wouldn't have allowed a reconnection into my personal life, social media or anything. It would be strictly about my child and that's it. Forgiveness does not require reconnection. If they showed you who they are before, believe them.

Also, privacy is power, what they don't know they can't ruin. Due to the fact she still seeks acceptance from and into Mack's family as their favorite baby mama that doesn't hold him financially responsible for his child and wants access to the "tea" of Mack and I and Moesha as she stated before, she fails to realize what staying connected and allowing them to be in her personal business and what it could do but that's a lesson for her to learn. In a new season of my life, I wouldn't allow any old to have convenient access to me. Boundaries would be put in place and they will be respected. It was funny to me that all of a sudden after Bryna helped ruin my marriage; all seemed to be well in her world with Mack and his family. The break in my marriage made the bond with Mack and his family closer with Bryna with her and their daughter when it should've been like that before I even got married to him. Bryna was telling me at the end of 2017 that her and her U.S. Marine boyfriend were going to be getting married and that she was changing her and Mack's daughters last name to his and that she knows Mack is going to be mad about it. However, that marriage didn't happen in that year or the following year. I also thought to myself, "You sure you still ain't bitter? Your daughter already don't have her dad's last name and you talking about changing it to a man who isn't biologically her father who could be here today and gone tomorrow just like you said about me being Mack's wife and all the girlfriends he's had." She told me that they live together and ain't have sex and she wants a baby boy and how she wants to get a house using her boyfriend's VA benefits. She sounded like she was in such a rush to get married to whoever would give her a ring after Mack didn't because she wanted the lifestyle she saw I had with Mack now with someone else but it didn't happen as quickly as she was hoping and yet she claimed she would be terrified if what I went through happened to her. If I was her I wouldn't be in such a rush for marriage not knowing what the end result of it could be based off of what she did to another innocent woman. I was also thinking, "Yeah right. It wasn't terrifying when you had my husband all up in your guts." Bryna had the nerve to tell me one day that Mack and I got married too soon. Like girl why is that any of your concern? You have yet to get a ring or a last name from him and besides you're just Mack's baby mama why are you even speaking on his wife? Whether or not Mack cheated I got the last name, the ring, the first son (the very gender you wanted) and truth be told you was jealous of me and and watching my Facebook page which you admitted to doing, plotting and praying on the downfall of my marriage because of what you did. She had later told me her parents were married for 20+ years and what happened to me happened to her mother with her dad and gave me the details of that. This was a perfect example of what I told her when I said it doesn't matter how long you're married to someone or the timing in which you get married to them, it can happen to anybody so her best bet was to humble herself from speaking on someone else's storm.

Getting back to the subject of the ultrasound of Mack's third baby, according to Bryna, Tamesha wanted her to beat Moesha in putting him on child support just in case Mack and Moesha broke up so she wouldn't short Bryna's daughter from getting support in the event she tried to file. Bryna and Tamesha were plotting on the fail of Moesha's relationship with Mack due to his history and because Mack's mother doesn't like Moesha. Like Bryna, if you're so happy and moved on why you would even indulge in his mother about his ex-wife and Moesha. Bryna asked me about Mack's social security number and how much I get in child support and I'm not sure what she was thinking but she couldn't have been serious asking me for this. Why would I give you his social security number and tell you how much I'm getting in child support? If Mack's mother gave you this advice to put him on child support and you and she are so cool, you should be asking her and not me.

Furthermore she stated Mack acted like I wasn't getting a lot of child support as a method to deter her from putting her on it so she wanted to know how much I was getting which I was not telling her period. The only thing I did tell her was I got quite a bit and it was fine with me. She would have to figure out the rest from his mom which she confirmed she would.

Bryna told me, "The last time I tried to file for child support South Carolina was moving so slow nothing got done so I gave up on it. So I make $15 an hour and don't how much he makes how would they calculate that?" I didn't have a legitimate answer to give her about that either. When Bryna decided to put Mack on child support after Tamesha boosted her up to it, Mack didn't want to talk to Bryna nor allow her daughter to while she was with her dad for summer visitation.

She said, "I'm texting him telling him to let me speak with her because he can't not let me talk to her it says on the agreement we have to talk four times a week, and I know he's going to ignore me. I'll just document how long he won't let me speak to her, she has that iPad but most of the time he has to tell her to get it from him when I text him and tell him I want to talk to her."

She thought Mack had changed because he wanted to be civil with her before child support became an issue but I warned her it was only temporary and if he really changed he would be cool with us both, child support being paid wouldn't be an issue and be active in our kids life.

She said, "Yeah I see now what you're talking about he's a complete asshole and he hasn't changed one bit I always try to have hope for people but all hope is lost when dealing with him. Referring to Moesha going along with Mack's crap Bryna said, "He going to do that girl dirty and she's just so in denial she doesn't see it."

When I told her that Mir and I were going to be moving closer to her and his sister soon she said, "I can't wait to meet him he's so freaking cute!" In regards to Mack's parents not coming to see Mir, she said, "Yeah I don't know why they won't travel down there here; Mack has visitation for our daughter every other weekend but he's never came down here to utilize that so if he ever tried to take me back for custody I'm going to be like he don't even use the custody agreement we have." In regards to why his family doesn't associate with me she said, "They scared of you because you don't mess around. I've always been too nice because I hate confrontation so much so I don't think anybody takes me seriously the only times I've ever snapped at that is if it had to do with custody"

Additionally she said, "When we first started talking, Mack's mom said she knows he's an idiot. One thing I can honestly say is, if y'all were still married I know for fact his life would not be as messed up as it is today because you kept him together as far as career-wise and stuff like he would tell me about it. I feel like he'd be in a much better position and actually have a chance at being happy because I know you really did love him but he cheated on Madison too so I guess he really doesn't know what Love is because he acts like that's his one true love and he still messed around with different women while dating her. Maybe Tamesha still needs time to get there with you but I definitely feel it can happen it's important she cannot have a relationship with your son and not have one with you it don't work like that. When I told her about the apology that Mack's dad sent a day after the divorce, Bryna said, "I'm sorry but his dad is full of shit and I don't like him but I tolerate him. Mack didn't seem to be on your level anyway like I always thought you were so well put together and he just wasn't." She told me how Mack's mom apologized to her for everything Mack did to her and met her new man as well as expressing that she's glad she had him and that she loves them both."

I was thinking, not once did his mom apologize about the situation with Mack and I with me being his wife and I thought it was bizarre. I endured the most pain and you acknowledge a baby mama's pain from six years ago and enabled her sleeping with Mack while he was married to me. It was just a backwards way of doing stuff to me. Bryna appeared to bragging about having a good relationship with Mack's mom after three years of having a bad one and how she can call and talk to her about anything. She told me how Mack's mom said she doesn't trust me because of everything Mack did to me and she feels like I have an ulterior motive and going to try to get back at him.

The only reason why she felt that way is because of her guilty conscience. She knows her son did a lot of wrong and they all disregarded and tried to downplay what he did and how I reacted as if I was acting irrationally. She felt as though I would be out for revenge for everybody so therefore she didn't want anything to do with me when it comes to my son. She basically wanted to cross me out so she didn't have to deal with the backlash of her participation as well. I thought to myself, Bryna did you enjoy feeling apart of his family getting tea on me? You and his mama both just baby mamas never married to the man you had babies with but y'all speaking on a wife, very interesting. She also said Tamesha can't stand Moesha because Moesha kept Mack from his family but forgot about the fact he had a wife and kid huh. When I reiterated that he didn't only leave his family, he left his wife and son as well she again mentioned how his mom was only concerned with Moesha isolating him from his family in Philadelphia.

Another conversation we had was when she claimed that she didn't want Mack back and I said, "Same but I think some may think I want Mack I think NOT. She said, "Yeah they probably think you still want to be his wife, I won't lie at first I did too."

I was thinking, "Even if I did still want to be his wife, I had all rights, we were married. What woman would get married and not want to stay married?"

She was so busy trying to plot against me and the marriage, worried about if I wanted to be with him again or not.

I told her, "I told them all, I never wanted him to begin with that nigga chased me not the other way around and I disposed him ain't no running it back for old times' sake, he trash and I'm too high class for his low class ass. Why would you think that?"

"Because usually when someone talks about somebody a lot it's because they are hurt and still wants to be with them , but then I see you were just in pain and what you went through has to be talked about in order to heal, she said.

"I don't want to be his wife anymore I have upgraded beyond him; if I did I would've never divorced him and would be stuck with him taking any and everything. I lasted less with Mack because I'm smart and I know what he is about. Why would I even remotely want to go back whether we have a child together; I love my child not him. Trust me if you was in my shoes and his family did the same, you would feel the same. Tamesha ain't been with Correll in a minute and still feels some type of way about his wife. I don't want Mack at all and yeah I talk about him because he's hilarious and I literally am smart enough to figure out his tricks, that's it. My corner of friends know for a fact I never wanted him to begin with he begged to be with me but I think they forget that. My last name still is his because of the military not because I want to be his Mrs. I mean Mack can't do a thing for me he's literally the bottom of the barrel period. How I was before is completely different, that's a boy not a man and all my guys know when I'm done that's its over period screw the history, I dispose quickly. If I did want him, everyone know he is not hard to get back and if I did I would invite him to my house a lot more, the fact I keep him away from the inside of my house speaks volumes. A woman with feelings would definitely not do that."

She said, "Yeah girl I feel you; I mean you didn't have to explain I know you don't want that nigga that's just what I thought prior to us really even talking. I mean if you went back to him I would be like girl really because I know you better than that. I wouldn't give Mack to my worst enemy!"

I said, "Nah I just wish they all knew how much I don't want their son. He got them thinking I do but no if I would have said fuck his girlfriend I still want to be with him and play the sides I would've. I respect myself, my body, and time a lot more and that divorce definitely wouldn't have gone as quick. Mack prolonged it not me like he got people thinking. He lied about the adultery and the date I kicked him out. I mean why you would do that if you're so "unhappy with me" but girl my phone be lit all the time with actual men I would be a fool."

"Yeah Mack always lies about everything it's truly sad!!! I say go for what's actually going to benefit you." she said.

I ended the conversation by saying, "Yes girl that's the continuous goal to grow and glow!" I learned a lot about Bryna's perspective of the whole situation combined.

Some of what I learned is Mack gets his ways from his father. Bryna's dad and Mack's dad, Correll went to school together and her dad said Correll was a dog just like Mack is. She said, "He be trying to brainwash every girl into believing his kids' moms are crazy and he's the poor daddy that can't see his kids. That crap use to piss me off so much when he was saying it to you! It's his fault just imagine how much easier life would be for him if he took responsibility for his actions at least."

When Moesha started texting her out of the blue, she was sending screenshots to me and I told her not to trust his girlfriend at all because she's up to something with Mack. Bryna said, "Girl this is strictly for information purposes I mean I don't hate her or nothing but I also don't see the point in building like a friendship because she's still connected to that boy, this is just the hook in the fish I'm sure she'll be texting me a lot more in the future and when she turn on him we got the tea. I think I'm going to be nice; you get more information that way!! I just want to see the motive behind this because this has never happened before I'm interested." Pause, if you in a relationship and claimed to have moved on why would you be interested in getting tea on Mack and her relationship. Bryna claimed she knew that Moesha was texting her to make a good impression to Tamesha and show that she can get along with his kids' mom and she was aware of that. She got annoyed when Moesha started asking her about her daughter and said to me about her, "It's just annoying because how are you asking if she need anything when her own father should be asking that. Furthermore, he sent her home with what five new shirts and two pairs of shoes. He should have been asking for her school supply list and brought all her new school clothes. He knew she didn't wear uniform. I mean if you really concerned you feel me. It's just mad fake. I'm sorry I don't like females hitting my phone about my child she has a father and one mom I could see if we was cool like that but we ain't so what are you doing."

When we got on the subject about Mack's family she said, "They want to pick and choose when they want to speak with my baby so I'll pick and choose if she sleep or not. They always show up late. We always got to send a picture or reminding text; it's just ridiculous. What she was saying I could definitely relate to because Mack's family acts the same way towards me.

When talking about the situation I went through, Bryna told me, "You're definitely stepping in the right direction, what he did to you was so messed up and the fact that nobody ever wants to acknowledge that is painful in itself. But you go and be bigger and greater and above it all. God doesn't let things swallow us whole, he knew you would come out the other side so there has to be a huge blessing in store for you. God is going to heal your heart and then send you some beautiful soul to take care of you and your son and love you both unconditionally. I really want that for you. What I did to you was so messed up. I can say I was going through this and that, but my pain and trials affected your life and I really am so sorry for that. I now have someone I want to marry and it would devastate me if someone did what I did to you. I should have never went there knowing that you were his wife it was wrong. I live with knowing I've done that. That was a secret I said I'd never tell my boyfriend but I felt like I wasn't taking total ownership of what I did so I told him and I felt free. Yes I did it but it's not who I am. Mack has a way of making you feel trapped but you have all the control in your hands it's nothing he can control and that's why he throws temper tantrums."

I don't feel like her apology was completely genuine at all, it was a situational apology. She waited until she got in a relationship with someone else to fill the void that she had from Mack to make it seem to me like she was apologetic just so it doesn't happen in her own marriage when that time came but not because she's actually sorry just how she pretended the last time her words were sincere and she was being directed by Mack. I found it hard to believe but I wanted to see how long she was going to keep her little act up. When we spoke about Mack being absent and not being the father he should be to our kids she said, "If I don't send pictures or say something to him about my daughter, he won't say anything and that's on him. I'm not doing anything extra. You want to know about your daughter then you ask for the pictures and you ask about how's she's doing in school. I'm not saying anything at all. You want to call her you do it. I won't be calling because she doesn't really ask anyway. Life would be so much easier without dealing with that boy."

In regards to Moesha advertising her and Mack's relationship on Facebook she said, "We see what she chooses to show social media "painting a picture" when behind the scenes she could be trying to hold together her "little family." We know Mack isn't a prize at all he isn't a father so I mean what is she really showing off and I'm not even trying to be mean it's just facts. Like your showing off a man that won't even take care of the two kids he already had. I would be embarrassed and if she was a real woman she would be digging in his world about it! Let my boyfriend have had a kid before we met and he wasn't being a father that is so unattractive for one and two that's unacceptable. Mack is a liar he wants everyone to argue so he can keep his lies going. It's when we come together that he gets found out and he doesn't want that. I always say if Mack had handled his business in a better way nothing would be the way it is, it's his fault."

When I asked Bryna about us not meeting up previously before she randomly blocked me on social media the last time we had talked she said, "I wasn't ready, it is hard for me to understand why you would want to talk to me let alone meet up because I mean I did overstep my boundaries when you and Mack were together and no human being just poof forgets about something like that. I mean if it were me I'd forgive still feel some type of way about it. and I wasn't sure if you had some motive behind it with Mack, I'm not judging you because I feel like you have every right to dislike him and you have every right to want revenge that's natural but I just wasn't sure if you were coming from a place of sincerity."

I replied, "I sensed it both times while trying to arrange a meeting; especially when you brought up telling your boyfriend you were going to meet with his dad which was really a meeting between us two. While I understand completely what you are saying, there are people in this world who can overcome and adapt to things especially if there are kids involved. If I did something like you did, without a doubt I would think that the same way, naturally and be afraid. That's the conviction process. Trust me I have too much to lose to have an ulterior motive and especially driving a hundred or so miles with my child, who I care about over any soul. I'm sure you know a lot of women honestly would've tried to take it into physical matters forever and a day but not Faith which I'm sure is hard to believe. Everyone that we all know who has knowledge about everything that I got through only because they know it was all wrong and I should've, could've and would've but I didn't. I'm sure it's hard to believe for everyone involved that I'm sane and still in my right mind but God. I got a present and a future and it ain't worth losing and doing time over no man or woman. I chose to use my mind over emotions because I've never been the fighting type. That's why I handle things through the legal system, in prayer and in God because both have a way of dealing cards that have been played and can do more justice then words or hands ever could. I've learned being kind to others who have done me wrong is the best pay off. Trust me it was and always has been sincere but that's perfectly fine, we can leave it in Mack hands. I've been told several times I am intimidating because of my strong no BS personality despite the way I look and the ability to move past a situation and I understand that too."

Bryna and I shared some personal details of our life such as the fact that she and I had similar childhoods with controlling helicopter mothers and downing dads. She told me her mother experienced the same thing I did after 20+ years of marriage and how her dad cheated on her mother with different women and the one he stayed with and married he also had additional kids by. She watched her mother attempt to fight the females while breaking inside and experiencing the motions of what her father did but exclaimed her mother found new happiness with someone else and that her dad is still cheating on the woman he's married to and getting money from other women as well. At one point she came to me seeking advice on getting a restraining order against her mother because she was talking to her in a threatening and demeaning tone and how she was always talked about because she had a teenage pregnancy. I gave her the best advice I knew from a legal standpoint and she also confided in me regarding her younger sister staying with her and not living up to her standards. Additionally, we both shared our plans for the future, well she did, I didn't say much about what I was doing except the fact that I was moving to Atlanta and I'm going to own business. I wouldn't go into details because I truly didn't know if our conversation was staying between us or if she was the information taker for Mack and his family to see how I'm moving along in life since he did what he did. Finally, she and I both acknowledge how Mack changed us into better women once we broke free from him and we both mentioned one day Moesha's going to see the same and realize how much better life is without Mack and his narcissism. Bryna and I arranged for us and the kids to get together and take pictures for Thanksgiving and Christmas 2018 together but when it rolled around all she had was excuses. We were going to share them with Mack because we both knew how he couldn't stand us talking. Aside from conversation with her, one day when I was cleaning out Mir's room of his old crib and thought I would offer his old crib to Mack for the new baby. After all, his dad's wife, Sherry bought it and I didn't mind passing it down. Moesha was claiming to be his wife and wanted to take his last name so bad so why not pass on a crib to her from one wife to the next. She was so obsessed with the idea of marriage. Moesha was in such a huge rush and I believe it was really a point to prove to me that she can keep Mack and have babies by him too and rub it in mine and Bryna's face. She was also all on social media talking about picking out wedding dresses and everything with her mother before we even got divorced, setting dates and everything that was within the same year. She even went as far as getting his initials tatted on her chest. What a fool she is, desperate for love.

As far as the crib goes, I also knew Mack was struggling financially being on child support too. I figured he would love a good deal and not have to pay anything out of his pocket for a crib and that it would irk the hell out of Moesha too since she would annoy me often. I texted him about getting the crib and he responded back and said, "I appreciate that, but I will be fine."

Later that day, he texted to confirm the time of him visiting Mir. We ended up meeting at a Children's museum. Mir and I had previously gone to it and enjoyed so I figured why not let him meet us there. I took pictures of him and Mir and sent it to his phone. He took pictures of me and Mir as well and sent them to mine. I was surprised he was being civil and started to think that their relationship must've been going downhill because this was out of his norm. I knew to just enjoy it for the moment for Mir because Mack was sure going to revert back to his usual ways after a matter of time when he and Moesha were seeing eye to eye again. I ended up figuring out that he was sneaking around to see our son he wouldn't even touch his phone and his phone would be on silent. His visitations continued every few weeks and the times in between where he wasn't seeing Mir he would not contact him at all via Face Time which I thought was pretty weird like if you really care for your child why would you not contact him on the days that you aren't seeing him. A normal parent that cares for and misses their child would. His actions spoke volumes. He asked me during one of his visitation if he could watch Mir get his haircut at his own Barber.

At first I was reluctant because Mir was already going to a barber and I didn't want to break that routine or that bond we had with him. But then I thought I would test it out to see how long and how often he would go to the barber with him and let him have that moment since he never volunteered to do before and consistently.   I also knew that he was doing it to please his dad because he always wanted pictures and also to stunt social media like he's super involved. I know exactly what that was all about. Earlier that week I had posted a picture of me and Mir at the barbershop on my profile picture so I knew they had to have seen it. Even though I had them all blocked I knew they were watching my page. I took lots of pictures and sent them I also thought it would be good for Mir to see when he got older. On one occasion we went to the zoo, I paid for my admission and entered with Mir. When I got past the check in line, he came up to me and asked if I had paid. I said yes why. He said, "Because I have service connected disabilities, I can get you in free and you can get a refund." I was like oh really and he was like yeah. So, I walked back and he told the lady and I got a refund. This day was a zoo day and Mir got a chance to explore all the animals. He enjoyed his time. Later that day, I texted Mack and asked him if any of the disabilities he claimed Mir has the potential to get. All he mentioned was asthma. I knew that he claimed more than asthma, but he wasn't going to reveal it to me. That information also was going to be useful in the event he filed to decrease child support again, I could tell them he gets disability compensation with dependent benefits and refer back to that text just in case he tried to lie. Since he was being civil, I figured why not share Mir's medical information and updates. I told him about Mir not saying a lot of words for his age which at the time he was 1.5 years old. He claimed that he noticed it and figured he would be saying a lot more words and I was thinking so why he wouldn't mention it to me as a concerned parent would or should anyways. He also asked about his next appointment. I happened to be getting ready to take Mir to the emergency room because he had a very high fever and the medicine was not working. He asked me to keep him updated but didn't even show up as usual. He hadn't gone to any doctor's appointments of Mir's and I always kept him informed but he would never follow up. I ended up spending a couple of days at home and he told me he had wanted to see him. I arranged for him to come and see him after the hospital visit but I didn't know if he was living in VA or PA. He was supposed to update me with his new address when he moved per court order, but he never did. I took this as an opportunity to ask if he had moved and he told me yes and also gave me the address.

There was just a little hope for co-parenting to be on track, but not much because he's known to be wishy washy, so I didn't hold my breath on it. I told him what time I would be home and mentioned that he could text me when he gets closer. He did just that and when I asked him to grab soup from the gas station, he actually did it. I told him that he would have to come to my house because Mir was lying down and not in a position to go outside. With no hesitation, he agreed and showed up. I opened the door and pointed him in the direction of Mir's room. I sat on my living room couch and didn't even go in where they were. He was in the room for an hour and a half. We said nothing to each other. He came out and was going to try to feed Mir the soup. He didn't want it. He ended up staying a few more minutes just attempting to get him to eat. After he got tired of trying, he put Mir down and tried to leave. Mir tried to follow him out the door, but he couldn't go. I took Mir back to his room and laid him down to go back to sleep. I wanted my baby to feel better and I wanted to as well since I was sick too.

About an hour later after he left, I got a text message asking, "How do you feel about me you and Moesha sitting down to talk?"

"She and I have nothing to talk about." It was very weird and uncomfortable for me and I couldn't understand why he didn't have the audacity to talk to me while he was at my house, so it grew my suspicion on if it was really him or not. I got a text back saying, "Well y'all kind of do. The fact that I'm married to her and she has our baby on the way. Eventually she's going to have to be around Mir. She doesn't have a problem with you. I don't want things to be like this once our daughter arrives."

I was thinking, "Married"? We just got divorced three months prior and he turned around and married her that quickly. I thought they were already married while we were married so why did I need to know this? I was like ain't no way, after he saw how things were in court for him and me. You would think marriage would be the last thing on his mind at this point and then the fact that it was said that she's going to have to be around Mir. First of all, you can't dictate alone who "has" to be around Mir and especially not over a chick like her. I had a current restraining order that protected me and Mir from being around her for two years. The last part really stunned me. The fact that it was said, "She doesn't have a problem with you." I'm thinking yes, she does. She was all on Facebook talking about how she wants to slap his baby mamas and obscene remarks, referring to me and Bryna and just making subliminal statuses about us even though she knew we couldn't see it. She would share and write statuses like, "Bitches that think we beefing because we fucked with the same nigga." When his baby mamas' trip on him and try to bring me in it and I'm minding my business for once."

Like first of all, I wasn't his baby mama I was his wife little girl. Second of all, it was only beef because you indulged in being the perpetrator to another woman's pain and you were the woman he chose over his kids and you were doing the most proudly boasting about a terrible husband I had and a terrible deadbeat father of Bryna and I kids. Then you was on Facebook posting things subliminally and even posted on Father's Day thanking him for everything he do for the kids, knowing damn well he wasn't doing anything for our kids but dodging child support and not consistently being involved nor visiting. Meanwhile Bryna and I was thinking what is she even talking about the things he do where are these things she speak of. We had also said the same way she got him; she was going to lose him. Girl, you were praising a deadbeat father trying to make him seem good on Facebook for his and your family and friends. It's almost as if she was talking to herself about her issues she had with us on Facebook. I responded back to the message and said, "Again, her and I have nothing to talk about. There is a restraining order for a reason. If she was civil and stayed out of our marriage and divorce from the jump things might've been okay, but you did things in a very bad manner. I don't trust her or you when it comes to Mir and although I moved on you just don't do the things you did when it came to Mir and me."

At this point, I'm thinking you can't make me talk to this girl. After all, she's done, and she is the reason you neglected your son and moved away to be with her just to make another baby. What a slap in the face! If the scenario was switched he sure wouldn't want to hear any of this so why was it any different for me

After I responded, I got a text back that said, "The court document states that she is allowed to be around Mir once she is my wife. Yes, I understand the restraining order. But she didn't have anything to do with our marriage or divorce."

I'm thinking this is such an idiot. A restraining order overrides a marriage certificate and she did have a lot to do with why our marriage is no longer one and why I got a divorce. At this point, I started to get very annoyed. Mir was sick and here Mack was trying to force and persuade me and this girl to talk. My last message I sent was "Please don't text me unless it has something to do with you seeing Mir, other than that I'm following the court order."

In that same time frame, I got a text that said, "This is Mack. Please disregard any texts before this one I'm sending. That is my fault."

I'm thinking wait just one minute. You mean to tell me that wasn't him and that it was her. Really?!

I texted back, "So you're saying that was Moesha texting me? This must be because you came over to my house to see Mir and she must be feeling some type of way. Was that her texting me?"

"Faith, Don't even worry about it, I didn't even have my phone and didn't know what was said. That is not her place to do what she did, so my fault on that behalf."

At this point I'm like nope, don't brush me off tell me what's up. I don't care the fact if they were married or not, if she was concerned about me by him coming to my house and scared about me wanting to sleep with or take him from her regardless I would've done it. The same way she interfered in mine, I would've had no second thought or sympathy to sleep with him during her pretend or real marriage, but I didn't because I don't like or have any type of feelings for him and I am not that type of chick. It has nothing to do with respecting her at all, I wouldn't care. If I was that type of chick, I would screw him when I want him and send him right back and she could not do a thing about it. I had him once, I could have him again. He isn't hard to get, but I really just don't want him, to be honest I never did. It was always him wanting and chasing me. I texted Correll the screenshots of her messages and I said, "Please talk to your son. I want peace and no foolishness, and I just want him to see his son without him involving this girl. I've been good without all of it."

He replied "I hear you. I think they're going through it right now; he called me all upset because I guess he found out she was texting you. I know he loves his son very much; don't let her ruin their relationship. You have been great through all this and I appreciate you for it." I didn't even respond back to his message. I brushed it off like whatever. He doesn't really love our son, he is just playing a role for right now while him and Moesha are not getting along.

I decided to call Mack and clarify why I was being dragged into the mess. He answered. I asked, "What's going on?"

"Yo she's crazy, she's out of line and won't stay in her place."

I heard him cranking up his car in the background and I said, "You need to leave that little girl alone." At the same time I was thinking she's out of her place because you never put her there, Mack. You let her come in between our marriage and say any and everything to me and now that you trying to get on to her about it, she's confused and feeling some type of way. I told him that she told me they were married and have a baby girl on the way. He quickly denied by saying, "I'm not married." Obviously, he knew that I knew she was pregnant so he couldn't deny that. He told me, "I'll make sure she doesn't contact you anymore. I said okay and I hung up the phone." He texted me an hour later asking, "Is Mir sleep?" Mir wasn't sleeping but I told him, "Yes, we're both going to sleep" because I know his next question was going to be if he could come over my house and I wasn't letting that happen period. I had my friend log into Facebook to see what Moesha was posting after all this had happened. I knew she was angry and would blast it all on Facebook because Mack was at my house and I think it was at that moment she knew that he was sneaking to see Mir and she didn't want that to happen. Shortly after this incident, she wrote a status saying "I never thought that I would be raising my daughter alone, but here I am preparing for it and I will not fail her." Bryna and I was discussing Moesha's reaction to Mack coming over my house and she said, "Why date a nigga with kids and get mad when he's with his kids and the mother is and whatever else you agree upon in place but because Mack let that girl mess with you the way he did he ruined that for Mir, himself, and his parents. That is Mack's fault! All the arrows point back to Mack, honestly but the reason I no longer argue with them about anything is because my child will be good regardless at the end of the day she wants for nothing! I make sure of that so when they have the little moments of being slack yeah I will be irked but I say nothing because it will not disturb anything my daughter got going on because I secure that. Children do grow up they don't stay little precious babies forever and then you allow your child to see it all for themselves at that point. Mack is the one who has to close the loop on all this mess because he did it period."

I agreed with her and she said, "I completely understand that you did everything the right way!! Yeah, Tamesha said she knew her son was an asshole and he did us dirty so I don't know. Girl, it doesn't matter how much you do for Mack you give him all the tools and he won't use it and still blame you for why he isn't doing something, it's pitiful. You're well put together, I don't feel he is. He just never really grew up. How he acts now is how he acted at seventeen. It's hilarious because they trying so hard to make you mad and jealous. I agree with you I would not have sent my child either especially with all that drama!"

The next day Moesha wrote, "I swear I should not be going through this much shit pregnant, but what doesn't kill you makes you stronger." The next day, I guess they were still going through it because he was being civil with me and she wrote "If I shed one more tear today" "If I could go back to two years ago, I would've chosen myself over you."

Like sis, how delusional can you be? The boy was married, and he has two kids by two different women that he wasn't even taking care of and attending to without being forced under the courts before you came into the picture. What made you think you were so special? He hasn't changed at all, he just changed victims and if you put up with him, he'll continue to do it. A man won't leave his dummy, that's why out of all girls he's been with and cheated on, she's been the only one to accept everything he does as long as she can have a piece of a man and a family with him regardless of how he treats her she's fine. Its pathetic honestly but that's her burden to bear and with time she'll see why I acted and treat Mack and his family the way that I do, with a long-handled spoon because the love she thinks he has, Mack is unable to feel and give due to him being a narcissist. He doesn't love the same way as a regular person does. As far as relationships go, he sees women as objects to use to stroke his ego and sexual desire due to him having a fragile ego. As far as kids go, he only sees them as an extension of himself and will try to live out his life by using them as puppets to do so as they get older. He doesn't care and it has been shown in many different ways. He's just willing to play the part as long as he can do what he wants. That's why every ex before me, never had anything good to say about him because if the benefit isn't really about him, it's a dead end. It's crazy because she didn't want to be with him if he kept being around me although it was only about our son. He may have her thinking it's something else or maybe when I'm brought up, she feels like he still has something there for me. She named herself a single mother meaning she was going to keep her kid from him or she knows he's a deadbeat already to his other kids and thinks it's going to happen to her too.

Bryna and I were texting back and forth talking about how crazy she was and the fact that she thought she was going to ruin a marriage and then come before the two kids he already had with us just because she had one on the way with him. That's insane and says a lot about her character and thought process. I don't know what made her think that she was exempt from getting hurt. Look at how she got with him. Did she think she was supposed to have a peaceful life and a peaceful relationship with him? It doesn't work like that. She felt super compelled to lie to his ex-wife about being married to him as if I was supposed to care or have respect or back away from him because of that. What's even funnier is when he started taking up for me, his ex-wife, and telling her to stay out of matters she kept writing statuses hurt because she couldn't understand. It's funny because my ex has been telling this girl all the bad I was and he probably had her smiling and thinking she's made it in life. So for him to switch up I'm sure it confused her because she was sure he hated me. I don't know what made Moesha think that she was exempt from getting hurt look at how she got mad. She thinks she supposed to have a peaceful life and peaceful relationship with him but it doesn't work like; that your karma is your karma, deal with it all. I ended up texting screenshots of the messages to Mack's dad. He texted back, "Shaking my head". I told him, "Please talk to your son. I want peace and no foolishness, and I just want him to see his son without him involving this girl. I've been good without all of it."

He texted back, "I hear you I think they are going through it right now he called me upset because he found out she was texting you. I know he loves his son very much don't let her ruin their relationship. You have been great through all of this and I appreciate you for it."

I brushed the statement off like whatever, yeah sure, but didn't respond because their problems are no longer my problems. She took a problem and she's got to deal with it. Mack continued to be civil and continued seeing Mir. I ended up having to take Mir back to the emergency room that night because his fever wasn't going down. I kept Mack informed and he continued to be civil. When we got back home from the hospital, I sent him a picture of Mir asleep and told him his body temperature.

He responded, "Sleeps just like you. Hopefully, he feels better than he did yesterday."

I knew the first comment was him trying to be nice, but I kept it about Mir and said that we were going back to the hospital again because he had just thrown up. When I got on Facebook later that day, I had a friend request from a blank page by the name of "Rose Mary". I had three missed video chat calls from the page and also messages asking for me to show myself if possible and to pick up the phone. I knew that it was nobody but Moesha and as soon as I said I know who it is and she better leave me alone, we have nothing to talk and if she doesn't that, I was going to contact the police. The next thing I knew was that she left the message on read and marked the page as spam and I never heard from the page again which confirmed that it was her and besides I didn't have any issues with anybody else especially the day after that incident of her texting my phone happened. When I sent the screenshots to Mack, he claimed he had never seen the page before and that he could only speak for himself. He told me to take whatever steps I needed to take, but he said, "I don't know who is calling you and I and Moesha don't talk." Mir's fever lasted a few days, so I stayed home.

After it was gone, Mack texted asking if Mir was free so he could see him and get his hair cut as well. We arranged for him to have his hair cut a few days later. When I asked him how much it would be for his hair cut, he told me the price and said that he may be able to come. I knew Mack's dad was supposed to come down on Mack's birthday, but he said his dad had to push his plans back. He didn't know that I knew but Correll and Sherry were going through marital issues at the time and she had changed her last name in Facebook to her maiden name so when I asked his dad if he was coming, he told me, "No Sherry can't come," and that was the reason why. Mack's visits with Mir started to dwindle a bit again. He wasn't having any contact with Mir on days he wasn't seeing him. Mack's dad texted a few days later telling me Mack had got something for Mir from him and Sherry. I had to correct him on the spelling of his name which is a shame. You don't know how to spell your only grandson name, just ridiculous. He laughed it off and said my bad, but I didn't think it was in the slightest bit funny. When I sent him a picture of Mir, he asked if I was going to, be in town on May 26th. Based on the screenshot of Moesha's page that one of my friends sent me back when I was trying to catch any more slick posts, she had said her baby shower was May 26th. I was already pissed because Mack didn't have decency or respect to wait until our marriage was dissolved before he got into a new relationship and got this girl pregnant. That was strike one and strike two is the fact that his dad really thought it was cool to come and see my child after being down here for the baby shower of another but yet he had never been involved with me and Mir when he was born or him and his family coordinating anything like a baby shower for me. I was pissed. How dare you put my son on the back burner for a pregnant mistress!! I texted Correll back and said, "Yeah I am but I have a duty. I know that's the day of the 3rd child baby shower. You're coming to town?"

Immediately followed by this message I sent another one that said, "I'm going to keep it 100% real with you, I do not like the things transpiring when it comes to Mir. Mir is almost two years old and you've only seen him once since Mack and I got divorced. I've been told several timeframes that you are going to see Mir and honestly I think it's pretty messed up that you are only seeing him at the convenience of being down here for another child's baby shower instead of taking the time out on a weekend to come and see him. I'm only five hours away from VA which is not far at all compared to my parents being twelve hours away wanting to see their grandchild often but can't. I'm moving closer to my parents in some months to have the real support and help and if y'all want to see Mir y'all will have to come to me. I did plan to come to Philly when Mir was first born but I don't have plans of coming to Philadelphia because I'm not with the drama of Mack, his "alleged wife" and his extra girlfriends that's completely out of the picture unless Mack changes his ways and learns how to completely separate his females from his kids mother and be civil for a long term and not just when theirs a spat between them. I have a bright future ahead of me and I will not let it be ruined over somebody that thinks I still want him, because clearly, I don't. I'm going to be twelve hours away. I've tried to be understanding but there is no understanding when it comes to my child and him being put off as an option. I'm no longer in the business of begging anyone to be in my child's life because it may be for the better good of the both of us anyway, however I could no longer hold my peace because I'm sick and tired of being cordial to people who make my child out to be an option and especially because we're so close or because they walked off and betrayed him. True grandparents that love a child would not make any type of excuse. I've prayed about the situation, tried to be humble with you, Mack and the rest of his family but I can't anymore. It sickens me that more kids are continuously being made and the ones here aren't even being seen and I know that's not you're doing it's your son's doing but it's annoying."

His dad screenshot my message and accidentally sent it back to me. I responded and said, "You sent my screenshot back to me. I know you meant to send it to someone else."

Correll responded by saying, "Yeah I meant to send it to my wife. But you act like five hours is nothing to sneeze at. I'm very busy with my work and it's really hard for me to take off on the weekend. I don't need to make an excuse, but I can't just get up and come down there. Yeah, the plan was to come down in March or April but I couldn't. I planned on coming on the 26th for the baby shower and I thought that's the perfect time to see Mir. Your parents come to you because you're their daughter. If my son was there the whole time, I would've been down there a lot more than I have. He just got down there. Yeah, the situation y'all in is between you and my son and if you're moving close to Florida then I will see Mir when

Mack can bring him to Virginia. But to be real you want me to keep coming down there more than I have but what can we do but sit in the lobby for like thirty minutes? So, I wasn't thrilled about driving down for that. I was hoping by now Mack would have been able to bring Mir back to his house so I really can spend quality time with him. I'm not retired I still have a lot going on you're not around the corner! So, will I be able to see him or not? I am not trying to be difficult with you and I understand your frustration but it's not my fault things the way they are.

Ps, me and my wife have plans to come down this summer to take Mir and his sister to Busch Gardens if that is possible?"

I started thinking, first off, five hours is not a lot of time compared to me moving back closer to home, that's even longer, 12-16 hours away from Pennsylvania to be exact depending on where I was moving to. Secondly, the reason he didn't come in March or April is that he and his wife were having marital troubles. That has nothing to do with him seeing my son but whatever; I don't know what that situation was about. Next, he claimed that he was very busy with work, yet he took time out to make sure he made it to the mistress baby shower for Mack's third child, but couldn't be there for my son when he was born up until he's almost two? I call BS. Then to think seeing my son after the mistress baby shower was cool and out of convenience instead of making special trips for him without their being not another occasion going on. Another thing is while he's mentioning his son just got back down to Virginia, his son moved during our divorce when I got a restraining order against his girlfriend which had nothing to do with him being a father but I see who was more important. What pissed me off is he brought up my parents coming to see me because I'm their daughter. What does that have to do with my son whether I'm Correll's daughter or not it shouldn't matter with him being able to come and spend time with his grandson? That was yet another excuse. He also thought that Mack was going to be able to have Mir at his house by then but apparently, he didn't know the truth of the story or Mack told him something completely different. Mack's girlfriend and her threats were why my son was not allowed at Mack's house. He chose to stay with his girlfriend who constantly was bothering the mother of his first son instead of separating her and our child so that's his fault. He mentioned coming down and spending thirty minutes in the lobby. He could come down and spend as much time as he wants it just wasn't going to be in my house being that I didn't trust Mack or his family based on their history nor did I want them to be in my personal life or give off negative energy in my space but he could very well get a hotel room or pick a more family-oriented place it's just the court order said the clubhouse, but it could've been like an indoor playground something that was centered around interaction and play with Mir. The kicker is that he thought he was going to come and take my one-year-old that he had only met once, no video chat, and no knowledge of anything about him or nothing else and thought that he was going to take him to Busch Gardens without me. He must've taken me as a joke because I would've had to be out of my mind for that to happen. I know he didn't want me to go to the theme park with them, but this was about the protection and safety and comfortability of my son regardless. The fact is Correll was basically a blood stranger and my son doesn't know or see him often so he would clutch to me anyways since I'm all he knows being so young. It wasn't in the court order so in my mind I wasn't following anything outside of that court order because if something were to happen I would be to blame as to why I deviated from the court order and then on top of that you already don't communicate with me. I've only met Correll two times in my life, and he knows nothing about my child nor did he ask unless he got picture reminders that my son existed. Busch Gardens isn't even a place for a one-year-old.

I responded, "My parents come to me because I'm their daughter, that's right and I have their grandson. Regardless if I'm your daughter or not and regardless if Mack is here or not, I have your grandson and I am his MOTHER. That's Mack's choice to come back, the same way he left, for no reason at all whatsoever but to play victim like I was causing problems with him and his girlfriend. So, I don't think you're clear on why Mack cannot have Mir in his care for visitation as he did before. I had to get a two-year restraining order on his girlfriend after she threatened and hit me up three times about her desire to cause harm to me. Three strikes with me and it's out. I took her to court got an order which includes Mir. Here we are a year later, and she is still contacting me from Mack's phone asserting her position as a wife that she wants to be, blatantly disrespecting the order. That had nothing to do with Mack coming over and seeing his sick son that day but I guess she's insecure and concerned that I want her man back. That restraining order does not expire until May 2019 and I will not be lifting it, I'm going to get it extended because I do not want to be contacted by her. The judge as you heard yourself in court did not trust Mack to keep Mir away from her, and neither do I. They are still involved and living together right by my job which is fine, but my child is not going to be in the midst of all that drama they always have going on. That is why Mir cannot be in Mack's care without me being present. He chose a female over his living child always. If you want to be upset, be mad at Moesha because she couldn't stay in her lane with our divorce matters and was mad because I had to pull all the proof out the bag so I can get the divorce I so greatly needed. She is the cause of him not being able to bring him to Philly unless I'm there, but I don't even feel comfortable there. My trust level is on zero. It doesn't matter how long you see him, or where it's at, just be happy to see him. And it doesn't have to be at a lobby, but it was put there so no more false allegations are made against me and there are cameras and staff to monitor. I'm a woman of business and I don't tolerate foolishness at all anymore. Mir will not be going to Busch Gardens unless I am present which I know you don't want. Mir doesn't even know you but saw you one time and the baby doesn't remember that. Yeah, you can see him at a park, a kids place, anywhere at this point in VA but Mir doesn't leave my sight and more so now because you all have to have an association with Mack and I cannot trust that. I will not give anybody jealous or mad at me the opportunity to put things in my child's head or mistreat him because of who his mother is. I am going to continue to go by the court order, that's why it is in place."

Correll said, "First of all I can give two craps about Moesha. I have nothing to do with that situation like I told you. Moesha is Mack's problem, not mine. Yeah, it does matter how long and where we see him at, I'm driving five hours away. To you, it may not seem long, but it is like I said for thirty minutes or so with you around are you serious? What we suppose to keep paying for hotels? No, it doesn't work like that for me. I'm supposed to keep driving there for you to dictate what I can do with my grandson. I rather wait until my son, his father, can get him so I really can spend time with him! Don't get me wrong I've grown to love Mir a lot from the first time I saw him but again you're five hours away! So don't involve me in this crap I'm getting down there when I can if you don't like it I don't know what to tell you."

"Well okay if that's what it takes for you to want to spend the time you want with Mir then so be it, your choice. Like I said that's the reason why Mir can't be in his care. Mir can't be around her so that's the only reason why I had to break it down in layman's terms for you. Don't be mad at me, I'm defending who I raised alone. That's fine. Enough said case closed."

"See you got everything messed up I told you I can give two craps about Moesha I'm coming down there for my son and grandson that's it. But if you don't trust me or feel like I would do something to hurt Mir then that's fucked up! You can protect him all you want but you the one that's keeping him away from us! I don't fuck with Moesha so really don't know where all this coming from but so be it peace!"

Here's the thing Mack is a huge liar and only tells his family what makes me or females look bad so I broke it down to Correll in case he didn't know the truth that's it. Never did I say he would or would not hurt Mir, there was a court order that stated supervised visitation for Mack and his family to be included in the visitation and I wasn't going out of that especially for these dysfunctional people. I don't even know them. I've met them twice and they've shown how disloyal and liars they are. I didn't want Mir going there and then something happens and I regret it and besides, he was young and attached to me and started showing signs of a developmental delay so I wanted him to keep close to me so I could see what's wrong. They wouldn't pay attention to the stuff I do as a mother and won't nobody else care and take care of my son like me. If they were so concerned about my son it wouldn't have taken so long for him to see him once. They just don't like me and wanted to be around me because I won in court against their son. He's used to screwing females over like Bryna said and he and the girl couldn't torment me by playing house and being petty. Another thing, I wasn't keeping Mir from them. They were freely able to come and see him in the state we lived in but of course, it's easier to blame me and I see where Mack gets his lack of accountability and blaming game from. I told Correll, "The lies and delusions, Lord Jesus and Nah, y'all keeping y'all self away from Mir. I have asked and told y'all you're welcome to come here and you choose not to for reasons and excuses like you stated previously so you got it messed up. I'm serving my country in another state. Good day, Correll."

He said, "You got it all messed up, it's whatever when it comes to Mir. I'll deal with my son because you've got some crazy shit in your head about this chick and bringing me in it. I told you I was coming down the 26th you have a problem because it's Moesha involved. That's your fucked up the problem, not mine! But peace out girl I won't be bothering you ever again."

Well first of all Moesha's crazy for all the shit she did and very questionable about any actions she could take out on my son due to jealousy. I had a problem because my son was placed on the back burner for nearly two years until it was convenient for him and to come to be there for another child but not Mir. That's favoritism and I guess it's because Mack was still involved with Moesha. Bryna said Mack's family was the same way with her. They didn't have anything to do with her until the baby got here but didn't come to her state in South Carolina when they moved and his mother and father would ignore her too. It's like the common denominator of all the drama which is Mack is not to blame for things and the females are wrong for reacting, protecting their kids and getting away from all of the mess and then trying to say that we keep the kids from them while they're doing no effort to come to see them. I said to Correll, "Nah I don't have anything crazy, I'm logical whereas you're not. You know you would feel some type of way if your child was in my shoes but you fail to see it from that point. Things would not be this way and Mir would be able to be there nor at his dad's house had none of what I previously stated been a factor. At this point, I feel like it would be better if I argued with a brick wall because talking to you is what it seems like. I can feel any type of way I want when it comes to my child and being betrayed. Fine, if you don't want to bother me that's cool. This is why I do not want my child around without me being around because you are pretending to not have a problem with me and I know deep down you do for no legitimate reason. You can't be reasonable understanding or civil. I can and I've been all three. Not one time have I cussed at you in this message which shows your hostility towards me about my child? Our convo is done today. When you can get your head out of your behind and grow into some real understanding. The line is always open." If you knew the things I know about her from people around town and things she puts on social media, trust me you wouldn't want your child around either."

He must've thought I was stupid, obviously if you're coming to Virginia where Mack and Moesha both live and you want to get my child out of my sight, of course, you're going to disregard what I'm saying and do it behind my back. I don't have time for that disrespect stuff. This is my child and I will protect him period.

Correll finally said, "AGAIN *I HAVE NOTHING TO DO WITH HER IF YOU DON'T WANT YOUR CHILD AROUND HER I COULD CARE LESS. I TOLD U I DO NOT MESS WITH THAT GIRL AND AGAIN I HAVE NO PROBLEM WITH YOU IF I DID I WOULD NEVER TEXT U ABOUT ANYTHING I WOULD JUST DEAL WITH MACK WHEN IT COMES TO MIR. ALL I CARE ABOUT IS MY SON & GRANDSON BUT U KEEP TALKING ABOUT MOESHA. I UNDERSTAND WHAT YOU'RE GOING THRU BECAUSE OF HER I WAS JUST TALKING TO MY WIFE ABOUT THAT HOW SHE CAUSE ALL THE PROBLEMS!!!! I'm GETTING PISSED OFF BECAUSE U*

*KEEP BRINGING HER UP FOR SOME REASON WHEN
ALL I ASK WAS WERE U GOING TO BE HOME SO ME,
MY WIFE & MOTHER CAN SEE OUR GRANDSON!!!!!
THAT'S IT!!!!"*

So at this point, I'm like see this is exactly why my
son ain't going unattended because you just said you could
"care less if I don't want my child around her" basically
you have no respect or honor for his mother and her stance
nor the court order. I also had told him I have a duty that
day so I was unavailable so I don't know what else there
was for us to talk about. Then here comes Mack inputting
his opinion, "I have given you enough respect to keep
things as cordial as possible, and I would expect the same
in return. I'm telling you straight up; do NOT contact my
family other than regards to Mir. My dad asked a simple
question as to if you would be available at a particular time,
not for your "thoughts." I could care less about anything
you have going on personally, but be advised and I'm
pretty sure you already know this custody arrangement is
set to change. I won't go back and forth with you as I'm
way past that stage, but don't contact my family to express
your personal opinions, only contact them if it involves
seeing my son." His family has expressed their thoughts to
me on several occasions and as soon as I do it and it had to
do with Mir it's a problem. These people are delusional to
think I have to listen to them and what they feel on this and
previous occasions but not to hear my mouth about their
hostility and inconsistency. In other words, they want to
dish it out but can't take it.

I told Mack, "Everything I have spoken about to
your dad is about Mir so what you're saying makes no
sense right now. It won't change because the courts are
already aware of everything. I have primary custody and
the judge already explained to you the reasons and factors
behind it. You have a lot going on to not have supervised

visits and Mir does not need to be involved in that. You have visitation I never denied you or your family visitation and that's that."

Mack always threatened to change the custody agreement like he had some type of magical power to do so. Truthfully, he doesn't care about his kids and even Bryna said he used to threaten her about custody as well and she didn't do anything wrong he just knows how precious our babies are to us and wants to make them, leave us for females, then strip them away for revenge even though he barely honored either of our court orders against him. She also said, "My daughter emergency contact is not them. I would not put my daughter's life in jeopardy like that and Mack mess around and not show up because he looking at a car or something dumb. I told him about her first day he didn't show up! I send him her weekly behavior he doesn't say anything that's his problem, not mine he doesn't care! They all on the "cannot pick my child up" list I take extra steps just in case you never know, Tamesha on that list too, I trust her but Mack is her son so sorry."

Mack responded and said, "Please reread my last message if you did not understand what I said about contacting my family. And yes, you may have the last word if that helps you sleep at night."

"Please reread my message if you did not understand everything I explained to your dad has to with Mir and I won't back down from what I stand by. You are too inconsistent and you always have an ulterior motive behind doing things and even the judge at the court said that." Even though I told Correll that I had duty that weekend, Mack still texted my phone asking about his family spending time with Mir on Saturday/Sunday. I informed him of the same and told him the next weekend is available.

He said, "Family doesn't Come up here often they're here for the weekend. I'm pretty sure something is possible, whether it be for an hour or ten minutes, doesn't matter what time, I'm sure it can be done this weekend."

I responded by saying, "Family should want to come up here more often. Mir is about to be two in four months and he has never seen any of them except your dad, one time. There's no excuse for not seeing him more often we aren't far at all. I can try to figure something out but this interfering with our life and my schedule with the last minute, back and forth, and cancellations."

Mack responded, "I'm honestly getting tired of the irrelevant extra talk, I just need answers to the questions I am asking you. You're not busy the entire day, if not then it is what it is but you're not even attempting an effort is a misunderstanding."

"I am free to voice my concerns when it comes to the choices of only wanting to be part of Mir's life when it suits others. That'll never change with me and it's actually great to be an effective communicator instead of being oblivious, I don't know where you get the "not attempting effort part from" but I have a lot of proof when I attempted for two years to get you and your whole family to see Mir since he was born but instead I get ghosted, blocked, and asked to give my child away to blood strangers for an extended amount of time. I know you don't like it, but I'm your child's mother for life and this is how I am."

"Not concerned about his mother, just my child. Feel free to voice your opinion, just not to me or my family. If you can make something happen this weekend, please let me know. Thank you."

His request was at the bottom of my list. I wasn't going to allow him or his family to force me to shift around my job and personal things for their rushed appearance to see my child especially after he's been put on the back burner multiple times until a new baby of Mack's came into the picture. What a piece of shit that family is. The last message I sent him after his remark was, "You could've kept that to yourself because that is a negative comment and not working towards maintaining a positive relationship with your child's mother whom your child will eventually see for him. I take care of Mir and my schedule and his schedule matters." He ignored. A couple of hours later I told him I could only do Monday since it were a holiday. If that doesn't work as I said, this weekend we can figure a time out for next weekend. He ignored my message.

A couple of days later I ended up finding a few minutes of spare time out of my schedule and told him but he ignored that message as well. He was angry he was not in control and couldn't get his way on the day he wanted to. When I texted his dad on Sunday and told him I was on call and could meet them with Mir, he read the message and waited about fifteen minutes to respond and say that they were headed back.

Mack texted a few days into the next month and asked to drop off clothes from Correll and to see Mir as well. I told him that I was taking Mir to the carnival and he could see him there if he chose to do so. He agreed and met me there. Mir's sister, my stepdaughter, was there and they met each other for the first time. Mack kept whispering to her trying to tell her where they were at for her to tell Moesha when they got back home. I guess he snuck out again to see Mir without her knowing so he was coaching his daughter to lie so she wouldn't say anything. I took a lot of pictures of Mir and his sister and sent them to Mack and Bryna. Bryna said when she had talked to her daughter she said she was going somewhere with Mack but didn't mention where. When I told her where were, she also figured he was sneaking to see Mir without Moesha knowing. When the carnival was over and Mack and Mir's sister went back home, her mother told me she FaceTime her later that day and asked her how the carnival was. Her daughter asked her how did she know and she mentioned my name. She said she saw Mack and Moesha leave out the room because Moesha didn't know about it and I guess it became an issue. Bryna posted the kid's pictures on Instagram and we talked about how pathetic Moesha was. She said if she had a problem with him having kids she should've dated someone else and not got pregnant by him. Bryna said, "I have no respect for either of them I just hold my peace because I will not let either of them think I care about what they do or have going on because I don't! I think she's a very insecure person and wants to look like something she's not! She's not a good "stepmom" what so ever! She sucks actually! She's not mature at all!!! She isn't mentally prepared to handle everything she got going on! This is why she's constantly making herself look stupid."

When she told me Moesha starting texting her out of the blue I told her not to trust her because she's connected to Mack and they are up to something as usual. She said, "Girl this is strictly for information purposes I mean I don't hate her or nothing but I also don't see the point in building like a friendship because she's still connected to that boy, this is just the hook in the fish I'm sure she'll be texting me a lot more in the future and when she turns on him we got the tea." She was looking to get info for both of us to see if her perfect relationship was turning out for her like it was for us and Moesha could expose him.

On another occasion, Bryna said, "I have no respect for either of them I just hold my peace because I will not let either of them think I care about what they do or have going on because I don't! I think she's a very insecure person and wants to look like something she's not! She's not a good "stepmom" what so ever! She sucks actually! She's not mature at all! She isn't mentally prepared to handle everything she got going on! This is why she's constantly making herself look stupid."

"You hit that right on the head. It's very visible she's not bright and it's been like that from the start. As a mom, I would be ashamed, if my child brought someone like that to me. Her mother ought to be ashamed but then again she may not even know all of what happened and I'm not the bitter ex but I was a bitter ex-wife I won't even lie but I had every right."

"Yes she reminds me of how I was when Mack was cheating on me I was doing any and everything to keep from making myself look dumb!!!! I was immature it took me a while to see who he was and hopefully eventually she will see it, because seeing his true character was one of the best things that ever happened to me. I mean, of course, you did look how he did you! I would have been mad too! It was harsh and so sudden "

"Yeah it's so freeing honestly I'm glad I didn't let him drag me with his false self and flying monkeys for years, they hate when you figure them out but adore you when you're oblivious"

"Exactly they love using people! But not today honey."

Bryna also said in a separate conversation because she was thinking about listening to Tamesha and putting Mack on child support after five years and when his mother told him about it, he was texting her trying to be nice and call her to talk about doing it without the courts and sending her $300 a month. Bryna said when she tried to put him on child support he cussed her out and told her he was not paying child support and that she had that saved in her email. "Money has always been important to Mack since forever!" Bryna said. "I remember when we were younger he brought me a sandwich and I didn't like it so threw it away and he literally cried real tears talking about he was saving that money and then let me have it to eat and I threw it out I was looking blank."

I laughed and said, "He does not have them all, he's crazy but will buy a new car or give gifts and money to females he wants to like him in a hot min She said, "Lol it's crazy !" I told her, "If I would've talked to you before lord I would've never entertained this crazy, this is embarrassing for me."

"Yeah and the crazy thing is he did me dirty way before we even really got together in 7th grade we liked each other and we were talking and this girl name Susie was my friend and she knew I liked him so she started flirting with him. Girl, he ends up dating her knowing she was my friend and then she "cheated" or whatever kids do and he was like I should have never done that to you like he was always toxic."

"Yeah Mack just wants to be with literally everybody. He got Moesha brainwashed girl; she lasting only because she's stupid and wants to be his favorite that don't get him on support and that won't move away but yeah he's very toxic he just puts on a different face when he first meets a person then the mask falls off and it's abuse and everything else."

"Yes he always had that hoe mentality! And I'm sorry but that was taught! Because both my brothers are married and are faithful because my parents didn't teach them to do that to women. Yup, that's exactly how it goes he lifts you up and in due time when he gets bored he tears you down and leave you to build yourself back up again."

"Yes it was taught by his delusional dad trying to act as if he doesn't know where Mack got that from and his wife lied to me back then and said his dad would never do such a thing like he did to you but I knew she was lying. Thank God I built myself back up; he's not worth the loss of self-esteem at all."

"Nah my dad said his daddy was a hoe to they went to school together. Yup. Becoming a teen mom has left a scar but I don't let it define who I am. It just hurts when you know you're better than the mistakes you made I let myself down when it came to Mack. My parents didn't raise me to want to allow someone to cheat on me over and over and stay they were so disappointed in me. I remembered my dad called me weak back then when he heard I went back to him and he was right it was weak."

"Becoming married and divorced in less than a year has left one for me, but when it happened and as I see how much of a mess he is I thank God for a second chance to get it right. I was surprised I took him back after he sent me to jail and cheated but I gave it one shot and after that, I was just done and had to kick him out. My parents didn't raise me to tolerate it either but sometimes we can't help who we love or attract to at the time it's okay, it's made us strong, our kids are well taken care of and not lacking at all."

"Yeah that's a lot happening in such a short time frame but I believe God was saving you from that fool."

"There is nothing good I can say about him honestly but that's someone else's problem to deal with and of course, nope and never will." Mack tried to make out like I wasn't getting a lot of child support to deter her from wanting to put him on it. Bryna said she would get more through the courts and last time he stopped giving her money because he got mad at her. She said to me, "He keeps forgetting I'm not seventeen anymore if I play dumb it's on purpose! If I'm being nice it's on purpose! If I tell him something, it's something that's not personal at all and if it's repeated I wouldn't care. His girlfriend has always rubbed me the wrong way, God shows me the inside of people before the person themselves show it to me. If I was a stepmom my stepdaughter's hair would always be done her outfit wouldn't be thrown the freak together; her nails would be done and she'd come back to her mother with a separate suitcase because I spoiled her that bad. That doesn't happen with her (referring to Moesha) she loves my daughter for Mack's sake but if she could she would choose to only have his child and say fuck our kids. Our kids are an inconvenience to him and her. Tamesha is trusted as far as my daughter's safety but I don't trust her with anything else but that Mack is her son. I would kill for mine so I know she would kill for hers that's just how it is and I respect that. But she just going to have to realize it goes both ways." Moesha had the nerve a few weeks before her and Mack's baby was born to say on Facebook, It's our last few weeks not being parents."

I sent the screenshot my friend sent me of that and we talked about that too. This girl disregarded our kids and acted as if her child was the only important one and as if Mack was not already a parent although he was not playing his role as one. She made it seem like he was becoming a parent for the first time. She's sick and delusional in the head to even think that was funny to say. We both were disgusted with it because he was barely seeing either of our kids. I told Bryna regarding her text message that she sent, "You hit that all on the head! When Mack and I were together, I didn't even have enough time with your daughter and by the time I would have, we were separated. I only spent maybe a week or so with your daughter before she left in 2016 and I was big pregnant and pissed with Mack. I bought her what I could at the time but had him. If I had somehow been together she definitely would've been beyond taken care of. I used to look up salon people for kids and I told Mack when she came I was going to get her hair done and for her to have an extra room set out for her. But it was meant for him and me to not be together and regardless of that I don't mind doing for her when I see things. I try to not overstep or try to be her mother or play that stepmother role but because of genuine care and concern. All of that foolishness they are doing, however, is just ridiculous and fake and you are right both of our kids are an inconvenience. She's only caring because she's with Mack and trying to hold on to every bit of him. I knew that she didn't care when she found cheap Wal-Mart clothes to buy Mir without putting who it was from but girl when I tell you if God hasn't done it already, he is going to put a whooping on them both. I'm starting to believe she is a female narc; she and Mack will last a while I believe now because they're similar but she's going to walk up on some bad situations, I'm not claiming it but that's usually how it goes with narcissists."

"Yeah and I can't lie at first I didn't like the idea of sharing my child with another female that's the only thing I wasn't looking forward to when I found out Mack was married, because some females start to think the child is theirs and they have said so in certain areas. My guard was already way up prior to you and during you I did everything by myself so I was like I'll be damned if some girl thinks they're going to playhouse with a child I raised by myself. Mack painted the picture that he was doing for my daughter when I knew he really wasn't but of course as his wife you had to believe him and that's why when you called and asked about my daughter when me and him wasn't talking I snapped. He was already doing a bunch of lying you just didn't know yet but I did so I was pissed but I feel like you would have been great to her. I wouldn't of had to worry about her being thrown together or anything and you wouldn't treat her any type of way. Yeah, she is feeling herself because she got him and I think since she's getting in good with Tamesha. She wants to show her that she can get along with his other kids' mom. I know what it's about. She might just be the perfect delusional girl he needs. She lets him treat her any type of way."

"That last part is on point. That's exactly what she's doing because that was too coincidental that she texted you right before they go to Philly. Mack trying to show her and you as good and that I'm just the bitter one who wants him back and can't be good but so much that his family doesn't know about has gone on. Meanwhile Tamesha has no idea the stuff that girl posted on Facebook before and how she just ain't no good period. It's like she helped Mack lose out on stuff out of course Mack is probably helping paint a picture that she's not that bad and when they were in Philly, I'm sure I came up and he talked crap but her time will come. I feel you on that not liking another female caring for your child part that's why I'm willing to fight about Mir only with Moesha because she is no good and I don't want to deal with her or him with Mir going there and teaching him how to lie so I think the courts would agree with a lot of my points because of the history and the likelihood of it occurring again. Yes she is super dumb and Mack loves that, he doesn't value or love her, he sees her as easy and no self-esteem and he has so much control over her. Do you know from your friend if she ever posts and tag him in pictures of just their child on Facebook? I'm really curious what crap he's going to say on Mir Birthday, we know him going to play victim and her going to follow up."

"Yup, of course, she probably hyped and feeling complete. I can't. She can have that headache if you got to do all that to keep a man it ain't worth it. Yeah, like even when my daughter came back she was singing songs that I don't let her listen to she was saying nigga and everything I'm like Whoa. I haven't talked to her in a minute .I got to go through a lot of hearing her complaining about her ex before I get the tea I need. I need to prepare to be annoyed first."

"That's crazy and it probably comes from her and Mack listening to Meek Mill. I know someone who is still friends with him but I haven't talked to her in a while either and she's the only one. I doubt she posted about the baby and Mack probably told her not to because it'll make her look bad posting only her child when he got two others and honestly she is only cool with him and have a father for her child because they are still together and she wants it to be that way while he fucks over her like a dummy. If they weren't together, it would be a different story and she wants to hold out until the order I have against her expires so they can keep the mess going again that's the honest reason they together, she don't want to miss out and thinks she has rights to my child but nah I'm going to permanently fix that. Mack has very little involvement with Mir and the fact he can't talk and he doesn't communicate with Mir now every day or so I doubt they let him go far away from me especially with Mir not talking at all and able to understand.

Bryna said, "Yeah she was singing Drake too, I don't listen to rap at all so I know I didn't do it she was singing gospel when she left girl came back a baby thug. That's sad he got her on the leash that much she won't post her child who does that. Mack use to tell people he didn't have kids at all when I was in Philly but my aunt bumped into him at his job at Wal-Mart and she was loud and was like Mack how your daughter is. Everyone was like I didn't know you had kids and he walked away embarrassed, that's when I knew he was really an ass-hole! Yeah Moesha dying to play mommy to your son, it actually pisses me off when she calls my daughter her stepchild; my boyfriend doesn't even do that and he's very active in her life but he said she has a dad and even though he's not worth anything he would never take that away from him. He is more than happy to play the father role in her life but he wants her to grow up knowing she does have a father. Now that's respect and she doesn't know to what that means. She ain't his wife like you; she's a girlfriend playing that role and sit down."

"Yes like that is so disrespectful and was calling herself a wife as well like his family got to know something wrong with her for her to have done that for all that time last year. Same here like Mir will know who his real dad is and who is his bonus dad and she don't know respect talking about, "Trust me now that I'm a mom I see things that you and Faith have mentioned." I've barely talked to her so I don't even know what she's talking about unless she was all in Mack phone. I honestly pray someone better can come in the picture but we know Mack is gonna brainwash them too. As I get closer with God than I have before he's been moving some things, so if we wait for something will work out and hopefully it's where we can deal from a distance. Hopefully, it's a military chick he marries and goes overseas."

"Yeah that's mad weirdo stuff to me like literally faking a marriage you got that much time on your hands' sis. I don't know but I'm going to keep both of them in my pocket. He would have to change for a girl with common sense to want him." I agreed.

After I told her Mir and I would be moving to a state and be closer to her and Mir's sister she said, "Oh you're going to be a lot closer! That's cool! Yeah we can do little trips with them and everything, yeah girl do what you have to do for you and your son, because you're the primary parent in his life, I wouldn't trust him with your child I don't trust him with mine, I have to stay prayed up just to keep sane with the fact that she's with him right now because he's unstable. Yeah I think we should definitely get him and his sister to do trips together. He probably has no idea how much we actually do talk but I like the idea he's completely clueless. I got him to run his mouth before and I know I can do it again. Just play nice for a little more and I'll get something out of it and I feel bad that I think that way but you have to dealing with him."

After Mir and his sisters' first visit together, a few days later I happened to be looking at the child support portal to keep track of payments made. I used those to pay majority of Mir's daycare expenses and paid the difference. I noticed that the payments were significantly less and reached out to Mack to see what was going on. He questioned why I asked him and I told him why. He was rude in his response back when I was simply asking a question. I ended up telling him, "So your smart remarks start helping the situation and you're making it worse overall when dealing with me and expecting me to work with you on everything. I just asked a simple question you aren't hurting me; you're hurting yourself. What is your problem? You never want to hear anything I have to say about Mir, check on him, or communicate about matters regarding him. I'm seriously at the point of wanting you to surrender your parental rights if you're going to continue to act this way towards me and play hopscotch in and out of Mir's life. If you do that you don't have to pay me child support and you don't have to ever hear from me again about him but ultimately that's not going to feel good for him when he gets older but this toxic counter parenting is bad. He ignored my message.

Two weeks later he asked if I was free and I told him exactly what times. There was a kids program going on that morning and I thought that we could meet there but he said he wasn't available until later that day whenever I was free. We ended up meeting at Chuck E. Cheese's later that day and Mir saw his sister again. They had a blast together and I took pictures and sent them to Mack and Bryna. I told her that Mack was being so cheap he didn't want to buy her daughter anything so I bought her a shirt and she was happy. I had Mack buy Mir a ball. Before leaving him and his sister took pictures with Chucky and then his dad as well. A few days later Mir and I went to North Carolina to have some fun at a children's museum there. We were always on the go. At one, Mir had already been to a lot of states such as Florida, Georgia, Washington, Pennsylvania, New Jersey, and South Carolina. I loved having getaways with my favorite little man. For me, it drowned out everything that was going on too even while still in the military and going through a divorce. . I felt so free, just my baby and me. When we got back Mack and Mir's visits continued and we went to museums, the zoo, the aquarium, and indoor playgrounds with Mir's sister included.

At one point I had bought Mir's sister a shirt and told her mom I could mail it to her or give it in person. I ended up giving it to Mack and he told her someone bought her a shirt but didn't mention who. She loved it and when she got on FaceTime with her mom later that day she told her she didn't know who bought it. Her mom told her I bought it and she said it loud enough so Moesha could hear it and there was complete silence in the house. I guess Mack didn't want Moesha to know he was seeing Mir and his daughter together with me around and didn't want her to snap on him, or try to leave him because she didn't like and want him around me if she couldn't be involved. I enrolled Mir in swim lessons and invited Mack to come along. I knew he wasn't going to but decided to tell him anyways. He asked questions as if he was going to show but never followed up with me about it. Mir ended up not going to swim lessons at all because he became sick. His sickness lasted a few days and Mack ended up seeing him at our apartment clubhouse.

A few days later I was checking my credit report I realized that Mack's second and newest Dodge Charger he bought a few months back, was appearing on my credit report under my maiden name. I sent him a screenshot of my findings and ask him to tell me why it was appearing on my credit report and if he used my old address or my new one. He mentioned calling me after he got out of class but I told him that I was working so it would be better for me to text. Besides if he admitted something I want it to be through a text not a phone call since I didn't have a phone recording app on my phone at the time.

He ended up asking me is it for an insurance quote and I told him no it was just on my credit report and he said he was not sure why but he's never used my address. It was concerning for me to see this car that I don't drive or never owned but it did help boost my score a lot. I told him I do not need fraudulent activity on my account and that the car was under my maiden name that was supposedly on his car and not many people had known that my name was that or if I still went by my married last name so I was really confused as to why. It ended up disappearing from my report weeks later. I asked Mack if it was his daughter's last weekend in Virginia before going back to her mother. He said, "Yes" and asked if Mir was available that weekend. I responded back with yes. He didn't respond back but the next morning I texted him and said, "For Sunday, you can have her bring a swimsuit and her and Mir can get in the pool together while you see him. He didn't respond back. I had no idea what that was about. The next day I didn't hear anything from him. I ended up texting him that afternoon because it was obvious he didn't care and I said, "Thanks for not letting me know you're unable to see Mir today. I don't know what your intentions were in telling me with this day but you could've given me notice like the court order says. I'm not available anymore at all today. Have a good one." Mack did this pretty often where he would just disappear and act like Mir didn't exist for weeks or sometimes months until he felt like it. He responded back to my message and ignorantly replied, "Hello is Mir available today. I didn't even respond because I had already said what I said and he was playing dumb or maybe he wasn't playing because it was actually in his character to act dumb all the time.

He double texted and said, "Thanks for the response. Let's make it clear, not once did I say I was not available on Sunday. But that's okay, continue to let your ego guide your decision, I will add this to the files. I'll see our child the next time "you" have an open availability. Enjoy your evening."

"You never gave me a time nor did you respond to Friday or Saturday's message to set something up. Like I said, court order says 48 hours so next time be smarter and finish the conversation the same day like usual so you can have "your visitation." Additionally, you can add it to your "files "but you're only working against yourself, not me."

He then texted back, "Let me ask you this, is Mir available today or are you unavailable today? I let an hour go by and I didn't even respond because it was obvious he was trying to have pointless conversation and start an argument. I got a double text that said, "O. That's all I needed, thank ya."

Bryna and I were texting and we was both said how it didn't sound like Mack and that it had to be a new girl stepping outside of her boundaries already. I know Mack and I know the language, punctuation, and words he uses so I knew it wasn't him especially because he admitted before that Moesha used his phone to text me and she's done it on multiple occasions.

I texted him back hours later saying, "Stop having your girlfriends and other people text my phone pretending to be you. I know the difference in the text language. If you continue this, I will file a harassment restraining order against you." You could tell he was bored and waiting for me to respond back to his foolishness because he responded back seconds later saying, "Goodbye, no time for the games. If it ain't about Mir don't contact me." Bryna and I were talking about how he was acting and she said, "I'm sorry but you can't disrespect the mother of your child and expect to have a healthy relationship with the child it doesn't work like that. She mentioned that Mack never thinks in the best interest of the child and the judge has already seen that this is all ridiculous." She also had mentioned, "I'm so glad you save everything. I wish I could testify for you or something but it's nothing I could really say I don't think but I just want them to see you need to be left alone and it's getting out of hand at this point. I feel bad that you have to deal with this; I'm really praying that you don't have to deal with his foolishness anymore it's crazy, nobody would want to continue in this. He acts so psycho with you've I've noticed and he's never ever been this bad to me that's why my mouth be open when I see how badly he treats you because it's ridiculous! Like the nigga has a mean streak and it's not normal and he has no evidence or you doing anything." He started seeing Mir again a few weeks after and started talking robotically like "Per court request, this is a 48 hour minimal notice message. When will Mir be available this weekend as I would like to exercise my visitation rights?"

I gave him times and dates and he started being condescending in a slick manner by saying Ma'am this and Ma'am that. I had originally set up for his visit to be at my clubhouse but decided to allow it to be in an indoor playhouse setting so Mir could play. Five hours prior, I pushed the time back thirty minutes which gave him extra time and I changed it to a playhouse. As complicated as he is, instead of accepting the extra time and enjoying the fact he gets to watch him play he said to me, "I would appreciate if a notice of this change of time in location was

224 | P a g e

provided 24 hours in advance to better prepare for this change. Your message was acknowledged. Thank ya."

"Your foolishness and robotic talk is really uncalled for. You're not co-parenting in any way nor are you really even concerned with Mir's wellbeing and things he has going on in his life and I'm not making you be. However, I know you have a problem that needs professional help, like our judge said twice at our divorce hearing. I would seriously advise you seek some out through the VA for NPD, like I've told you before and co-parenting if you aren't already. You are the only one in the court order who is provided to give a 48 hour notice if you're exercising visitation. You ought to hush and be happy that it's not a cancellation and you get to see Mir in a public setting while he plays, period. This change is not negative nor is it even an inconvenience for you at all; you just want to be complicated as usual, making it more difficult on yourself, not me."

"Thank you for your concerns, but if it's not related directly to our child, as I have previously and extensively requested before, refrain from contacting me. I would like to assure you that your negligence in following that request can and will be used to further present to a judge. Thank you for your understanding and cooperation."

"Your behaviors directly can affect Mir and co-parenting with me and that is why I address it and highly recommend you seek help because Mir does not need to be around you unsupervised which is why the judge has it in place because he is aware of your behaviors and actions and continued harassment from your baby mama #3 on your phone of whom I have a restraining order against and will be extending. I have told you to stop having her contact me as well as your inconsistent job hopping, state, and house hopping, and your inconsideration of Mir overall period. I have done nothing wrong, I've obeyed the order and I am not one bit worried about you going to court and using what you think is "evidence" to a judge. Trust me; I have a lot of valid evidence against you. Mir will see you at 430p.m. This is uncalled for. You want to cause chaos and I'm not entertaining it, just see Mir and make sure to pay the $4510 to me by December 7 so you don't go to jail and can continue seeing Mir."

He said, "I will add your messages to the files. Please do not contact me further if it is not about Mir as I have continuously stated or harassment charges will follow. Thank you for your cooperation."

"I'm only contacting you about Mir and co-parenting. I've done nothing wrong. Only contact me about Mir and how you can contribute to him."

"Please do not contact me as previously and continuously stated if it does not directly concern Mir as further action will be taken. Thank you for your cooperation."

When the time came to take Mir to see Mack I replied, "I'm here." As soon as I sent that message, Mack said, "Its 5, this place closes at 6."

"I know what time they close which is why I moved the time to 430 instead of 5, however Mir was napping and had to eat so that took precedence over arriving on time for today. We're coming in."

"Why he was not prepared earlier to 4:30 knowing I am seeing him at 4:30, you had plenty of time. That makes no sense."

"Mir fell asleep and he had to eat."

"Right. Okay. I'll be in shortly."
1"His best interest over ours and okay."

"Plenty of time, but okay."

"I know you may not understand things happen last minute with kids, I hope you do in the future."

"Still waiting to begin my visitation as I've been waiting since the agreed upon time of 4:30pm."

"I told you we are here. You stated you'll be in shortly. You're holding yourself up. We are leaving at 6. Come on."

"You have yet to walk into the location. I can clearly see both of you in your car. I am walking in once you walk in. I know this. I've been waiting on you this whole time."

"It does not matter, we are here and you know it takes time to get him out. I'm here inside and you've yet to come inside." He came inside shortly after.

I got a text later that said, "Per the 48 hour minimal notice prior, when is Mir available tomorrow, Sunday August 11th, as I would like to exercise my visitation rights."

"We are unavailable tomorrow, however you can see him on Friday at 4pm. If that doesn't work you can see him on your every other weekend schedule visitation for the 25th and 26th."

"Acknowledged. I will review the court order and get back to you. Thank you for the response."

"Sounds good." I don't know what was going on in Mack's kiddie brain, but he texted me the next morning at 548 a.m. something he doesn't usually do and I know he was trying to be funny and disturbing. He already knew that we weren't available the current weekend of the 18th and 19th but I was willing to allow him to see him on Friday afternoon which was the 17th. In knowing that he still facetiously texted me; "Per the 48 hour minimal notice prior, when Mir is available this weekend of August 18 & 19, as I would like to exercise my visitation rights."

"Please do not text me until after 8 going forward. Thanks. Per, last week's message, I gave you the option to see Mir today at 4 and told you if that did not work, we would continue your every other weekend visitation like we normally do on the 25th and 26th."

"The court order does not state time restrictions of communications about our child ma'am. Per our last conversation, what is the location for a visitation today?"

"It may not be in the court order; however I am requesting you do so. I don't think a judge would even agree with you texting me so early. Mir is not in your care, he's not sick, and it's not an emergency involving him so you don't have a logical reason to text me at 5 in the morning, a time when people are normally slept. You never texted me that early before, so please cease it. You're only making matters worse, for yourself, not me. You can meet me at 4 to see Mir at the library on the 2nd floor. Have a good day!"

"Thank you! I'll be there at 4:30 as life does not revolve around you! Have a blessed one as well!"

Every time matters have to do with Mir I always get personally attached. There was no need for him to say "life does not revolve around you" to me. At this point he was showing me full blown narcissistic individual behavior aka being a dickhead for lack of better terms. I told him, "The court order is based off of Mir's best interest and me, the plaintiff and custodial parent; either we come to a mutual agreement or a sole agreement on my part. I did state 4pm, not 430pm."

"Did I agree to 4pm, or did I just tell you that 4:30 is the time I'll be there? That's where you have it twisted, it's not about you, and never is/will be. It's about him. Last visitation I recall you appearing 1 hour later than the agreed upon time. 4:30 works best for me, and I'm pretty sure 4:30 will work for you. And thank you for the reminder of the "plaintiff/victim/custodial parent.""

"Let me remind you of the many times you have been late to visitations while not having a child with you to bring because you did not plan properly. Last time I opened up an extra 30 minutes for you to see Mir and in a playful environment which is free for you within a short distance of us both, before they close and you were unappreciative of that. While I was late, I had a legitimate reason and I informed you and for no other reason than what I stated. Things happen with kid's last minute; I get it you don't completely understand, maybe you will one day. Yes, I matter, my schedule matters and without me and my schedule Mir wouldn't be taken care of and he wouldn't be able to get himself to you, to see him. He's one and depends on me. I am the one who makes it possible for you to see him. Your continuous hostile and not understanding ways are insane and I'll be printing this stuff to add to my binder, when we do go to court. You shouldn't be mad at me for you having to go through me because of Mir's age and development as well as additional factors that were not caused by me. We will be there at 4, like I said. I have somewhere to be at 5. Next weekend you can see him for your normal 1-2 hours you only normally take."

"Not reading your book, I'll be there at 4:30."

"Well before 4 wasn't a problem with you, you had asked about 4 on the weekday. I'm guessing this is because you switched jobs again and you have a different schedule?"

"See the above message please."

"Failure to communicate."

"To you. If I was able to make it at 4 I would be there, 4:30 is more realistic."

"If its work related or traffic, I can work with that but if you rescheduling to be complicated, I cannot. I still have an appointment at 5 so this will be a short visit."

"Traffic."

Hours later I told him, "You can see him at his door in my car at the library. I do not have extra time to take him and out of the car seat to go inside. If you're not there by 440, we are leaving."

"Is seeing a child for 10 minutes and leaving beneficial to the child? I don't think so and I would hope you wouldn't think so too. I'll see him at 4:30."

This conversation went way past what it needed to be but obviously Mack was stuck on stupid and lacked understanding, consideration, and respect as a whole.

"Mack, I told you I have an appointment at 5. Last Week on Saturday, I told you, you could see Mir at 4pm today and you said you would get back to me. Your choice to wait until Friday at 5 in the morning at that, not 48 hours prior to ask about seeing him on the weekend which I told you would resume on the 25th and 26th. You act like you won't see Mir another time. I have things I must do and because your visits are supervised Mir comes with me. The judge and the order is saying in basic terms it's a mutual agreement or I lay out the parenting time and place which can be anywhere and anytime. I believe your purpose in things is more so not to see Mir, but to build some irrational case against me and I follow all court orders and you waste the judge time because you're unhappy with the terms in which you see him. Leave me alone, this conversation is done for the day. I have to repeat things and break it down for you to understand basically your way of extending the conversation and playing dumb. See him at 430 and just go on with your life. You choose to take 1-2 hours with him. That's your choice. Obviously you know you can't have him overnight or in your care. Frequent visits for Mir's age are recommended but overnight with a restraining order is not. Does some legitimate research please and take a co-parenting class. It'll help you a lot with your mental state. This is concerning for Mir to be around you unsupervised."

Bryna had told me before that she didn't think Mack was really coming to see Mir and that he was trying to get away from Moesha to see me. I knew his intention wasn't real and that his dad was in his ear trying to get him to come around so he can get pictures sent to him to act like he's so involved in my son life.

He replied, "I honestly could care less about your opinions, truth of the matter is you're toxic to Mir's growth and his relationship with me. Give it time for everything to be exposed, this custody thing can go on for years for all I care, just know it won't stop until wrongs are turned right. Let me stress this as well since you haven't gotten the hint, you will never have to worry about interactions with me other than about Mir, I have no need to contact or see you otherwise nor does it benefit me in any way so don't worry."

I'm not sure where my being toxic to Mir's growth came from. After all, he doesn't see or check up on Mir via FaceTime when he's not visiting him, he had never came to a doctor's appointment asked anything about Mir's likes, dislikes, basic information so whose really the toxic one or is it that he is using projection towards me because of his own issues. Additionally, when he said that the custody thing could go on for years for all he care, it definitely is him being spiteful and refusing to think logically outside of the courts. He never mentioned anything about me being an unfit mother, on drugs, abusing Mir or anything which let me know that him choosing to take me through court was not about Mir because he was seeing him when he felt like it and I wasn't denying him of that, but he preferred to use the court system to harass me and make my life a living hell to be of an inconvenience to me and also cause me to pay more money for attorneys. There's a name for people like this and it's very common in narcissists. It's called a "vexatious litigant "which is legal action that is brought solely to harass or subdue an adversary. It may take the form of a primary frivolous lawsuit or may be the repetitive, burdensome, and unwarranted filing of meritless motions in a matter which is otherwise a meritorious cause of action.

Mack had a history of this in court and the judge as well as my attorney knew it. We were always in court pretty much every month because he was holding up the process or trying to manipulate the court system to make it seem like the evidence and proof they saw was not what things really was and basically he was painting me as a villain or something unstable. I also don't know why it was important to him to let me know he would never have to worry about interactions with me outside of Mir which was his way of letting me know I have been discarded yet again, also a narcissistic tactic. I had already divorced him not the other way around and I wasn't going backwards so the feeling was definitely mutual.

In addition he said, "Revisit the restraining order as well, last I checked it included you only, not Mir. I reside alone, so what's stopping him now? You should look into seeing a Psychologist on base since we're on the topic of mental states and for military the care is free, it'll help you a lot with your emotional intelligence. I'll see him at 4:30 as I stated, thank you."

"Do you think leaving the state for 8 months during our divorce with your girlfriend to make another baby when you can't afford the 2 you have now and no contact and blocking me and Mir for those 8 months were beneficial, I didn't think so either. Please don't come for me, I'm a mother, a great mother. I hope you work on being a father, a better father to Mir. People have sent me a lot of evidence to do with you because we know you don't think about the best interest of the child."

"Your lack of emotional intelligence is showing with this one Faith. You're absolutely right, you are a mother, but your parenting is to question for various reasons such as Mir's clothing choices, explanation as to why his face is covered with old food when I see him, and his interactions with other outside of the "bubble" you have created for him which in reality, will have negative impacts on his life. I can sleep easy, Mir knows me and who I am even with the short time I spend with him due to this unrealistic order, but just know I'm from Philly, and I play for keeps. It won't end until Mir receives the parenting time from me he TRULY deserves, that simple. "Anything else you'd like to share? Enlighten me."

"You don't live alone. I have your ultrasound of you and Moesha child y'all share together and proof from Facebook posts that y'all moved together and are in an active relationship with a yellow Kia and a blue Charger right outside the base. I've seen you both. You know that court order states no contact me with me or my family member and Mir is my family household member. I'm not toxic to Mir's growth I'm very beneficial. A toxic person is one who makes multiple kids with multiple women and is on multiple child support orders in different states. The judge didn't think you were best fit; you can barely take care of yourself switching jobs so often, switching cars so often. You've had ten jobs since May of last year. Mir has been doing very well with me and in a stable environment. You dropped your daughter off to strangers whom are not her family, ignored her cry to go home to her mother because you have mistreated her and a list of other things. I'm very intelligent. Mir is well taken care of. Like I said before you're angry because you have to go through me and you can't stand it. Mir is never covered with old food. The judge is the one who put the order in place because you definitely lie and try to cover up things and you can't do so, so well. You can keep fighting by yourself because I legitimately look at the best interest of Mir and you only look at it for yourself. Please take your anger elsewhere. We already know that you can take it to court a million times and it still will remain as it is. You've been to court multiple times with many mothers because of your lack of everything to do with parenting skills. Goodbye, see you for your visit. You have a child with Moesha. You both post everything on Facebook for people to see and send, you have a newborn baby born in July and I will not give you the opportunity to bring Mir around someone a restraining order is against and if you read it the right way it does cover Mir and you have a lifetime association with her and I will be extending the order like I said before only because she has broken the order and will not leave me alone. She is irrelevant to our case and is the main reason your visitation is the way it is."

The funny thing is literally days after this conversation he made a post that said I just love waking up to these two every day. (Referring to Moesha and their daughter). He lies, tries to get me to believe the lies, and when it's revealed he's mad.

He replied, "Lol is that current? You show a lot of interest in what goes on in my life and that very weird and concerning. All you have is the military, a few child support payments, and a scarce education; you think you're better than the world? Sit down. You communicate with the mother of my daughter because you're sick, eager to stir more drama that I don't have time for." Let's stop right here.

Mack doesn't want Bryna and I to communicate with each other because we both know how he is and he doesn't want us to tell others or his girlfriend and ruin his game. He didn't want me to enlighten Bryna so he could continue to manipulate and use her to get his way, although she already knows how he is, yet he wanted me to talk to Moesha because no matter what she's going to stay but I'm sick for talking to Bryna and not sick for talking to Moesha. He continued by saying, It's just sad that Mir is the victim to your selfish and self-centered ways. I don't have to sit and insult you all day; everyone truly knows who you are and what you're about. As I said, enjoy your "court order" and "protective order" while you can, it won't last very much longer boo. You can stop texting me now as well, you're irrelevant". Ps thank you for that tip, I may have to have an order put in place if I feel I'm being stalked."

The top part of the message was Mack and the last part of the message about enjoying my protective order and calling me boo, was definitely not Mack, it was Moesha. She had called me boo in a condescending manner before. Mack never referred to me as that. First, there was never anything wrong with Mir's clothes, he was always dressed nice so he was just throwing something into the mix or it was some foolishness he was feeding his girlfriend to say in the message because on a couple of occasions he complimented Mir's outfits. He never mentioned anything negative about the way he dressed nor did he buy his own outfits if it was a big deal so that didn't add up at all. Then, for him to lie and say Mir's face was always covered in food was so untrue. I never would keep my child in food. If anything in route to visits with Mack he would have gold fish or fruit snacks and that's it but he would always be wiped off. All of the stuff Mack was saying about me was him engaging in a smear campaign. It's a narcissistic tactic where there is a plan to discredit a person by making false or dubious accusations. Also, when Mack says negative things about me or people I always have to remember that he is notorious for projection meaning he's talking about himself but pinning it on me which is a narcissistic trait. Projection is the process through which they reveal who they are and what they're doing. Through projection, they call you what they are. They accuse you of doing what they're doing or planning on doing. They throw all the uncomfortable feelings onto you because they don't want to deal with them. They throw their shame on you so they don't have to deal with it. They make you feel guilty for who they are and what they're doing because they're unable to feel that guilt themselves. So, essentially projection is an unconscious way of denying the existence of something inside oneself and attributing it to others, externalizing it. This could be unacceptable or unwanted characteristic, flaws, thoughts, emotions, actions, feelings. It's a defense mechanism.

"I told Mack, " No I actually don't have an interest in it I have people that care about me and know as well as the courts know you are a liar and have been to jail for perjury and kicked out the navy for lying as well. Now this is all. You can communicate by yourself. I'm not stalking you period. We have mutual friends on Facebook and people talk. You're harassing me continuously. This conversation was to end a while ago. Leave me alone and just see Mir. That's it!"

The conversation ended by him discarding and devaluing me yet again by saying, "Lol what's there to be angry at? You? You honestly think I care about the things you do or try? You're at the bottom of my concern list. I will tell you my son is at the top. Your 26/27 years old and still to this day do you act as immature as a teen, grow up one day. Carry on miss; you're a waste of my time." I didn't respond to that message and he double texted me saying, "Stop messaging me then ma'am, I'd very much respect that you stop messaging me."

Again, he was trying to be condescending by saying Ma'am. Mack knows my actual age so the mention of the estimation of it let me know that it was his girlfriend texting me expressing her thoughts. I didn't realize it until later that the day he was arguing back and forth with me was what would've been our three year marriage anniversary. I guess he thought he would ruin that day when in reality I didn't even care. When I arrived for his visitation later that day at the library, I noticed he was not in his car. He knew that I told him to meet me outside in my car because I had to go and he told me he was inside. I told him I was outside and he came out. I began recording especially because of how highly conflicting communications always were with him. He opened the door to my car looked at me and talking to Mir. He began asking him, "where's mommy going" which I don't know why that was a concern of his. He tried to get Mir out of the car seat but had trouble. Mir had a bottle of water he was drinking and I believe while I was driving he took it and poured it on himself. Mack noticed it and started saying, "Why didn't your mom change you and why you all wet." Basically, down talking to me trying to get me rattled up. When I tried to tell him about the water bottle, he cut me off and said he didn't care and didn't want to hear it. He continued to make the same remarks and I got tired of it.

He continued to see Mir for a little and then one weekend decided he didn't want visitation with him. The next time he asked I gave him a heads up that we would not be in town for Mir's birthday weekend so if he wanted to see him, he would need to let me know beforehand. He asked where he would be for his birthday and I told him about our family. I arranged for him to meet us at the library later that day and he tried to change the location to suit his convenience.

"Select a different location than the library that is not suitable for a location to play with a two-year-old."

"We met at the library last time in the play area. This time will be no different. See you Sunday."

"I would like to meet at a different location than the library Faith, someplace more suitable to play with Mir."

"This library has a play area floor just for kids too so I don't even know what you are talking about right now."

"He screams and runs around when playing, it is a library. Can you please select a different location for me to play with Mir?"

"Mack, he is a kid; I mean come on. He's going to run and play and make noise. I don't know what you expect. It's not about you it's about him and Mir loves the library and no one complains about him being a child. You can read a book to him or if you're that self-conscious about it, get a private room brings books and toys and play with him there. My final offer is the library or the clubhouse for this day. Besides, it will be raining that day so outdoor activity doesn't make sense at all."

He left the message on read and responded the next day indicating his choice. "Library. Please be considerate and give a heads up on time before that day, I would appreciate it, he said."

A couple of days later as I was looking at the weather forecast, it was supposed to be raining. I said a couple of hours before his visit, "Between now and 1 is better for you to see him after 2 it will be raining." He mentioned not being able to meet them and said if it was raining by his original meet time that he would see him next week and if not, he would see him the same day. A couple of hours later I said, "You will just have to see him this Friday or the weekend. It's a storm coming and we are not leaving this house. You always have the option to FaceTime him."

He replied, "Sure." but never attempted to do so.

The weather appeared to be improving so I texted him and said, "So the weather appears to be improving therefore if you would like to have your visit today at 4, you can do so. Let me know if you will or will not be exercising visitation at the previously agreed upon time and location."

"No."

"Okay."

So from the end of August 2018 until a couple of days before Mir's September birthday he did not see or FaceTime him at all. I took Mir to take birthday pictures a week before his actual day and sent Mack the proofs. He didn't acknowledge them at all. The next morning he texted saying, "Mir Birthday is approaching. Do you have anything planned for him and where will he be? I responded, "Are you ok? I notice when I tell you things you ask a second and third time and blatantly disregard what I already told you. We will be with our family for his birthday. Also, you did not see Mir on Sunday, Friday, or Saturday like you were supposed to and completely forgot about him that is pathetic."

"Thank you. When will Mir be available next?

"I'll be available next week for you to see him."

"Now was that so hard psycho lady? Thank you very much."

Mack would always use names such as "psycho" and "crazy" which is a form of gas lighting a victim. Gas lighting is when someone is manipulated by psychological means into questioning their sanity. At this point, I began to think I must be talking to multiple people and not Mack because I was repeating and slowing down everything I was saying to him and it's like it didn't process through his brain or it was one of his girlfriend's texting me, Moesha to be exact.

"I'm not sure if this is Mack or if it's one of his girlfriends with his phone again because Mack doesn't talk like this in text message nor does he talk in person, he's admitted to having his girlfriend texting me and violating the order before. I know he has told me he would refrain from having his girlfriend's text me anymore; it appears to be a pattern and problem again. I will be documenting this for court purposes. Have a good day."

A shrugging shoulders emoji was sent back and I thought to myself this is it. I've had enough of the insults and Moesha using his phone to take jabs at me right along with Mack. I went down to the courthouse and filed a violation of a restraining order and included the information from where Mack and Correll both admitted she texted me before from his phone. In a criminal complaint, I was very detailed. I knew Moesha did not know that Mack and his dad ratted her out because they cover things up and lie so well so I figured I would put it in there so she would know and the courts would know. She got served a few days later and on the same day, while I was at work, Mack blew my phone up. I declined one call, just for him to call again. One call turned into four phone calls in a matter of five minutes. I knew something wasn't right at this point and it has nothing to do with Mir. I texted him because I didn't have a way of recording the call at the time and I said, "What's the reason you are calling for? You can text me, I'm busy right now."

"I prefer a call. I cannot text at the moment."

"I cannot talk on the phone just text me."

"I would like to speak to Mir."

"I am busy. You don't usually blow my phone up calling me or FaceTiming to see Mir which leads me to believe you are contacting me about something else. What is the issue you have blown up my phone about?"

"Have Mir give me a call today when he gets a chance. He added a winking eye emoji face which was very unusual and I knew he was playing a game.

"By the time I get home he will be sleep."

"Are you sure?"

"I am at work."

'If he's up when you get in please let me know." I indicated thumbs up. He double texted after that and said, "Oh and lawyer up; 1 actually got two."

This is where his real motive for blowing my phone up was revealed. He was referring to the violation of a protective order I had got against his mistress. I didn't even respond. Of course, when Mir was picked up he was already sleeping and I got him ready for his normal nightly bedtime routine. Mir's birthday was a few days later. He asked me at midnight if he was up and I told him no. He FaceTimed the next morning and wished him a Happy birthday. Of course, he had to say something negative about Mir's hair not being cut. It was cut, but it was too dark outside and the light was not bright enough for him to see it in the car. He asked Mir, "Where he was going for his birthday and he just looked at Mack and smiled." Mir wasn't verbal at all for him to be turning two. I brought it up to Mack before and he said he noticed it and thought he would be talking more for his age but never said anything to me about it. Mir and I got on the road and we headed to Atlanta to spend some time there for his birthday and then saw our family in Florida. I was planning for us to move to Atlanta once I was discharged from the military. I was actively working on getting out of the military on account of being a single mother with no real help or support from Mack and being away from my family as well. When we got back a week later, Mack asked when Mir was available on the weekend. I gave him a time and date. I knew that because of the current violation of restraining order against Moesha being filed, Mack was starting to be a little less hostile and more acknowledging of me having to bring Mir for visitation instead of him acting like Mir could bring himself. He was more civil and Moesha was upset because she had read in the criminal complaint that Mack and his dad told on her and she unfriended Mack as well as wrote a status saying, "I don't want a man who acts right when you're scared of losing me. Save that shit!"

She was pissed about it because I guess she thought they had her back and the fact that he was continuing to see Mir without her around. Mack and I met at the library after Mir and I came back. The next day I bought Mir a tablet and sent Mack a message saying "Mir has his tablet so if you ever plan to video chat with him, you can call that. You just had to download the app and add his Username.

"Cool beans, does he play on it a lot?"

"I just bought it; I'm teaching him how to use it."

Days later, after I had made my mind up about where Mir and I would be staying when we moved to Atlanta, I went to the post office after typing two letters that included the 30 day notice that we were moving and the location we were moving to as well as getting it in certified mail format to where he would have to sign to acknowledge that he had got it in his hands. It was court ordered that anytime either of us moved we had to notify each other within 30 days before the move to get each other a chance to reject the move and go to court. I said to him, "I sent you a letter in the mail today to both addresses."

"In regards to?"

I said relocation and our new address it was delivered to Norfolk and Philly since I don't know where you're living.

"Cool."

A couple of days later he texted me saying, "I will not be seeing Mir this weekend."

I continued to send him normal pictures of our son and he didn't respond so I stopped. Stop asking to see our son completely. The relocation date I told him was November 5, 2018, so he had plenty of time between when I sent him the letter and before we moved to see our son. For whatever reason or his continued anger, he decided to take it out on Mir and not see him. A couple of days before it was scheduled my address changed and I updated it to Mack as I was supposed to according to the court order. Again he didn't respond. He didn't see our son from the week after his 2nd birthday in person up until we moved. He didn't even see him the day we moved but in my head, I was like whatever you want to be mad that's you on you. Before this move was planned there are a lot of events that led to me being able to do so.

CHAPTER EIGHT: Motherhood Mattered More

For me, September 2016 my life changed forever. I welcomed my son Mir into the world. He became my entire world from the moment I first saw him. I spent eighteen weeks on maternity leave and when it came to an end at the end of January 2017, I went back to work. I enjoyed my off time so much I didn't want to go back. Even though I tried reaching out to Mack to make amends as far as him seeing Mir, he wouldn't budge, he ignored me. The one time I had asked for space, got that space, and took my attorneys advice about not denying him any longer, he chose to continue to go longer without seeing him instead of giving it another try and taking up the fact that it was on the table for him to help out and visit. I had to pay for the cost of daycare on my own. Not one time in the first 4-6 months of Mir being born did Mack give me any money to help out with daycare or even try to figure out the facility he went to, to do it automatically if he didn't want me to have it for fear I was out for his money or something. He didn't ask if I needed any help with Mir if I wanted a break or anything. He was so engulfed in his relationship with Moesha, I and Mir was a thing in the past to him. He was living his other life, with his new woman.

The times that he did help, it was like his family was in his ear as always directing him on what to do and so they could get pictures of Mir from him and he would leave. None of them came to visit, offered help, or nothing either. They just wanted to see pictures and post all over social media in awe of his handsome and take credit for him being their grandson, that's it. In the military, there is a Family Care Plan you must have on file that outlines who will care for your child while you're onshore or sea. There is an instruction in black and white ink that outlines the details of it. Everyone with children must have one, no exceptions, and if circumstances arise that prevent a sailor from having a solid plan, and all options have been exhausted they are to be administratively separated. I kept that in mind for a while but did my best to always make sure I had a person available to watch my son, which resulted in me having multiple childcare providers on speed dial. I had tried to stick it out for as long as I could. My son went to about 6 daycares on a rotating basis during my time in the military to accommodate my crazy schedule.

Some sitters were available on times and days that the others weren't. I hated it. It made me feel bad as a mother because I had to please the Navy and leave my son with different people. I was spending hundreds of dollars each month for work and personal related matters on weekends. You may ask why I did all of this when my son has a "dad?"

I'll tell you it's all because my son's dad abandoned him and left everything up to me, went to jail at one point for committing perjury, and moved back to his hometown and made a 3rd child with the female he got kicked out the military for. Due to him in and out of our son's life and going eight months without speaking to me or seeing about our child because I got a restraining order on his girlfriend for her repeated threats of violence during my divorce. The judge ordered supervised visitation which means every time he sees him I have to be there. He just can't be trusted with the best interest of our child and it's not hard to see it. After all of this, I had reached my breaking point. I spent a lot of days crying about the mess I got myself into. Work issues and verbal altercations with my shitty leadership were at an all-time high for me. I had a hard time coping with the challenges of being a single mother and they weren't really of help but more so a burden.

Believe it or not, the worst experience I've had in the Navy is dealing with the crabby and two-faced ways from people of the same skin color as me! You would think since we all go through the struggle and know how hard it is to be a black female in the military, they would have our back right? Nope, not at the command, I was at anyway. All I heard on a daily basis from different people is, "You're a sailor first, you're in the Navy, you aren't the only single mom, It's plenty of people doing it with more kids than you, why did you get married, why did you have a baby, when are you going to be done with court." Those were just some of the low blows I've heard. Every week, I was angry and belligerent to anything my work center leadership said or asked of me. I would be open and honest with them about my continuous problems and they would brush it off. I decided to file my paperwork to be administratively separated for parenthood. I discreetly did everything because I know based on other's experiences in similar situations that were the best route to go about it. I printed instructions outlining Navy policy and had my parents write a letter about them being unable to watch my son due to my mom recovering from cancer and my dad recovering from seizures all while they are in Florida unable to provide local help. Sure enough when I turned the paperwork in I just knew that something was going to go wrong but I knew I had all my ducks lined up so I was ready for war. The military, well some of the people in the Navy tend to retaliate against sailors when they use the instruction on their leaders, step on toes and those who try to get out early. Sure enough, they couldn't accept all that I gave them and came to me asking for additional information that was not required by instruction and I refused to give it to them because I knew they were doing it to complicate and prolong matters even longer. I used to get dirty looks leaders that knew I was trying to get out. They justified every way possible without that information they wouldn't be able to help me further. I knew that they were trying to dig more personal than they needed to. I told them they are not my child's parents and don't tell me who they think I should have watched my child nor will I listen to them at all period. I also told them I don't care about the millions of others in the military doing it and to stop comparing me.

So I decided to take it a step further and get legal involved. Before my Chief knew I filed a complaint of wrongs against her, It got to the point that my Chief stopped responding to any messages that had to do with my separation and those under her followed suit which I guess they thought that I was going to let them ignoring me stop me but it didn't. I printed all messages and filed charges against her for failure to communicate with me as well as interfering with my request for discharge. Things started to get very shady at work and I documented it all. I also requested to be removed from my work center due to the amount of hostility and toxic work center she created all because I decided to put in a request for parenthood separation. I talked to my Master Chief about it and he dared to insult my intelligence by telling me that the Navy wasn't processing anyone out of the Navy unless it was for medical reasons. I knew it was bullshit because there was never a memo put out that would interfere with a single parent getting discharged. He just wanted to throw me off thinking that I was going to take that for an answer and sit stagnant. They took me for a joke and they didn't learn their lesson from the last time I stepped on their toes and fought to get what they were preventing me from making my rank so I went further and went to the highest chain of command, my Commanding, and Executive Officer. I was in tears choked up talking to them about what was going on. The only thing my CO could say was we will file the paperwork and whatever decision the deciding authority would make I would have to deal with it. I told him that my mental health was affected and what I was supposed to do with my son being that I was drained and parenthood was affecting me and is more important than serving.

I couldn't even focus on work while I was there and barely did my job. I was so down and out, some nights I had crazy dreams and woke up in tears. Single motherhood and dealing with a crazy narcissist ex and his girl toy affected me because I didn't think I would ever be in the situation I was in. Truth be told, I was still healing and had to encounter this narcissist daily until he went ghost again. I had to focus on the military and their expectations and then I had to focus on my son while neglecting myself and the things I had once enjoyed. I lost myself, I won't even lie. I covered everything up with a smile, at least I tried to anyway but my real friends could see I was breaking inside. I decided to finally talk to a mental health counselor about my problems and ask for help because I needed to get out of the military. The person I spoke with heard me out for everything and gave me some suggestions on coping mechanisms. I gave that a shot and it did work however it was a temporary fix. I was begging for their help to get me out of the Navy because I was all burnt out and couldn't deal with it anymore. Every chance I got I kept telling my chain of command my son mattered more to me than staying in the Navy.

"I ended up being removed from my work center and had a much better leader helping me along the way with my process. Two months later after talking to the chaplain, new leadership, a counselor, and most importantly God I was able to break free. I fought this battle for months, trying to keep myself together, anxiety and depression through the roof just counting down the days to being at peace. To be honest, I felt and knew in my heart that they were fighting to keep me in because they wanted to set me up by pushing buttons so I could snap and react in a way that would get me in trouble and possibly a bad discharge. Just in time, new higher leadership came in, took care of it all and assured me I was on my way out. Others also knew and admitted that my Chief and LPO's and some of the old higher leadership were fighting to keep me from getting out so they could set me up using my situation to gain leverage upon me to make it seem like I'm a rebel, when realistically I was suffering from depression and anxiety causing me to lash out. Of course afterward, they acted salty that their game plan against me did not work and I got that honorable discharge I needed simply by fighting my way to the top, stepping on toes, and didn't stop. It's crazy how many levels I had to take to get what I needed. I found so much strength in fighting my way to the top it was because of God I made it out and I can't thank him enough. Two weeks before I got out the Navy I was given 10 days for house hunting leave to find a place to live after discharge from the Navy. I was also allowed to apply for unemployment and receive it for up to 6 months. This gave me time to move, get settled, rest, and prepare for Mir and I's new journey. Originally I wanted to move to Dallas, Texas but realistically I knew nobody there and would've been further away from family for Mir to be around so I canceled that out.

CHAPTER NINE: New Beginnings

I decided to act on faith and move to Atlanta, Georgia, November 2018. I wasn't too sure which were the good and bad areas of Atlanta so I had a cousin of mine give me direction. Mir and I ended up getting an apartment in one of the best places to live in Georgia, the Sandy Springs area. It has an overall A+ rating and good for young professionals and families. When he got to Atlanta, I decided I would stay at home for six months to get myself together and spend time with Mir. He and I had endured quite a bit so this was our time to enjoy the newness of a new place. The unemployment helped a lot and had money saved as well as still consistently receiving child support so that took care of Mir's daycare and daily living expenses. Daycare in Atlanta is expensive and started at $205+ weekly but I enrolled him anyway. I didn't want him to not be around other kids and miss out on learning besides that's what I am getting child support for, to support him. I enrolled myself in online school so I could continue my Bachelor's in Criminal Justice. Unfortunately, due to going through an extremely contested and nasty divorce I had to stop school because my focus and grades were declining. The income I got from school had helped with expenses as well. A few weeks before starting school I started to explore the area of Atlanta and decide what type of work I wanted to do. I had applied for a few jobs just for the heck of it, not putting too much pressure on entering the workforce so quickly. I ended up receiving offers from federal and state employment agencies. I took a chance on a couple, but realized that I needed to be a mother first and being at a job all day long helping the employer get what they need done and putting appointments with my son and I to the side wasn't beneficial. I started thinking of ideas on how I can become my business owner and came up with three ideas of which I will not disclose until they are official. When I left Virginia, my slate wasn't completely cleared there. I had ended up getting a violation of a protective order taken out on Moesha because she was still using Mack's phone to text me and I could tell just by the language of the text it was her again. A friend of mine saw a Facebook post of Mack's where he posted an old picture of Moesha before she had her daughter and the caption said, "This woman here can do anything she sets her mind to, and I will be there to support her every step of the way! I love you boo!" I knew based on Mack's previous history of only doing things with ulterior motives, that this was probably a declaration of him on a social site he knows would get back to me somehow, that he would be at court. I followed my gut and when I logged on to the portal of the court site to look up the witness information, sure enough, I saw that Mack was a witness on Moesha's case to testify against me. Of course the delusional duo sticking together as always against the ex-wife they both envy and hate so much because they got caught cheating and it was revealed to me through the Navy, Moesha not being allowed to be around nor play house with my son as they thought, and the fact that I appeared to be living my life and not letting all of what they did drag me down. When I went to court, Moesha was already sitting down and while Mack was coming through the door, he opened it for me. When we got in front of the judge and I showed the evidence from April when Mack and Correll admitted Moesha was texting me from his phone as well as the most recent piece of evidence, she plead not guilty to the recent piece of evidence since that's what the judge was focused on due to me not filing a violation for the earlier one. I told the judge that I knew Mack very well and the names he was calling in the texts did not sound like him and the judge looked at him and told how his ex-wife knows him pretty well and appears to be a reputable person however when the public defender Moesha had, told the judge as well as Mack that she was not guilty the case got dismissed. Had she been found guilty she would've served time in jail and I did not care at all period. This girl had already reached out to me on at least three occasions harassing me so I didn't care what they did to her; I wanted her out of sight, out of mind. The baby they had together he would've had to figure out to care for her on her own since obviously, her mother didn't care when she was harassing me so much. Bryna and I were talking about the post and she was saying how she guess the thoughts of being a single father make him shutter and he wanted to save his relationship so he can continue to use her by going to help her case. After that was over, I decided to download a co-parenting app to speak with him on and sent him letters stating such. I told him that my number was no longer active and that he could communicate with me regarding Mir and to schedule appointments via the app. I said it is highly rated and works perfectly fine for iPhone users like him and me. If the app does not work, an alternative to contact me would be via email. I mentioned to him previously about Mir having a kid video chat account on his tablet and to message me in advance when Mack wants to video chat with him. Instead of going along with communication in the co-parenting app like he had previously stated in a message months prior that he wanted to do, he asked for my current phone number and stated that the court order does not include any enforcement on communication through a specific app of my choosing. He also asked where I wanted the $4510 in attorney fees he owed me to be sent to. The attorney I had for my divorce had mentioned a co-parenting app before, Mack just wanted to have control and have my phone number even though he doesn't ever use it just to be difficult as usual. I responded to him informing him that the court order stated contact information it was never specific to how that communication is carried out. He has my address and the messenger feature and the best part is messages can't be altered and reports can be printed for court purposes. The purpose of the app wasn't because I had communication issues it was because Mack had been very hostile and threatening since I found out about his adultery and when I beat him to filing the divorce papers because I had grounds and he didn't. I told him that the app as a means of staying on the road with healthy co-parenting measures and eliminating further conflict. I reminded him that he mentioned it before so I figured it would be no problem for him. As far as the money goes, I told him he can meet me at a designated Navy Federal with a cashier's check from his bank account since it was a large amount of money. He got mad I wouldn't release my phone number and mentioned another co-parenting app that he wants included in our custody agreement for the future for all communications to be court-monitored, not Faith monitored. He sounded dumb. I can monitor text messages and messages on an app. He just doesn't like the fact anything outside of Mir that he has texted me I have screenshot it and took it to the courts and now he's playing the victim as if I am the one who did him dirty and I'm so complicated to talk to. The thing about Narcissists is they will push all of your buttons and boundaries and as soon as you catch on they go from villain to victim and shift blame onto you as well as project the things they are doing wrong to be your fault as well. Mack is very notorious for this. Of course, he had to throw a jab at me by saying I will not meet you in person, I do not need to if I am not seeing Mir and for me to send whatever information was needed to transfer attorney's fees to my bank account. He acted as if I wanted to see him for my pleasure and I'm not sure who he thought Mir was with because as always Mir is with me. I ended up giving him my app phone number that he already knew from when I lived in Japan. I also told him that I wasn't opposed to talking to him on a co-parenting app, I mean it's not going to change Mack and his hostile ways and we're still using the same type of device so why couldn't he just be an adult or man and communicate like regular human beings but of course he's not regular, he's very conflicted and difficult and all of his family I met has admitted to that. After I gave him the number I told him that I do not want force, hostile, or harassment from his phone. I told him it was fine if he does not want to meet with me to give me the money, that's the only reason I was meeting him and I have Mir with me like I always do but because of his issue with me, he chose not to see him. I told him I was noting it for court documentation purposes. Instead of responding with something like Okay, I'll meet you to see him or I want to see him, he said afterward that he was never notified that Mir was in the area. Regardless, thanks. I had just told him Mir was with me and he tried to play the victim card and also disregarded him as a whole by saying what he said. I made sure I informed him, we didn't leave the area until November as I stated in my relocation letter and he stopped seeing Mir when we were living in the area in September 2018. The court order doesn't say to notify you each time I am in the area but I just did. I won't force you to see Mir, he has a father figure daily and even though you didn't ask, Mir is doing fine and you're more than welcome to always come and see him. The last thing he said was, "Irrelevant information, like I said thanks." This man is so heartless and bitter he doesn't even care about our son because he can't stand me, it is crazy. I'm not keeping our son from him, he just doesn't like the boundaries I've set in place nor the rules the court has set in place due to his behavior and absence. He treats me terribly but I overlook it because he's miserable and won't make me be miserable or feel guilty for what he's done. I left Virginia and went back to Atlanta and on the day in December 2018 that my attorney fees were due to me he paid them. I was surprised. Mack is very stingy about his money unless it's on him or has something to do with his car or photography. I believe when I told him if he didn't pay he could be found in contempt of a court order and serve time in jail that scared him to pay up his dues.

Since September 2018, he's had no contact with Mir through any means of communication I have provided to him. I have even FaceTimed him for Mir and sent pictures and he still would not respond. Christmas rolled around and Mack didn't call Mir nor did any of his family get my phone number from Mack and reach out or send gifts to Mir. On another note, Bryna and I had made plans a few months prior to my move that before Thanksgiving and Christmas, we would get the kids together and take pictures, all four of us. After I moved and settled in, I observed to see what was going to happen between the interaction of Bryna and I and if she was going to lie again like she did before when it came to her and our kids being around each other. She would watch every post I shared on social media and like things from time to time. I didn't hear anything from Bryna at all. I brought it to her attention that it seemed like the only time, she cared about her daughter being around Mir was if Mack was involved and I pointed it out to her. Instead of taking accountability and admitting that she didn't want to meet up with me for the kids' sake then or ever, Bryna blocked me before the day before the new year of 2019. Of course she never intended for her and I to meet and have the kids around each other because she still has feelings towards me about my marriage to Mack and the part she played in ruining it. She knows what she did is wrong so she was still afraid I'm out to do something to her. Honestly, when I did find everything out at first, I wanted to murder her and Moesha because of how foul they both were but those feelings died down just a bit after time had passed. I also have too much to lose behind some baby mamas and a husband that ain't worth nothing. I believe she portrayed wanting to be cool with me to get information and tell his family but there was nothing I told her that I didn't care about getting back to them or that I wouldn't repeat myself. I didn't switch up about how I feel about the situation as a whole. A few months after I realized she blocked me, she added Mack and his parents and Moesha on social media. I was thinking girl, you just told me a few months ago, "I talk about him because I can, and it be funny but I really don't care. His life literally doesn't faze me and he's literally irrelevant. He doesn't belong to me, he belongs to my daughter and that's that." I thought in the back of my mind, "Quit lying, you still got a soft spot for Mack, you love him, and he knows you're his one of his boomerang baby moms that he can manipulate when it comes to money, sleeping with him, or a stroke of his ego." "I'm not adding Mack or his family ever on social media and giving them a window into my personal life for them to chat about. They showed me their true colors, none of them are loyal and trusting people at all, they are very deceptive and not people I would want in my circle keeping up with. Besides, by remaining friends with the narcissist, they get to keep all of their former partners on a carousel of convenience: they can create a harem of people to use for sex, money, praise, attention or whatever else they desire, at any time. I'm not about any of that at all. I keep it professional and business like when I do communicate with Mack and his family that's fine enough for me. She wants to be a favorite and the one his family adores because she goes outside of the court order to cater to them and she wants the tea on his other kids and their mothers. It is what it is though. I'm done with that situation as a whole. As far as Bryna and Moesha I have nothing in common with either of them. One commonality they share collectively is that they sleep with men who are married. I don't. I'll let them all wallow in the foolishness as I continue on with my life and let it be cheers to new beginnings.

The New Year of 2019 came and that meant new blessings in store for Mir and I. As the months have gone by with me being in school and Mir at his daycare my focus shifted a lot positively. I began to feel very comfortable and at peace. In February, I decided I didn't want to continue on the rollercoaster of choosing when Mack wants to be a parent and be civil. In February, I emailed him since he wasn't responding to any of my text messages and I said, "I'm not trying to start anything with you, however due to you not seeing or showing any interest in Mir as you should've when we were living in VA and abandoning him since September 30, 2018, until present and even now that we live in GA, I think it would be in the best interest of our child if you sign over your parental rights. Due to your continuous child support modifications, since Mir has born, and your added responsibility with two additional kids it would only be fair to do so since you're already not there."

He responded saying, "No thank you, custody and communication changes pending."

I knew he was lying. First of all, custody was not going to change due to the factors against his third baby mama Moesha, his absence for basically two years of Mir's life catering to Moesha's insecurities and jealousy as well as him being hostile towards me in communication I knew it wasn't going to change. He hasn't been willing to co-parent with me since he got in a relationship with Moesha and a lot of it is because of the amount of control they have on each other when it comes to him being around me and my son. I didn't even respond to his message because it didn't scare me at all, he sounded like an idiot going to court to fight for the absence he is responsible for. Correll and I communicated but you could tell he was being very short with me and just trying to play nice to stay involved because his son wasn't.

One day his dad happened to ask me what size in clothes my son wore and spelled his name wrong and I had to correct him. How do you not know the correct spelling of your grandson's name? Just pitiful. He didn't even say no hey how's he doing or anything so I corrected him by saying, "Can I get a Hey how is Mir doing before just asking me a question like this? I don't mind giving you his clothing size which I just gave your son the other day but I think it behooves Mir's family to at least check on him instead of coming at me randomly asking questions. It's sad enough that we are only hours away for now and y'all don't come see him maybe because y'all don't like or want to deal with me and that's fine but Mir is an innocent child out of the situation. Time is more precious than material items." Correll claimed that it's hard for him to get down there because he's got so much going on in PA and at work. He said, "At one point you were sending random pictures to him, his bed, and him with Mack so since I haven't heard from you in a few weeks and I was thinking of him I wanted to buy him something. Again I have no issue with you I'm very happy you're raising my grandson I know you're doing a great job I just hope you keep sending me pictures because I do put them on Facebook as a proud grandfather." First of all Correll, I heard what you said about me when I wasn't around and I'm far from stupid with you only playing nice for this sake. Energy doesn't lie to me and you're telling me it's hard for you to get down to see your first and only grandson at the time but yet it was no problem you making time for the baby that Mack had on the way after my son, it does not make sense and sounds honestly like a bunch of bullshit. Never had any involvement with me and my son because I and Mack weren't together, but because he and Moesha were together you want to be involved. Honey, please run that by someone more naive then me. He then asked me where I was moving too but ain't no way in hell I was going to tell him before my plans were set in stone so he could run his mouth to Mack. Mack was a piece of work and hell on wheels why would I advertise my next move before I make it just so he can go to court and try to interfere although he wasn't seeing Mir just to make it complicated for me by playing the victim. Correll thought I owed him pictures. First of all the phone goes both ways. I got tired of the one-sided mess sending pictures and not caring or asking about my son's wellbeing. Just trying to be a social media grandfather like your son likes to be a social media father on birthday, holidays, or when he's sleeping with the mother.

Correll and I went back and forth for several months receiving pictures and, never once asked to FaceTime or anything. Yet Bryna was telling me how he was always Face-timing her daughter which was very weird to me of why my son was excluded.

In April 2019 I was supposed to appear in court for a child support modification Mack had filed, but due to the distance and Mack's repeated filings I asked that a telephone conference occur.

Before the court session started the child support worker called and asked about my employment information which I told her I had a job offer letter and I would be getting it the following day. I could've provided the pay and hours but she refused to do so. She was focused on the fact that I was receiving unemployment compensation overlooking I had a federal job pending. She asked if I've been receiving unemployment why is Mir in daycare. I looked at the phone like Lady, he still needs to learn and that's what I get child support for. The call ended and she told the judge I had no job and Mir was still in daycare and they gave Mack a decrease. I didn't have to be there to know that he felt victorious because he finally had won a reduction while my presence wasn't there. After I had got information about the decrease, I filed an appeal via mail to the courts. I knew for a fact and it was confirmed later that Mack had hidden his veteran's affairs money, trying to short me; meanwhile I gave honest and accurate information.

The appeal court date occurred in June 2019 and I had to fly back to Virginia because now it was in my corner of the courts to prove why the amount needed to stay the same it was before or increase if necessary. The day before I went to the courts in Virginia, I went to the courts in Georgia and filed a request to domesticate the previous custody order in the court system being that Mir and I were officially residents after six months of living there and at that point any future custody proceedings would occur in the state of residence where Mir lives. I did this because I knew that Mack was going to try to be vindictive and spiteful by filing a frivolous custody petition knowing he had visitation rights and I wasn't denying him of them, he chose not to use them. From what Bryna told me before, Mack likes to use the courts to stir up anxiety within you to make you think he's going to win custody but he never does. He does it to harass the mother when they no longer want to put up with his foolishness. There's a name for these types of people, they're called a vexatious litigant. A vexatious litigant is someone who persistently begins legal actions but doesn't have sufficient grounds for doing so. Vexatious proceedings include cases that are stated or pursued to abuse the process of the court, to harass or annoy, to cause delay or detriment, or for another wrongful purpose, and without fair or reasonable grounds. Mack had already proved he was this type of individual during our divorce proceedings that cost me $10,000 because of his continuous delays and erratic behaviors. There was no way for any reason that I was going back to Virginia for court for false allegations to be made against me with no evidence of me interfering with Mack's visitation and no evidence of him trying to exercise it within the past year.

When the court date for the appeal came around, I took a flight that cost me about $490 round trip. I did not want to pay this but I refused to miss another court date and not be able to defend myself and something goes wrong again. When I arrived, I waited until the court doors opened and then I saw that there was a child support attorney there to represent for Mir. She sat down and talked to me about the last court hearing and made the remark that Mack might not even show up because he got a decrease but we waited to see if he would. Like always he appeared about thirty minutes late as if he wasn't fazed at all. I provided my accurate employment information and told her this was the job I was about to start right after the child support hearing and she didn't understand why the caseworker present didn't take that information, however, she assured me that we would refigure the amount of child support with the correct amount. I also revealed to her that he was hiding a lot of other income.

He ended up telling them he receives $3700+ a month in Veterans Affairs disability money and some of which there is an amount out of that chunk that is supposed to be for Mir in addition to his $20 hour job so he had plenty of income and no reason to keep filing for reductions other than he didn't want to pay. When my income and his income were added up, it was warranted for an increase, not the decrease he requested. He told on me and said I was getting school money from the military, which I was previously months before, but I had taken a short school break that was going to resume a few weeks after court. I went ahead and gave them the information anyway since I would resume getting school money for housing again. Although it was specifically for housing, it was still counted in which was fine. I had nothing to hide. Little did he know by me providing my income information and his that the new figures warranted for an increase in child support. The child support attorney went and told the judge what she came up with and he told her to determine the new amount in three different ways. Each way there was still an increase of $200 more than the original child support amount from our divorce decree. When the attorney spoke to Mack, she told him that the amount he would pay would be a few dollars short of $1000. I saw his eyes get very big out of shock. When he saw I was paying $205 a week for daycare he questioned them about it and looked so angry. The attorney went back inside the courtroom and informed the judge. He came to an agreement that Mack can choose to go along with the increase in child support or he can withdraw his previous plea for a decrease and the child support would go back to the original amount it was before. Of course, Mack chose the lower amount. We all went into the courtroom and the judge and attorney told me what Mack chose to do. I didn't have an issue with it going back to the original amount even though an increased based on a rise in his income but I didn't care. I asked the attorney if this meant that Mack owed back pay for the three months of the decrease that happened before and she said yes. I saw out of the corner of my eyes that Mack was unaware and angry about that too with pouty lips and all. They mentioned giving him a child credit and I asked which kids because that was going to affect the amount, the one before mine or the ones after mine and they clarified the one before. Mack looked so sick. He didn't want the judge to know he had other kids but it's on record now that even though he keeps filing for decreases, he keeps making more kids which makes no sense at all.

Before court ended Mack asked the judge if he could ask me a question. The question he asked was completely relevant to our son and it was him being nosy trying to keep up with me. He asked where I work at questioning me as if I lie about my income when in reality that's him he does that. He's been convicted of perjury for lying about his employment I have no reason to lie. After he asked me that question he asked the judge if he files for custody will the amount of child support decrease. The judge said I can't answer that and dismissed Court. I'm not sure why he thinks that he's going to get custody of Mir when number one he's been absent for nearly two years of our sons life, has never been to any of his doctor's appointments that I have invited him on multiple occasions, he has little to no contact with me, I've never been found unfit, hospitalized for anything crazy nor am I an alcoholic or drug user, nor has any signs or reports of abuse been a factor. Mack just does it out of spite and he doesn't like watching a kid he's the type that will get custody of his kids and drop the kids off at his mother's house. Bryna told me before that is what he does with their daughter. I watched him attempt to do get primary custody over Bryna's daughter before by turning a situation where she was a victim to a serious crime and making her out to be a criminal and he went to court and lost. Mack loves to file continuous court motions for custody to spite the mother to get up under her skin and rip the child away from her to hurt the mom's feelings even when he's been absent for several years but he overlooks and doesn't take responsibility for that. His fourth child came about a month after this court hearing so that makes 2 girls and 2 boys for him and I doubt he's done yet. He already can't afford to pay child support and Bryna talked about putting him on it before too so what sense did it make to create more. You might as well call him the impregnator; seriously it's like the only thing he is best at. Bryna and I had said before our kids are going to have so many siblings and we were so right. I thank God I got out of dodge with Mack because I was going to be up again for pregnancy again according to him after I had Mir and I wasn't going to let that happen. After court, I hung out in Virginia for another day and spent time with my friend and her kids. I boarded my flight the next day and headed back to Atlanta to get ready for work the next day. Anyways, as far as new beginnings in Atlanta, I enjoy the city as a whole. There's so much to do, the scenery is nice, not too hot or cold and no snow and I'm as far as possible away from drama just what I needed for Mir and I. The businesses I plan to open are going to flourish so well here and I am excited for those to take off. It's something unique and stands out from the rest. In addition to those, I also want to become a Certified Life Coach of topics of Narcissistic Abuse to help inspire and empower those who are dealing with Narcissistic individuals to remove the chains of bondage and serve as someone who is caring and compassionate to give a listening and understanding ear. I want to also help those who have kids with these individuals and how to navigate through the court system using steps I have also used to protect myself and my son and combat the lies, slander, and abuse after choosing to walk away or being abandoned by the narcissist. I feel this is now my calling and I want others to be set free as well just like me. I am glad I made this move out of the military and to Atlanta. My focus has shifted, my peace is restored, my blessings are flowing, and I'm looking forward to what's next in store for my family.

CHAPTER TEN: Not My Baby!

On June 27, 2019, my life changed forever in a new way. I wasn't mentally prepared for the news I was about to receive. I woke up and I got Mir and I dressed to go to a doctor's appointment, I kissed and hugged him and we both walked out the house front door. While driving to the appointment, all I could do was drown myself in gospel music. This wasn't just any ordinary appointment; it was a special one for Mir. When we got to the brick facility, on the inside it was colorful and full of other kids. The lady at the front door greeted us with pleasure and directed us where to go next once we checked in with her. We got in the elevator to go to our designated floor. When we arrived, Mir spotted out a place to play with other kids while I talked to the front desk and waited for the doctor to come and get us. I fiddled on my phone scrolling Facebook while my mind raced. Ten minutes later, we were called into a room with a psychologist and a psychologist intern. They brought us into a room with an array of toys, a desk, a kiddie table and chairs, a couple of cameras, and glass windows. I was instructed to sit in front of the psychologist for her to ask me a series of questions. I was warned the visit would last about 3-4 hours. My heart sank because I knew this was going to be challenging for Mir and I to stay in this same room for so long.

The reason for the visit was to discuss a neurodevelopment assessment due to my concerns regarding Mir's cognitive development, language development, and social/emotional functioning and to assess him for a disorder. I had concerns about him lining up toys, rocking back and forth, hand flapping, being extremely aggressive, and speech delays. The psychologist started off the assessment by going over family history which included the fact that I am divorced and his father is choosing to be absent as well as family medical issues that

I was aware of. When asked about his birth and history, I told her that I delivered at 40 weeks and had a healthy vaginal delivery with no complications during delivery. Mir had no known allergies and he passed a recent hearing and vision exam. As far as Mir's developmental and behavioral health is concerned, me and our family have been concerned with his development since he was about ten months old.

I recall my mom telling me as a baby the possibilities of Mir having a diagnosis but I went off on her because I felt she was being negative and he was too young to say anything. I felt he was going through a phase that would pass away; at least that's what I was hoping. Mir used to have a ritual of flapping his right leg as a baby and babbling. I believe it was a soothing method for him and sometimes while he would listen to baby music and flap his leg, it would put him right asleep. Mir's early speech milestones were delayed. He began speaking in single words at twenty four months. He had approximately ten different words he would say verbatim each day. He knows a little sign language that he learned from speech therapy he was receiving before this appointment. He is able to follow one step directions and understands lots of questions he just doesn't verbalize it. His eye contact at times is described as inconsistent and avoidant at times. His motor skills were within normal limits. He sat up at about nine months, and walked after he turned one year old. I have no concern about his motor skills. With regard to his adaptive functioning, he is able to self-feed using utensils and accepts help with dressing. He does require assistance with bathing and brushing his teeth and also has sensitivity to his hair being washed when he has to place his head underneath flowing water. Mir is a picky eater who only eats certain foods according to texture and taste. Like myself, he does not like vegetables and scarcely will eat fruit but when I put them in smoothie form he enjoys that.

He has food texture issues. . Mir generally sleeps well, however sometimes it is very difficult to get him to go to sleep. He enjoys snuggling in the bed with me, but periodically, I will allow him to sleep in his own bed as he gets older. He's a very wild sleeper and sometimes I get kicked in the face by his feet or hit in the face with his hands. I've learned to adjust to it as much as possible because I know he can't control it.

Mir's social skills are normal. He has interest in playing with other children and enjoys chase games. He does become aggressive if a child takes a toy from him or won't share. Mir has an assortment of toys he enjoys such as Legos and Cars. As far as behavior is concerned, I had a lot of concern with his difficulty in managing transitions and changes in routine. He demonstrates rigidity, such as needing his toys to be a particular way. When disturbed, he has a huge tantrum. When Mir is angry, he screams and becomes very strong and begins throwing things, he will bang his head against any surface if he's in a sitting position, and he falls and flails on the floor. He is sensitive and cries if he is yelled at, loud hand dryers, and sounds that are extremely loud. I have a huge concern about him walking off with a stranger and running away in public places because he attempts to especially when he's angry. This is literally the biggest fear I have in dealing with Mir and it's very common in kids with a specific diagnosis. The technical term for this type of running is elopement. I have to place a tight grip on him or place him in a cart because if not, he will playfully run off not knowing the risk of doing so. Mir is an emotional child and is very accepting of and a giver of affection. He feels everything so deeply. He is literally the sweetest child I could ask for. He is very embracing in my happy and sad times. He'll come up to me and give me a random hug or kiss, he tells me off that he loves me and whatever it is I am stressing about, he will literally take those feelings right away.

After my interview with the psychologist was complete, she instructed me on what was getting ready to take place with Mir. She went to another room and watched and listened on camera to how Mir reacted to the psychologist intern through play and learning. This happened for about an hour. The psychologist came back into the room and allowed Mir and I to go on a short break while she prepared for the next part of the session. We walked out and I gave Mir his tablet so he could watch his favorite shows. I wanted a breath of fresh air after being questioned and having to give so much sensitive information about my baby. We walked outside and basked in the sun that was coming up and enjoyed some snacks. Mir was very happy and in a refreshed mood. I started breaking out in tears because I knew what was next. I started battling in my mind how was I going to handle this news, how was I going to get through this being a single parent with an absent and nonchalant ex-husband and father of our son. So many questions yet so few answers, but I had to look above to God and just ask him to keep me in his wing and not let it break me. My baby means the world to me, he really changed my life in a good way, and we've experienced so much together in a short amount of time, I couldn't imagine life any other way.   After our break was over, we went back inside the clinic to wait to be called back in. When this happened, we were escorted back to the same room. At this moment, the psychologists had some snacks and tried to see how Mir would react when presented with the snacks. They went over colors, shapes, numbers, and alphabets as well as how he played with certain toys to gauge his response and rewarded him with a snack when he responded positively. This continued until the assessment was complete. Once everything wrapped up, the psychologist sat and explained everything they observed to me. All of my concerns were validated within the four hours we were there. They got a glimpse of everything. Their behavioral observations I was told is that "Mir is presented as a sweet child, who displayed a relatively cooperative approach to the testing experience. He was dressed appropriately for the weather and testing situation, and was accompanied to the testing session by his mother. Rapport was easily established as he took the examiner's hand to walk to the assessment room, and he immediately sat in his seat at the table and engaged with the assessment materials. However, rapport was not easily sustained as he became preoccupied with playing with certain toys in his own way, rather than imitating or following the examiner's instructions, and he became upset on several occasions when transitioning away from preferred items. Overall, his eye contact was reduced, and he inconsistently coordinated his eye contact with other forms of communication. However, when activities were preferred, he demonstrated relative strengths in directing smiles to others, and he frequently requested access to desired objects. Mir's expressive and receptive language skills were significantly delayed given his age."

Overall, results indicate that Mir's is showing significant delays in visual reception, language (expressive and receptive), and motor skills. Visual reception refers to nonverbal problem-solving abilities. Mir's visual reception abilities are in the very low range equivalent to that of a 20 month old child. In terms of fine motor skills, Mir's abilities were also in the very low range equivalent to that of a 23 month old child. Mir's receptive language is below the 1st percentile and is equivalent to that of a 9 month old) and expressive language he ranks in the 1st percentile and is equivalent to that of a 16 month old. Scores both fell within the very low rang.   In the cognitive and language development area an assessment using the Mullen Scales of Early Learning indicates that Mir's development is significantly delayed. His Visual Reception, Fine Motor, Expressive Language, and Receptive Language skills all fall behind his same-aged peers. After all of this was explained to me, the next words uttered to me were that, "Mir is being diagnosed with Autism Spectrum Disorder. "I burst out into tears, crying uncontrollably, looking perplexed, so many emotions filled me at one time. The ladies brought me a box of tissue. In my head I was screaming, "Not my baby, NOT MY BABY!"

I knew he displayed characteristics of a child with autism but for it to be confirmed by a professional broke my heart into a million pieces. In reality, I was just hoping I was wrong. So many questions clouded my mind like, "is it my fault," "should I have gotten out of the military earlier to spend a lot more time with him"," was it the extreme stress I endured while pregnant that his dad put me under, those days where I used to beg him not to do things to stress me out or put me under immense pressure, was it the days and many nights that I cried while pregnant and didn't feel Mir move at all, did that cause it, does his dad have autism or someone in his family? I knew I was doing everything right by Mir except giving him the time I wanted to because the military had drained me of all of my time with him to the point when I got home after work, I was burnt out but I had to get him and make sure I did what was needed and on weekends I tried to make up for lost time and teaching him things he needed to know. I didn't have any help from Mack after he left town to be with the mistress Moesha. I couldn't just quit like a regular job or I would've gone to the military jail for escaping. I had to stick it out, there was no other option.

This news really hit me like a ton of bricks at once. As if I hadn't already been through enough, I was given yet another battle to bear. The psychologist gave me tissues and let me know there are resources to help me cope through this. She told me most parents give the same reaction I give and it's totally normal. They said a report would be made and I would have access to it in a few weeks but they gave a lot of information to start working on getting Mir the help he needs. Mir had five therapies he was recommended to take which includes speech therapy, physical therapy, occupational therapy, nutritional, and behavioral therapy. I thought to myself, how in the world was I was going to juggle working a job in one area of town, his daycare on another side closest to home, and taking him to all of these therapy sessions. That day we walked out, I felt like my heart was literally broken in two. Mir didn't have any idea what was going on but I could tell he was burnt out from all the testing and assessments they had done. I embraced him with a smile, a hug, and kiss and we left the building to go grab some lunch and enjoy the rest of our day. I sent Mack a text message saying, "Hello Mack, Today Mir was diagnosed with autism and he has 5 different therapies here throughout the week and some on weekends. I'm unsure why it's been 9 months since you've had absolutely no contact with Mir but I'm letting you know that whenever you do decide to see Mir, you would have to come to Atlanta or we could meet in a state in the middle and decide on a place for you to see and interact with him. Right now Mir is developmentally delayed and at a 9 month baby level overall and he needs to not be interrupted from his daily learning at daycare and treatment process so overnights away from home and his familiarity with me is not recommended either. Best, Faith"

He did not respond at all nor call, anything. He wasn't really concerned with Mir at all period but for court purposes I always made sure I did my part so later when he decides to start his court chaos and when he lies on me, I have the proof to show I've been attempting to co-parent with him and he blatantly refuses to because he's extremely hurt and bitter over issues he caused to be the way they are. A week before Mir was diagnosed, my mother had called me stating Mack's mother, Tamesha called acting like she wants to see Mir and crying and lying about me cussing her out the last time I talked to her. I have text messages to prove that's a lie. I don't know why she felt comfortable contacting my mom about me when they've never communicated previously and Tamesha's son is the one spreading lies, causing issue, and she's going along with her son's foolishness. She felt comfortable because my mother answered the phone for her which was also an issue. I take care of my child and I have say so on what goes on with him, I didn't need my mom speaking for me or coming in the middle of it to give me recommendations. I'm Mir's mother; I know how the other side of the absent family is however, I didn't always inform my mother about how they were. That was for me to deal with. I texted Tamesha and told her, "Please don't contact my mother and involve her in matters that have nothing to do with her. She doesn't want anything to do with you calling her. Thanks. I'm saying this because when I used to contact you and Mack's other family about matters I was always told by Mack to not contact y'all at all regarding issues that I had so that is why I'm saying from this point on to not contact my mother." Besides, my mother never told Tamesha she was welcome to call her but Mack's family had always told me I could talk to them until Mack started messing up and they couldn't take the heat so they didn't want anything to do with me, that's when the hostility and don't contact my family came from Mack because they hated that he didn't get over me with his lies in court. Fine, they can hate me for life. I'll always reveal Mack's lies via text messages, emails, phone calls, whatever, I do not trust him.

After Mir's diagnosis and texting Mack with no response, I let his family know as well since it's about Mir and to see if they wanted to improve their prior inconsistencies towards Mir and communicate like an adult with me. It had been about six months since I heard from Correll. The last time he had randomly asked me if Mir needed anything out of the blue after not hearing from him for months. I ignored it because I was beyond tired of the inconsistencies and I was taking care of Mir, I didn't need Correll's help. What was necessary was for his son, Mack, needing to be a father and do his part while being civil with me without blaming me for his shortcomings. His dad responded back, actually it was Sherry responding back using Correll's phone and I could tell by the text language and properness used in the text. Correll doesn't use such fanciness when he texts.

She said, "Thank you! I appreciate you sending me a picture of my grandson. He's getting big. We heard about his diagnosis. But we don't know any details. Can you please fill us in? Also, we'll be in Atlanta the week of July 22nd and we would love to visit with him. I responded back, "He was diagnosed with Autism and he has to go to 4 therapies. I don't have anything planned as of yet on the weekend of the 22nd, however I have a trip that starts on the 25th so I will not be in town. Sherry passed off the phone to Correll and he responded, "What type of therapy he needs? We will be in Atlanta the 22nd or the 23rd. I told him, "I do not have his official report as of yet but as far as I know speech therapy which he's been going to before that. Correll responded back, "Oh ok hopefully therapy goes good for him. I have an event July 14th for Autistic kids to play football and now my own grandson is diagnosed with it. Sad. Right now I'm praying everything works out for him if you need anything for him please do not hesitate to ask. Also if you get time can he FaceTime me please?"

"Yeah it's sad and stressful and okay." A few minutes later, I facilitated FaceTime between Mir and his grandfather.

After the call ended he said, "Thanks for the FaceTime he's getting so big. Please have him call me a little more and if you need anything please don't hesitate to ask."

I ended the conversation by saying, "Ok you can FaceTime and if he's not available I'll let you know it's a lot going on and ok."

My thing is this. Mir is two years old and doesn't know how to operate a phone let alone FaceTime. Why should he be responsible for calling and reminding Correll that he has a grandson to see about instead of Correll taking the initiative to check on him? Furthermore, I'm juggling a lot of things as it is and remembering to call some distant family members who want to play hopscotch in and out of my son's life isn't a priority for me to remember. If my son was old enough to make the decision if he wants to call, sure, I'm not opposed to it, but he's young and should be checked on by them. I sent Correll pictures of my son, being the bigger person as always, but really didn't ask or initiate any conversation first outside of that. Here or there he would make small remarks about how my son looked but other than that he barely asked how he was doing but maybe once or twice if that unless I sent a picture or video of happenings with my son. As far as Tamesha goes, her and I hadn't talked at this point for two years since she had the audacity to ask if she could have my son for a week, two weeks, or a month and had never met him before and knew nothing about him nor was she even working at the time which she had admitted to me, so how could she even take care of my son with all these factors involved and especially because of her interactions with Moesha.

I sent Tamesha a message with a picture of Mir attached and said, "I don't know if you know it or not but Mir got diagnosed with Autism yesterday."

She responded back saying, "Oh wow, No…I don't get info from Mack. I'm driving now but wow. *sigh* Now he's my little Buzz. No limitations…to infinity and beyond!

I responded back saying, "Exactly."

One time I video-chatted her to see him on Duo and she was telling Mir's sister about going to Florida to visit. I know she gets a lot of info from her son although she likes to play reverse psychology and claims that she doesn't. I guess she assumed seeing Mir in Florida since my parents are there and she was trying to go through them although they don't dictate or raise my son, I do. I would periodically send her pictures of Mir and just like Correll it would be small remarks but never any initiation on her behalf or checking on Mir.

It was getting tiresome dealing with Correll and Tamesha sending pictures reminding them they have a grandson yet little to no effort with Face-times and sending him anything in the mail at all. Tamesha went on to tell me about family members of Mir that have concerns with their kids and autism and such and how some of them have yet or avoided getting their child checked out.

At the end of our conversation, I told Tamesha, "We are in Atlanta, GA, and are permanently living here now so you're welcome to visit. I know you mentioned to Mir's sister on Duo video chat about visiting in Florida so I wanted to clear that up. If you want to send things you can send it to this address for now but that will change at the end of the year when we move to our house."

She responded back with so much shock saying, "Oh wow, okay thanks."

I knew Tamesha wasn't going to send anything because she never did except once when we was living in Virginia when she gave two little outfits, a hat, and sun glasses to Mack to give to Mir. That was the only thing she ever did for my son and he was about six months at that point. I continued anyhow sending pictures and videos of Mir trying to gauge her true interest in my son and sometimes she wouldn't text back for several hours or days later. That was the number one sign the fake interest she showed my mom was just purely an act to play on my mom's soft and less informed spot.

A few weeks later I texted Tamesha and said, "My mom told me how anxious you sounded to see Mir and I was wondering when you were finally going to meet him? His 3rd birthday celebration is being planned at a theme park in Florida and I thought that might be something you, Mack, and his granddad would want to participate in. Speaking of which, I haven't heard from nor has Mir had any contact with his dad in nine months so can you pass the message on to him too so you can both make advanced plans."

"I was just about to ask if you'd heard from him. I'd love to attend his celebration and I know his granddad would like to as well! Mack would too. He was emotional when I tried discussing things with him. He wouldn't respond so I just talked to him."

Tamesha is a liar and fake just like her son so I see exactly where he gets it from. Mack didn't show any emotion nor follow up with me about Mir's autism diagnosis. His mother just was trying to say whatever about Mack's response to make him sound good. If he was so concerned and emotional why hasn't he seen our son in person or on FaceTime for a whole year? Sounds like lying and a bunch of fake love and care to me but I didn't allow that to even be a thought I believed for a second. Their actions spoke a lot louder than their words ever could as it is.

"No Mack hasn't talked to me or reached out since about a month before we left Virginia and when I had Moesha back to court for harassment. I believe he's still mad about everything but I just want to co-parent at this point. It all is what it is." I said.

She said, "WHAT?? Never mind. I'll try to talk with him. There's still a lot going on. You'll hear from him soon."

When she said I would hear from him, I knew it was something behind it. He hadn't contacted or seen Mir for a year; he didn't suddenly change and decide to do so. Of course she had something to do with it as well I just wasn't exactly sure what it was. Tamesha, Mack's family, Bryna, and Moesha are what I refer to as his flying monkeys of him being a narcissist. Flying monkeys are those of who are against the target. They are enablers, accomplices, and entourage of him. They contribute to the narcissism by using abuse by proxy. It's when they get other people to abuse you and are often fed lies by the narcissists to do their bidding. They attack your character and you as a person and in turn this makes the narcissist feel good and in control. The phrase, I would be hearing him soon, I just knew had an ulterior motive behind it.

I responded to her saying, "I can only imagine and you don't have to make him talk to me. I would rather it be natural than forced and its okay. I understand a lot of this with him is stemming from her not liking me because when she and he are on bad terms he's civil and co-parents when they're back on good terms, it's bad to silence and absence."

She said, "I can't force him. He wants to but said y'all don't see eye to eye. I think me telling him Mir had Autism sent him back into depression. He's moving back home soon. I thought y'all were talking and he already knew."

I said, "He was able to see Mir before when we weren't Seeing Eye to eye and nothing happened, I just let him have his visits. It doesn't have to be eye to eye seen on nothing other than Mir and his interaction with his Dad though and his best interest given the current circumstances. Yes he knew because I texted him first before I texted you. He just never responds."

Tamesha acted like she was the first to tell Mack about Mir's diagnosis, she was playing the reverse psychology role.

She responded back, "Oh wow!"

I'm not sure what she was referring to but I'm guessing she was shocked because I told her that Mack and I don't need to see eye to eye on anything outside of Mir and she's used to females wanting him back and/or still sad over him cheating and then end up sleeping with him and I guess I was the only one who didn't want any of that. I said, "But anyways, I just wanted to let you know about Mir's birthday celebration and when you planned to come to see him. She replied, "I'll be at his birthday celebration God willing. I'm out of work this summer because of my Multiple Sclerosis and the heat." I said, "Well you've never met Mir so it would be cool if you're able to or if y'all could plan trips throughout the year to see him." She replied, "Here you go."

She didn't want to hear the truth but I'm tired of her pretending to want to see my son, it's been three years and she has no valid excuse at all and anything she tries to tell me I know is bullshit. I replied, "Huh?"

She said, "Texting gets confusing after a while. I'm silly. Send me the dates as soon as possible so we can start planning. I'm excited!"

There was nothing confusing about what I said, she obviously didn't like what I had to say, hence her smart remark but tried to do reverse psychology and play it off. I ended the conversation saying, "Alrighty."

I know she wasn't going to show up. A lot of empty words with no substance are all I really ever hear from Mack's entire family. Sure enough a few days later I heard from Mack. Lord was it some foolishness as always. He wrote me an email instead of texting me and it went like this, "Hey Faith, I know this is very short notice, but if you are in the area this weekend my daughter is having a party this Saturday at the infamous Chuck E Cheese and I just wanted to reach out and let you know that you and Mir are more than welcome to come, my dad is headed down that same weekend, I know the distance thing is kind of crazy. Also, I'd like to set something up to see Mir soon, I'm not sure when you are usually available but it can be planned out a bit out and not something really close. When you have a chance please get back to me, and thank you."

So first of all while this sounded like a genuine and true email it was not and you'll see what I mean shortly when I break it all down. You could tell he carefully construed the words to make it seem like he means well but he does not. First of all, this man had not seen or reached out to see our son for a year, no video chat, no physical contact or nothing. He never once responded to any of my messages or pictures regarding Mir and his wellbeing nor his diagnosis. He knows that I do not get along with his third baby-mama and I have told him on multiple occasions I don't want anything to do with her. Why would he think that I would come to the first birthday party of a child he made during our marriage and that he stopped seeing our son for to cater to that child since he is still sleeping with and in a relationship with the mother.

Third of all, I had just had a restraining order against this girl and we both do not like each other. She doesn't like me because I had the wife title she's been lying and dying to have, and every time she threatened, harassed, and lied on me I took her to court and got her criminally prosecuted for it on multiple occasions. I have nothing nice to say or do to her period and because I refuse to go to jail for putting my hands on her and beating her black and blue which I've desired to do after all the disrespect and hell I went through with her and Mack, I'm avoiding her. He didn't even include a location in this email as there are plenty of Chuck E Cheeses in Virginia so this was definitely a bogus email that he was only writing and seeking a reaction he already knew was going to occur from this.

Fourth, He knows Mir and I do not live in Virginia and even if we did I have no reason to go to that party whatsoever. What made him think I was going to be in Virginia on that particular weekend?

Fifth, he mentioned that his dad was coming to Atlanta which I already knew that same weekend to see Mir so Mack obviously knew we weren't going to be there or else his dad wouldn't be coming to Atlanta nor will his dad have mentioned coming to see Mir.

To conclude, he said, "It can be planned out a bit out and not something really close." Like wait a minute, you have already not seen our son for 9+ months yet you want to see him further down the line? Mack had no valid reason as to why he was not seeing our son. He couldn't even say us moving to another state was the issue because he stopped seeing our son a month and a few weeks before we moved, so that was not a factor for his absence at all nor was he in the military any longer. So this all calculates to none of what he was saying was logical and he was trying to be funny and hurt me as he has still been trying to do in different ways since I've divorced him. This is a narcissistic tactic after the divorce is over to harass you through the court system or by throwing their new victim and family in your face. He wouldn't have even paid me or my son any attention and I'm sure it would've just been funny business and extra petty foolishness had I been dumb enough to fall for that party. I responded back by saying, "No, thanks. We will not be in attendance to the party. I don't wish to have any contact with the mother nor my child to have contact with the mother either. We also don't live in Virginia and won't be coming back there for any reason. I will be doing something for Mir's birthday in September. More details to come. Any other time you want to see him you can meet me in Atlanta on weekends as it would be more convenient given his therapy schedule for me to not travel with him. In the future, you can reach me on my cell phone that is more direct contact than emails that sometimes get overlooked. Best, Faith" He replied back saying, "Thanks for getting back to me and that's understandable. I do not want Mir to grow and not have a relationship with those around him. I would love for him to be around my daughters but I'm hopeful that will come with time. Atlanta is a distance so it's not really feasible to come for just a weekend and have him for a short period of time given we both have our own set schedules, which is why there needs to be a change in how things are currently set up. But it is out there, and that's all I was looking to do with the first email. I guess I will be in contact with you some other time via email, the last time I contacted you via phone you claimed it was not me, so until an alternative is set up to where that isn't possible to happen again I'd prefer to just email you. Thanks again for the response; I'll talk to you later. He was sending, this email to show or prove something to somebody because it didn't sound like it had true intent nor was it the type of language Mack uses when he talks. Someone coached him on how to portray as he's being civil in this message.

Another thing is Mir and I was in Virginia when his third child was born and he never had any type of priority with bringing her around, he never even mentioned her existence until this email. We only saw Mir's oldest sister, Bryna's daughter, not his youngest sister. The baby was born and several months old before we left Virginia and he never brought her up or made one attempt to bring her to meet Mir. I had a restraining order against the mother, not the baby and he could've brought her if he was so concerned about the relationship between them then, which he was not so I knew this was just word salads he was saying which are ways to manipulate and control by inducing that confused addled state I know so well. It is a form of gas lighting, the "go to" method for brainwashing to foster loss of trust in reality and you. This was basically his way of sounding like he's mature and trying to do the right thing but I'm sure this was something he did to show Moesha so she could feel validated or have something to laugh at because I want nothing to do with her. If the shoe was on the other foot that girl would be cussing him out and everything but because she hasn't fully been in my shoes yet, she too is an enabler in the background of continued drama between her, Mack, and I. Also, Mack previously stated that if it had nothing to do with Mir to not contact him, yet he contacted me about coming to a party to be around a child who was once my step child in an affair of my marriage who is not my kid but a sibling Mir has not met yet due to Mack never doing so the entire time we lived in Virginia.

As he continued in his message he said, "Atlanta is a distance so it's not really feasible to come for just a weekend and have him for a short period of time given we both have schedules, which is why there needs to be a change in how things are currently set up."

Pause, before Mir and I moved, I told him we could set up a visitation plan to accommodate our move before I found out Mir got diagnosed with Autism, but he ignored my text message and never responded. Mir now has a life changing event and several therapies to go through and with an absent and uncaring father with no experience in dealing with this diagnosis he has a hard case to prove and most likely he's going to have to come to Georgia to see Mir without interfering with his therapies.

Second of all, it doesn't matter where your kid is you should always make time to travel and see them, at least that's what a real and caring parent would do. His real concern is trying to acquaint my son with Moesha to make her happy because she's always been the main concerned about playing a stepmother role but to be petty not because she actually cares or is even a real stepmother by law.

Third of all, Mack has four kids by three different women and one of us is in South Carolina, Virginia, and I'm in Georgia. How in the hell can Mack say Atlanta is a distance when he has babies all over the globe. South Carolina is seven hours from where he lives in Virginia and Georgia is only three and a half hours away from the part of South Carolina where Mir's oldest sister lives.

So basically because of distance, you don't see her either on your scheduled every other weekend visitation? Oh yeah that's right. Bryna told me previously he never once come to visit their daughter on his scheduled visits on weekends. The two babies in Virginia are Moesha's and obviously he is involved with those kids because he is still in a relationship and sleeping with her trying to avoid child support with her and everything else. If she and he were not together, I'm sure Moesha would haul ass and not let him see the babies. She already made that clear when they were having relationship problems and when she found out he was sneaking around to see our son with me present that she was going to be a single mother, basically implying he wasn't going to be in the picture and had also posted a meme picture on Facebook of a single mother and a baby saying she doesn't see anything wrong with the picture and that's another subliminal message that when and if they break up he's out the picture unless of course she wants to be like Tamesha and stay with a man for sixteen plus years, give the man babies, just for him to leave off and marry another woman a few years later.

Mack also travels from Virginia to Philadelphia a lot to see his other females and see his family and that's a five and a half hour drive. I also have proof and admission statements from a source with Mack's full name where on two occasions in the past couple of years, he admitted to driving from Virginia to Philadelphia and flying from Philadelphia, PA to Detroit, MI to purchase a vehicle. This was the same time we were in divorce court and he had owed me arrears for child support but was purchasing a new black Dodge Charger and showing it off on Facebook as if his several months of arrears didn't exist. That's a lot of traveling for a car.

On a second occasion, he admitted traveling from Virginia to Tennessee to buy another Dodge charger, this time the color blue a year later from him buying the first car. So you mean to tell me you can do all of this for a material possession when you had a good working car before both of these but you can't travel to see your kids? He's straight up pathetic and very trashy for that! The last part of the message was him saying, "But it is out there, and that's all I was looking to do with the first email." This was his hint that he was going to try to pull some court mess again. He continued on to say, "I guess I will be in contact with you some other time via email, the last time I contacted you by phone you claimed it was not me, so until an alternative is set up to where that isn't possible to happen again I'd prefer to just email you. Thanks again for the response, and I'll talk to you later."

He was basically blatantly telling me he wasn't going to reach me on my cell phone so basically like I told him before if he does that the emails will get overlooked as I don't check them often enough to have conversation and he rarely contacts me anyways unless it's with an ulterior motive or underhandedly causing drama or creating a conflict. He was trying to dismiss me from the conversation but yet he did not schedule anything about our son like he originally said, nor ask about him, he only cared to tell me about the party and play a disappearing act again. Mack was also trying to shift the blame on me about another person using his phone as if he and his father didn't admit to me Moesha texts off his phone, and that's in a text that I have saved. He was using reverse psychology but I made sure I texted him back to set the record straight.

I responded back saying, "Mir doesn't even have a relationship with you because you stopped seeing him before we left Virginia. So I'm confused as to why now you are concerned about his relationship with his other siblings when you haven't had any contact with him for 9+ months and this is the second time you have went nearly a year of no contact with him around the same times I filed a restraining order against your third baby-mama. It appears to me that you were more primarily concerned with inviting us to a birthday party knowing we hadn't had any contact from you and we don't live there and then threw seeing our child in there to cover it up. I don't see any change honestly occurring with this order given all the circumstances and evidence I have to present as well as Mir's recent diagnosis Also, as far as the communication on the phone, you admitted as well as your father that your phone was being used by your third baby mama on occasion before violating a safety order. You're using your phone to text me this email so how do I even know that it's even you even with a signature the same way a message that wasn't you came from your phone. I have a concern about you not having our child's best interest at heart due to you not showing any concern and being that you have been continuously absent and the communication from your end has not been the greatest and the safety of him being around your third baby mama. Being that I am the primary parent, the court relies heavily on my evidence and my judgment. Lastly, you and your family are more than welcome to schedule arrangements to see Mir preferably on weekends to allow more time being spent with him. I've invited your mother since Mir has been born and she hasn't made an honest effort and as far as your dad, there hasn't been much frequent and in person contact. Best, Faith."

He responded trying to act all mature but really it was again another mask of his for show off to somebody. This is him playing victim by saying "Faith, being mature adults that response really wasn't necessary (I did not read that entire response).

Pause, what I was saying was valid. Anybody whose child father abandoned the child and came at them about a party for another child made after their own child and absolutely nothing or no contact about their child for a long period of time would be upset and tell them about their actions. Mack doesn't like knowing or owning up to the fact that he is wrong to his actions nor does he like to be corrected. Also, he read that message, he just wanted to let me know he didn't to make me feel small and unimportant which is a form of disregard by a narcissist basically implying that nothing you're saying they care about or care to hear.

He continued on to say, "No hostility, no smart remarks, keep it short and simple without bashing the other person."

I wasn't being hostile, I was being truthful, there were no capitalized letters or any punctuation marks that indicated I was being hostile, I wasn't giving smart remarks, I was speaking facts. I wasn't bashing him. Bashing a person is defined as striking them (referring to a person) hard and violently. He continued on to say, "It's not that difficult, that's what I aim to do whenever we are required to communicate, because we are beyond the age of communicating the way you would like to. He concluded by saying, "Again, thank you for taking the time to respond about the party, and I will talk to you some other time."

Here's the thing, Mack doesn't even communicate with me so his statement was contradicting, also it didn't make any sense when he said beyond the age of communicating the way I would like, it's as if he was referring to me we wanting to talk to him in another way or he was basically saying he was blatantly not communicating with me in the healthy or logical way I would like. That's what I gathered from that statement. He also admitted what I made clear of that he was doing in earlier texts and that he only was reaching out to me about the party. He made that very clear in the text which pissed me off because I knew his intent had nothing to do with seeing our son at all. Again it was bullshit as usual. The next day I wrote him a message about his address since his mother had told me he was moving back home.

I said, "Your mother told me you were moving back home soon and when you have your new address make sure you update me with it for court purposes in the future in Atlanta."

He said, "If I moved, you would know. Otherwise, don't contact me further about it."

Now I could've easily snapped back and said, "All you had to say was Okay, I will" the same way he tried to correct me about explaining his absence and stuff in the email but I didn't. Things apply to me only, but when it comes to him, he's exempt. This is another narcissistic trait. Instead I said to him, "When did you want to schedule to see Mir in Atlanta? You mentioned wanting to set it up but I noticed you didn't say anything further after I declined the party invite."

He said, "I answered this question yesterday; I will talk to you some other time."

He was trying to brush me off as if I was a disturbance to him, but he felt he was totally okay and it was justified in his eyes to write that email he knew was upsetting to me.

I replied, "Okay, I just wanted to make sure it wasn't overlooked since you mentioned yesterday that you wanted to schedule a time then to see our son at a future date. This was just a follow up from yesterday when you wanted me to get back to you about it." He didn't say anything else. He knew he was caught and it was revealed that his real intention for writing me was only about "the party" and not about our son. I never heard anything else about him scheduling to see our son. It had already been a long time already at this point. The messages ended at this and months went by before Mack came at me again, but not on a positive note surrounding our son. As always, it's on a negative note that I will hear from him or that he will respond to my messages if he's on good terms with Moesha. If he's on bad a term, that's when he's civil, understanding, and responsive, at least he "acts" like he is anyways. I knew Tamesha had a lot to do with Mack even reaching out to me being funny like. After all she gave me a heads up that I would be hearing from him soon so this wasn't a spontaneous act of his, it was carefully planned with Moesha and Tamesha to do this to upset and get a reaction from me because they knew Mack hadn't been seeing nor having anything to do with our son. You might as well call Tamesha "Messy Mammy" because she truly lives up to her name and has for the past four years with all of this foolishness she has had a part in along with her son instead of taking the high road past his unacceptable behavior. Still, I continued to send Tamesha and Correll pictures. Usually when Mack would pull petty crap like this, I would stop talking to them all because I know they have a part in it, but I continued sending pictures anyhow. I wouldn't let them think for a second it was going to stop me from being the bigger person. I noticed that both of their response times started to get longer, they were saying less and you could tell they were both distancing themselves. It's as if it was scaring them the fact I could continue on knowing they were egging Mack on.

I stopped sending Tamesha pictures of Mir a couple of weeks later because it continued to be a one-sided effort for me, she clearly wasn't interested in initiating video chat at all since the first time I did it a couple months prior, and it took her days to a week to respond to any pictures and videos about Mir so that let me know she wasn't into it at all and that I should really stop because I was draining myself trying to get her to care about my child in a genuine way. Correll would pop in my messages periodically wanting to FaceTime Mir but still going weeks in between doing so. That was annoying too because it seems like the whole family knows nothing about how important consistency is with a young child whose memory isn't completely formed and especially within an autistic child. Literally, a few days after the emails between Mack and I, is when court in Georgia was being held for all of the custody matters to be handled in the court system in which we lived in since Mir and I were established residents beyond six months. Of course, Mack requested a phone consultation but I still had to appear. When I arrived at the courthouse, I went to the floor I was designated to be on. The officer directed me back to the female judge office and I had a seat at her table while he sat in the corner. She confirmed my name and then dialed Mack's number from her phone.

When Mack answered, she confirmed it was him and told him court was being conducted. He told the judge I've been calling the court house requesting a phone consultation and I was trying to see if it got approved. The judge looked at the phone with a scrunched and confused face like yeah this is why I'm calling you. Court is now. He was like, "Oh okay." She said I have, Ms. Faith here with me, do you know who that is? His voice sounded really shaky and he said, "Yeah" She said, "Today we are here because Ms. Faith filed a petition to domesticate a foreign judgment, did you get those papers in the mail." Mack said, "Yes but I didn't know what it was for." The judge said, "Mrs. Faith and your child live in Georgia. All matters will be handled here. You do know that she lives in Georgia right?" He said, "As far as I know. I thought that all matters would be handled in Virginia?!" The judge said no they are no longer a resident of Virginia where ever the mother and child goes that's where the order will be heard at for any changes." I whispered to the judge that the only thing left in Virginia is the child support. She told him exactly what I said and he was silent. She said, Do you need some time to review this domestication order?" He said, "Yeah I guess I can get a second opinion." She looked at the phone very confused as to what he was even talking about. She reiterated the fact that Mir and I live in Georgia and whether he get a second opinion or not it would be domesticated.

He said, "So that means I have to come all the way to Georgia if I want to file something in court she said, "Yes, this is where the child is."

He sounded so disappointed because he couldn't take me through the usual in and out of court anymore he would have to drive several hours away to pay to be seen in front of the judge as well as include travel and food expenses. Mack had planned right after his child support went up to go and change the order for no reason when he is the reason that he isn't seeing our son. He wanted to make it inconvenient for Mir and I so we were coming back and forth to Virginia for his games. It's also a method of control for him to feel like he has the upper hand.

The judge said to Mack, "She's just here to certify she lives in Georgia and for matters to be held here. Ms. Faith do you plan to file anything?" I said, "No, there's no point in me filing anything but this. He has chosen to not see our son for nine months."

"Did you hear her?" The judge asked.

"Yes."

The judge shook her head and he knew then he couldn't lie about his absence nor was I lying because it would've been perjury yet again when all the proof I have to show for his absence is in text messages where I've attempted to coordinate physical and video visitation. In the lowest most shaky tone he said, "I guess you can go ahead and domesticate it."

The judge said, "Okay, this matter will now be domesticated and you both will receive copies."

I was so relieved. No more flying back and forth to Virginia in his web of games. I thanked the judge and walked out the court room. Court ended.

A few days later Correll came to town. He texted me, "Good morning what time will you be home today?"

It didn't matter what time I was going to be home because he and his wife were not welcome with their energy in my home. I'm not sure why they thought I was going to be friendly enough for them to be in my place where I lay my head at for them to scope out things and go run telling Mack and Moesha. There was nothing to hide; I just prefer to keep it as business and professional as possible especially with the false allegations, games, and hostility all of them had a part in previously. I didn't want to give them any type of ammunition to where it was just me against them two and because of how they personally feel about how I handled Mack. I didn't want things to suddenly go left while they were visiting and my son being snatched away because of their plot or something. I have extreme trust issues with Mack and his entire family when it comes to revenge and setting me up.

Besides, It had been way too many negative vibes amongst them since the beginning of our marriage and when our divorce trial had occurred, I don't trust them especially if cameras aren't around to monitor.

I ended up telling Correll, "I wasn't going to go back until later on. I can figure out a place for us to meet so Mir can play as well."

"Ok let me know."

I sent him the address for an indoor playground that was not too far from the place Mir had to be evaluated at. When we arrived at the designated time and approached Correll and Sherry, I spoke to both; Sherry said not one word and Correll barely spoke. I asked Correll if Mir's older sister was here with them and he said, "She was originally supposed to come but Mack didn't want to come."

I didn't have anything to say. Mack was so bitter, he didn't want to nor did he want Mir's older sister to come to see Mir. This goes back to what I mentioned earlier about him really not caring if the kids have a bond not even with himself, especially because he didn't at least allow his daughter to come see her brother. That message he sent me before Correll's dad came, was literally just a message he sent to appear like he cares but really he was doing it for show to somebody like I had said. I let go of Mir's hand so he could play with the toys and bounce houses in sight and Correll followed after him.

I went over to some chairs, sat down, and used my laptop to do my school work. Sherry sat at the café tables with her face balled up looking very stank looking at her phone. Not one time did she attempt to interact or play with Mir. He came near her and she ignored him completely I mean she was very cold towards him. We were at the indoor playground for two hours and she sat in that same spot all in her phone. Honey Mir and I was looking fly, fresh hair cut for him, my hair was done as usual, my nails and toes done, pretty outfit, just glowing all over and the energy and look all over her face was all bad. It reeked of envy. This is exactly why I did not want them in my house.

Of course Correll tries to play it cool because he wants to see Mir, but he's not good at hiding his animosity either until it benefits him. While inside, I took videos and pictures of Mir and in one of the videos you could see Sherry's angry face. She really looked like she did not want to be there and I wondered why did Correll even bring her. It's all positive vibes with me and Mir; she can take that mess elsewhere. It's funny because this was the same lady who was all for me at the beginning of this mess sending positive aspirations and used to talk a bunch of shit about

Correll and him enabling Mack's behavior acting like Mack was innocent when he was not. She used to talk a lot of shit about Moesha and how her and Mack were immature for things they did to me and how karma was going to come for them, but as soon as matters ended up in court and I presented all text message proof of Mack's adultery with the witness from the Navy, hostility, restraining orders against them both, and false allegations they've put on me as well as proof of Mack's absence and refusal to co-parent as well as the car's he purchased while in arrears for child support they began to hate my guts. She actually helped me out by sending screenshots of Mack's page as well when he was posting things on there. I should've known it was a façade. She and Correll had a hidden motive of pretending to be nice to me while Mack was dogging me out so I wouldn't cut everyone out of the picture from Mir for their messy participation.

The visit ended after two hours of play and Correll said he might attend Mir's birthday party and for me to let him know the location. I told him, "Ok." He and Sherry left. Mir and I left followed shortly after as well. I continued to send pictures here and there of Mir so they could see he's happy and well taken care of and show them who they're missing out on. Besides, my son is way too handsome to not share his fashion and his lovely physical features.

Here and there Correll would FaceTime but it was once every few weeks. In between this time, I found out how much Mir's therapies would cost me out of pocket due to the insurance I had through my job. It was a total of $3000 that I would have to pay first before the insurance company would cover 80% while I take care of the other 20%. It didn't matter what company or facility I chose to use, it was a universal cost I would have to front first before the insurance kicked in and this was a cost every new year that I would have to pay. I looked over my divorce decree to see what percentage Mack was ordered to pay towards medical expenses. I sent Mack a message that said,

"Hello Mack, Mir's autism services are going to require a payout of $3000 deductible and 20% copay before services are rendered. Per our divorce decree clause number five you are required to pay 44% of medical expenses which would equate to $1320 for the deductible. I am texting you in an effort to see if you would willingly provide your percentage before I request an increase in child support through Virginia being that Mir has special needs. Please let me know as soon as possible as this is very important for Mir's development. Thank you. Best, Faith"

Mack didn't respond back and I'm thinking to myself like damn you're extremely bitter at this point you refuse to pay for your son to get the treatment he needs. Its apart of our court order and is not counted in child support. I remembered when Correll told me if there was ever anything I needed to not hesitate to reach out to him. I knew he didn't mean it but I figured this would be a perfect moment to try to see where his heart and intentions really was. I texted Correll and said, "Hello good afternoon, I sent this message to your son about Mir and his autism services and he doesn't respond back to any messages that have to do with Mir and his development. He hasn't seen Mir in almost a year but found it important and petty to invite me to the baby birthday party that he made during my marriage knowing we don't live in VA but nothing legitimate about Mir. I know you said hit you up if I need anything for Mir, well here I am asking you to talk to your son about money for Mir's medical needs before I have to go before a judge about it. Thank you."

I knew after I sent that message I knew Correll wasn't going to do anything at all but stir up more drama and not even contribute even though he said a couple of times to reach out if I needed anything for Mir. He was probably saying if I needed anything materialistic, but Mir's health is more important. I gave it a try anyways. He responded back being very short with me and saying, "I'll call & talk to him." If he was such the caring grandfather he portrayed periodically and if he had my back so much with my son he would've took up for his son's slack, not that it's his responsibility but as a grandparent you should want to since you want to be involved by posting on social media like you really doing something in his life and you not. After he said he would call and talk to him I said, "Great! Let me know because I will be moving forward with a decision soon." He read it and didn't respond. I also had sent the same message to his mother, she never responded at all.

This is the point where I said to myself, since my son getting the help he needs isn't important to none of them, I'm not nor am I obligated to send pictures so they can post my son all over social media but be deadbeats in real life. My child is not a toy that you put on the shelf, and play with when you're ready. It doesn't work like that so I blocked her a few weeks after that message. No need for me to keep her updated when she doesn't ask about my son anyways nor has she ever made an actual effort to see him whether it be physically or electronically. I didn't hear back from Correll but of course Mack responded the next morning and said, "I've been telling you this for too long and a too many times, stop contacting and getting my parents involved with YOUR personal issues that don't pertain to my parents PHYSICALLY SEEING or TELEPHONIC COMMUNICATIONS with Mir, those two things are the ONLY things they or you ever need to discuss, all that extra stuff, DO NOT CONTACT THEM about, they don't want any involvement in it just like you said not to contact your parents as your parents want no involvement either.

Secondly, I will not be thrown some random number with no knowledge of what Mir needs with any documentation etc., and no I will not be sending payment to you if it is not COURT RECOGNIZED, so I'll see you in court. Regardless, I'll see you in court, we'll clash it out. I do not nor will not contact you via phone unless communications are court monitored so I will not be responding to this message as you have a history of false accusations. Thanks."

Mack showed his hostility very well in this message and his refusal to do anything unless we're standing in front a judge. As far as when he said I have a history of false accusations, he's projecting what he has done against me which is a narcissistic trait and refusal to take accountability for what he's done. When I take matters to court, I have everything documented from text messages, to letters, to videos, and pictures. I don't go lying in front of the judge knowing I have no evidence to back it up. Everything that I have ever brought in front of the court with Mack has always had proof and all of the false allegations he made against me, every time the judge asked where his proof was he never had any but I had the proof to show that what he was saying was a lie.

I responded back to Mack saying, "This message you sent me contains nothing about scheduling to see Mir, no follow ups about his wellbeing or diagnosis. In regards to the contact with your parents your father has admitted in a text message dated on June 30 at 8:10 pm that "If you need anything for please do not hesitate to ask." Your father has also stated to keep him "updated" on things with Mir. I have proof of said messages. Your mother has inquired on Mir's care regarding his diagnosis on July 2nd at 8:14 pm about calling me. Instead of calling me, she asked about Mir's diagnosis on July 4th at 2:22pm. Both of those inquiries from their text messages are outside of the realm of what you're saying about only contacting them regarding "physically seeing or telephonic communications with Mir" It appears that there is a miscommunication on the opposite end but due to you admitting that they want nothing to do with Mir outside of physically and telephonically communicating with him, I will not contact them moving forward upon your request. Nothing in my message is personally about me; it's specifically about the wellbeing and care of and for Mir. It's okay, if you do not pay for it to me, I will take it up with my attorney here in Georgia and in Virginia and also in court. I will continue informing you of Mir's medical status as it is a part of the court order to keep you informed." At this point it's just ridiculous, Mack refuses to comply all the way around with co-parenting because he's just so angry at his actions and how he could not hide behind them any longer and has been for 4 years. I have put my feelings to the side about him cheating and abandoning myself and my son to be with other women enough to co-parent about our son and our son only. I don't bother him about anything else and it's a problem to him for that.

At this point he's already two month in arrears, owing me over $1500+ dollars in support so he's really digging an even bigger hole for himself but of course, like always I'm the blame for everything. If his family don't care about nothing outside of physically or telephonically seeing my child but nothing with his health, they need to be banned period and for my baby I'll go to war in court about these evil and spiteful demons within Mack and his family. How could I trust these people with my son when I'm not around to take care of him outside of flashing photos for social media?

I decided to send Mack screenshots of the documentation outlining everything so he couldn't say I was just lying which I have no reason to lie and I don't want Mack's money for my own leisure, besides he doesn't have any and I've been holding my own weight since 18 before and now that I have a child he just needs to do his part and get over the divorce he caused me to get, that's it that's all. I sent him screenshots of the documentation and said, "Hello Mack, As you stated earlier about "not being thrown a random number with no knowledge of what Mir needs with no documentation" I have attached to this message a copy of the email I received from the therapy place here in Atlanta, Ga. You are more than welcome to make your payment directly through them and I can have it arranged for a statement to be sent to you where they will deduct your percentage for unreimbursed medical expenses as outlined in the divorce decree for each visit he has but you would have to let me know if that's what you choose to do. They did not include it in the email but I was told by the coordinator via telephone that an additional $10 fee is also assessed per visit, per therapy for them to render services while he attends school. I don't mind calling them to get that in an email as well you just have to let me know. I am also going to honor your request to bring this matter to court by filing a Contempt motion for medical expenses in the event they do not get paid by you to the facility or reimbursement to myself and I am going to file an increase in child support through Virginia for his special needs. Best, Faith. He responded back, "Okay."

A couple of days later I sent him more documentation and said, "Hello Mack, I have attached a screenshot of additional costs associated with Mir's therapies. He will need three evaluations at this facility which will be an additional $500 for each one along with a cost of $10 per visit per therapy if traveling to his daycare. As previously stated, you are more than welcome to render payment to the company, you would have to let me know or you can provide reimbursement to me, your choice. Once he starts services I will provide you with a more accurate amount that you would pay including everything and if you still refuse to pay until it is "court authorized" although it is already outlined in our Divorce decree the percentage you're supposed to pay, I will file a contempt of court motion, ask for interest, and attorney fees to be paid. It would be best to keep these matters out of court and coordinate payment amongst each other while prioritizing on Mir and his needs. Best, Faith."

He never responded but I keep him informed anyway because he's going to lie in court like he always does on me and say he had no idea and that's when I have to pull out the proof. He makes himself look bad and of course every time I'm going to cover myself. He's a narcissistic pathological liar and if you don't arm yourself with truth and proof these type of people will try to get over on you and sometimes the judge will get duped into believing them hence the reason I only communicate with Mack and his family via written form of communication and if it ever comes to a point of phone communication, I would record the entire call for my sake.

Moving forward, the video visitation between Correll and Mir didn't last for long before another turn of events occurred and it was for the worst. One day, Correll asked me to have Mir FaceTime him. He knows my son has no understanding of how to do so but wanted to disregard acknowledging me doing so for Mir, a trait exactly like Mack. I can see through it. This particular day he asked, I was out doing a photo-shoot for this book cover and enjoying my day being baby free. Mir was with his babysitter at home enjoying his day. I didn't respond for hours and when I did, I had to brace myself because I just knew it was a particular reason his dad wanted to FaceTime Mir so late in the day.

When Correll answered the FaceTime, Mack was holding his newest one year old daughter and Correll was holding Mack's newest two month old son on camera. Mack looked so miserable. He looks like he gained a lot of weight and like life has really hit him like a ton of bricks.

He didn't appear happy at all, but more so like he was going through something over there. I'm thinking in my head, this is new. You could tell it was all staged and it looked like Mack's daughter didn't even want to be in his arms. This is the first time Mir had even seen these kids, as I said before Mack never mentioned their existence at all.

Mack and Correll were so occupied with those kids that they weren't paying attention to Mir. The focus wasn't even on him, it was really to show off Mack's other kids, the ones he got abandoned for. They also made sure these kids was on camera, not so much to show Mir them but because they know I was holding the camera for Mir and it was a reminder to me of what I got cheated on for and the kids that came during my marriage and right after my divorce. They also wanted me to know that they are active in those kids' lives. Trust me, they knew I was holding the camera for Mir and they were definitely trying to be funny. Correll was being extremely extra, more so than he's ever been before when Mack and the other kids aren't around. He was yelling and acting very frantic for Mir to take a picture showing they were on video chat trying to get him to pose, Mir appeared very confused as to who these people were and what they were saying and doing. Out of anxiety and for soothing purposes, Mir began to rock back and forth. This is something Mir has been doing for a while and its apart of his autism spectrum disorder. Mack didn't appear interested in talking to Mir at all, he didn't say he missed him, loved him, nothing at all. Mir had on the most basic outfit ever and Correll said, "Oh I like your shirt and Mack repeated after him."

They were obviously being facetious and trying to make out like they are into him but they weren't and it was written all over their faces. Mir was continuing to rock and Mack made funny faces at him, he looked confused at him and then looked at me. Correll on the other hand came out of nowhere saying, "What you doing crazy man?"

At this point I'm thinking in my head Oh no the hell he did not just call my child crazy. Has he lost his mind that fast coming for a kid, my kid at that? I didn't want to make a scene in front of Mir and he end up crying so as soon as they said their good byes, I hung up the phone and texted Correll saying, " I was reading through my divorce decree and it says nothing about you FaceTiming. It only has a clause for you to be included in parenting time which is in person so in other words don't text my phone asking for a two year old to call you on FaceTime. It's annoying when you know he got things going on in his life, you're inconsistent, you continuously lie talking about you going to call him back and never do, you pick and choose when you want to do for and talk to my son. You don't have any conversation of substance anyways and it ain't helping. That remark you made about my son being a crazy boy on FaceTime which I got recorded is just negative and not building him up. Nobody will talk to my son like he different. He needs a life and family of consistency and honesty not continuous neglect and favoritism which I have noticed is prevalent. Mir has always been on the back burner to you and the whole family and I'm done dealing with it. My child has more important issues to be addressed in his life other than some few minute of a phone call every blue moon by somebody who plays hopscotch in and out of his life. I'm grown and nobody can tell me what to say out my mouth and in a text. I don't have to deal with this foolishness or nothing that's not in a court order. That being the bigger person is gone out the window when it comes to my boy. I'm sick of the entire BS. Good riddance!"

After that message I placed him on the block list. I got tired of talking and draining myself dealing with these toxic people who always claim they going to do things and never do. As Mir gets older, I don't want to tell him anything about somebody doing something for him unless I know for a fact it's going to get done because I would be the one to try to console and mend his heart if he starts feeling a certain type of way about people misleading him and I don't want him to ever feel inadequate or like he's not important. Less than an hour after I sent my message, Correll's wife, Sherry, the one that used to be on my side so much, sent me an unwanted text message. She said, "I really hope you get the mental help you very much need ASAP. Your instability isn't beneficial for Mir's development. You're all over the place. One minute you're upset because you feel Mir's paternal family isn't "doing enough." Then the next minute you're upset because the family is trying to keep in touch, and that's too much for you. Why FaceTime a two year old, you ask? Because he lives six states away! And why aren't the conversations of any substance, you ask? Because he's two. You're being utterly ridiculous! Your immaturity and jealousy is very obvious. Like I've told you before, functioning and making decisions primarily based off your emotions only hurts one person. I'm praying for you to one day be able to move on past all the hurt you've endured in these past few years, for Mir's sake."

First of all, this message she sent defending the husband she would talk so much trash to me about all the time was not even about me needing mental help it is about the fact that an innocent two year old autistic child was called "crazy" by the man who is said to be his grandfather.

Second of all, me defending my child and the name he was called, the favoritism that Mack's entire family shows towards the other kids, and the ongoing pettiness they continuously are doing since I have divorced Mack. There's nothing wrong with the way I chose to write Correll addressing and correcting the issues and my choice to dismiss him from having any contact or verbally abusing my child ever again. I wouldn't be a real mother if I didn't stand my ground for this stuff and for her to come at me talking about I'm not good for Mir's development, like what girl? I was thinking, you and Mack and the entire family can never come for me as a mother. I'm a damn good mother, my son is always eating good, living good, and well taken care of regarding his health and medical status so how could you even fix your lips to be absent and speak on my motherhood. In reality, by saying I'm not good for Mir's development, what she's doing is using a trait of Mack's by projecting her insecurities on me. In reality, Sherry, Correll, Mack, and the rest of the family are not good for Mir's development and they've shown that many times in their lies and lack of everything to do with Mir, it's just completely ridiculous. I'm not even all over the place.

I got out the military and before I did that I divorced Mack, cleared everything out in court that was rightfully deserved after I all I did endure, and I moved to another city. I don't bother Mack or blow up his phone about what he did to me, nor do I constantly move back and forth like Mack does from state to state, I've only moved once. I maintain all of our standards, Mir is never unkempt and neither am I so at this point she was just saying stuff to defame my character to make her feel better. As far as me being upset because of Mir's family, I have never even showed an ounce of upset about them being involved with Mir, the problem is they are inconsistent people but they forget that part though. Being upset because the family is keeping in touch and that's too much for me? Okay, at this point she's making assumptions because I'm not sure where this is coming from. I would send pictures, allow Correll to see Mir on FaceTime, keep him posted when he asked so how would that cause me to be upset? If I was upset and it was too much for me, I wouldn't have done any of that. I don't like any of the situations because of how foul and fast everything happened but I am over it enough to be civil and keep them involved until they do some out of the way type of shit. I have boundaries and apparently they don't mind crossing them and that's where the problem is. See Mack's family is used to him dealing with young, immature, and females that have no boundaries. Ones that have allowed him to boomerang in and out of their life, treat them bad, not do for the kid, leave them, come back, and take his mess. I chose to kick him out and walk away and handle him with a long handled spoon, no kissing ass, no messing around, no manipulating or duping me any longer and they aren't liking my wall I built so every attack is at my character and never about Mir like I try to keep it at. Unless she knows what they are doing is being extra and not what it should be, again she's making up stuff about what she thinks I am to defame my character. As far as me being utterly ridiculous, I'm not. This grandfather of Mir's claimed he wanted to FaceTime with Mir. He was barely paying my child any attention because they were so busy trying to flash the other kids in his face and Mir was looking overwhelmed and confused. Then she wanted to say, I'm being immature and jealous? Sweetie, immature because I'm addressing an issue without cussing, fussing, or none of that? Jealousy? Over a man who hasn't been paying his child support for over two months now. A man who dogs women out all the time? A man who looked super miserable on that camera and like life has hit him very badly. Mack was looking so rough. That's the roughest I have ever seen him. His hair was not cut he was looking old in the face, just aging poorly from all that dogging and lying he's been doing. Jealous over other kids? No, that's not the case. I'm fine with my one. It only took me one time to learn my lesson. I'm good on having anymore right now. Lastly, for her to even mention that I'm functioning and making decisions primarily based off of my emotions which is only hurting one person was ridiculous to me. Like what are you even talking about? I'm living life and raising my son, not chasing after his Dad to be with him, not knocking on his door for his help. As far as conversation with Correll he doesn't talk to my son as if he's normal. He talks to him like he doesn't pick up vibes or understand things. Mir is very smart he doesn't always verbalize what it is he wants or sees but he understands and even I understand him and I'll never treat him different because of a medical diagnosis. He is not that diagnosis. He is the same Mir I have laid my eyes on when he was first born. The most handsome, lovable, sweet, caring and smart little boy I ever want to know. At this point, I know I don't want another child. I'm too in love with him, I couldn't imagine sharing my love for him with another child of mine besides I want to dedicate all of my time and focus on making sure he grows up successful and well because really and truly, I'm all he's got for sure. When I tried to respond to Sherry's message I realized she had already blocked me. She wrote the message and then disappeared. This lady is damn near 50 playing games and so is her husband speaking negatively on a childlike how dare he. I have another number connected to my phone so I copied the message and sent it to her through there. I said, "Girl if you don't get off my line with you want to be relevant self and texting my phone. I don't need any help I'm perfectly fine, stable, and doing well taking care of my son. Yeah, as a mom I feel some type of way about the treatment and favoritism about my son. He's innocent and it doesn't matter how many states away we are, what matters is the fact that he unfortunately has a sorry paternal family who mad and always trying to do whatever they can to get back at Mir's mother because she's excelled at everything y'all thought was going to stop. I never had a problem with the keeping touch, the inconsistency is a problem. Who the freak only thinks of a child every couple of weeks or every few months and hit them up sporadically? You're not sounding logical, you sound like you're brainwashed honestly. You was all for me just a few

304 | P a g e

years ago until I peeped how fake you was playing both sides between me, Mack, and the mistress. I'm not being ridiculous period, jealousy over what and who? Honey I have moved on in life and I'm doing new things with my child, while all y'all still doing the same thing. You can't talk about me being jealous about anything when you were salty when Correll wanted to see Mir. Always throwing shade to his ex and all that extra jazz. I got a video of your stank looking face when y'all was just down here in Atlanta. You so mad you ain't even speak, I spoke to you but I'm jealous and insecure. About my child I ain't playing this favoritism stuff period Pooh. I think you got it misconstrued if you think I still want Mack. Honey he is no prize. He's not a good father to our son and only plays right when it's of a benefit to him. He only being a father to those kids because he don't want to be on child support for 4 kids and believe, trust me I know Mack and I don't got nothing to be jealous of. My child hasn't had his father because he was neglected and that's the only thing I have to be mad about, a DEADBEAT. That's it that's all now you take your outta shape, outta place self to bed honey and get off Faith line. Everything in court has played out exactly how it's supposed to, not because I lied but I told the truth and the judge saw it to. You keep talking about me functioning and making decisions based off of one person but yet you fail to realize your husband's son caused all this foolishness. He's bitter. He ain't seen Mir in a year because he's bitter, I'm not. He moved before I even got out the Navy. You mad I'm doing well in life yeah I saw it all over your face. Now Go play with one of them other baby mammies honey since you want to be so important but not over here. You don't run anything over here sweetie."

She responded back, "You sound crazy! Speaking of things you know nothing about. Get help real soon."

I knew exactly what I was talking about and had witnessed it before. If what I was saying wasn't true, why was there even a need for her to call me out of my name and mention me getting help trying to play reverse psychology as if I'm imagining things for my own desire?

"Honey I ain't crazy. I got my entire receipts sweetie and I ain't deleting a thing. How about you get help? You need it badly coming for me about my child because you're miserable and jealous of my child. You're brainwashed. (I said this because obviously Mack and the family have fed these folks a mouth full of lies and they believe everything he tells them although his actions show a lot different.) I also told her I'm going to pray for you because I got out of that mess you in." She knows exactly what I'm talking about. When she was trying to play cool and get on my good side, she spoke of a lot of things negative to do with Mack and his behavior and she admitted it was his fault and Moesha's issues but now she's changed sides by attacking me like I done something to her personally and revealing her true colors. She used to hype me up about things being in my favor too She responded back, "Jealous of a child?! Crazy again." All while laughing."

Apparently she just thought everything was funny and missing the whole point of the message to Correll. I think her texting me definitely wasn't about my son, it was more for her to project her anger towards me and tell me how I feel and I haven't talked to this woman in a couple of years. I told her, "Girl bye before I get harassment charges on you, you already know I'm not like those others I don't play period pooh. Now hit the treadmill and get off my line." She laughed and lied by saying, "You texted us from multiple phones! Who's harassing who here, you're a clown."

First off, she texted me first but here she was again lying on me, projecting, and name calling as if that really was going to bother or make me feel bad. I said, "I actually have two numbers connected to my phone. You text me first, I got the proof but you dumb so I understand. Goodbye lady your games won't work with me or court." She's acting just like a flying monkey for Mack, someone who lies and buys his foolishness and tries to inflict whatever necessary to cause a ruckus without taking accountability for one's actions. She responded back, "Yeah Yeah, Yeah, you have so much proof. Proof of what? That you're still crazy and bitter and angry and mad and obviously bored. It's a Saturday night, shouldn't you be out enjoying your oh so fabulous life instead of going back and forth with this old, overweight, jealous woman? Clown. Oh and you have pictures of me that I didn't authorize you to take? And if I looked miserable it was because nobody wants to deal with you crazy."

First off, the proof I have is the continued harassment from Mack and Moesha, the messages Mack has sent me that are extremely rude and hostile, the messages where I have invited him to doctors' appointments, invited his family to see Mir, given addresses for them to send gifts, Mack's refusal to co-parent or talk to me without downing me and reminding me he left me, the talking about other children that have nothing to do with Mir's health or diagnosis, Mack's dismissal of Mir's diagnosis, refusal to set up visitation, admittance that he cheated and brought Bryna in my house, arrest records, bogus restraining orders with proof of lies, I have everything Mack has ever done in a text message, video, picture, I can pull the thousand dollar transcript of the divorce hearing and how nasty he acted towards me, the judges, and attorneys, I literally have everything to show that I've been civil, have tried to encourage a relationship between Mir and Mack but everything is literally an attack on me personally instead of taking accountability for his actions, correcting their absence, and the reason things are the way they are. She's angry because I covered and armed myself so they couldn't lie on me and get away with it like demons. They hate that I'm smart. Too smart to fall for their BS. Like Bryna had said before, Mack is used to getting over on females and he couldn't on me without taking accountability in court and that's why they hate me. That's perfectly fine but it's also not my problem because Mack caused so much hell, he should've braced for the consequences of his actions but instead he likes to throw rocks and hide his hands as if he did nothing and I'm the blame for everything. Also, her continued name calling only proved that she was everything she was calling me. I wasn't cussing at her or name calling her, I was irritated and wanted to of course but because all of their actions will be used in court to protect my child from verbal, emotional abuse, and absence I have to remain civil in a text and allow them to look bad since the damage is coming from them. I'm not giving them the opportunity to shift blame on me. Another thing is why is she so worried about my Saturday night? I'm not worried about hers. For her to say, "shouldn't you be out enjoying your oh so fabulous life" this statement let me know that she is very envious of my life and the fact that I have moved away and on with my life from Mack. For her to go above and beyond to add in "going back and forth with this old, overweight, jealous woman" I only said she was jealous, I told her to hit the treadmill because yes she is overweight and instead of coming for me about correcting Corell for calling my child crazy, she needs to focus on her weight loss journey and leave me alone. She really thought I took pictures of her. The video I was speaking of where she's in the background looking stank was the same one I sent Corell where Mir was in the forefront playing and she could be seen looking how she was looking. I don't know why she thought she was important to me for me to just snap pictures of her when clearly my child was running in the vicinity of her and Corell but she wasn't acknowledging him. The crazy thing is she saying, "If I looked miserable it was because nobody wants to deal with you." I've literally done nothing to these people. Their anger with me is so displaced because of the lies Mack has told them. He won't tell the part of what he did to me, only how I reacted so they look at me like I'm the villain when I am the victim. They should know by now he has victimized several women by getting into relationships with them, getting them pregnant, making them have abortions or if they decide to keep the kids, he runs off with another woman and makes the child's mom a living hell by throwing the new victim in their face to taunt them that he cheated on them. I've been nothing but civil and inviting of them into my child's life so all of the animosity towards me is so unnecessary because of how I chose to handle the divorce, custody, child support, and how I chose to grieve what Mack did to me. He inflicted a lot of pain, what was I supposed to do, continue to take his foolishness like all of the other girls did in the past, allow him a free pass to walk all over me and open and close the door repeatedly on me being his wife, and abandoning our son. If that's why they don't want to be around me, then good stay away. I don't have to tolerate them if I do not want to. I have done my part; they are barely and have not done theirs. I'm done being the bigger person. They don't know how to distinguish my reaction from what Mack did then that's beyond my control. I ended up responding to her and saying, "You're saying I'm all these things huh, all of them are inaccurate. You're basing how you feel about me because of what a liar said out of their mouth. You seem real concerned about my Saturday night when you texted me first, you're irrelevant, been irrelevant, I dismissed you a long time ago but you just had to hit my line because you feel left out. Not my problem. I'm glad things are how they are because honestly my child doesn't need to be in any of this foolishness. He's got a loving consistent family right where he's at. I told you goodbye several texts ago yet you kept bothering me. Get a life, goodnight." She kept going on by saying, "Which makes you crazy. You texted us, you crazy bitch." I told her "Nah you texted me first, I corrected Correll about my child. You're a liar and a narcissist too. Now let me go save and send all these to my attorneys for court. Toodles."

I let her get the last word in but I was over it when she first texted me. This last text is where her hostility and continued true colors came in. She said, "You and your attorney can kiss my ass. Next time, think twice before you text anybody's phone over here talking crazy. I've been quiet long enough. Text my husband phone again and we'll be right here again. Now tell your attorney that! I don't know who you think you are."

My first thoughts were I am someone who left and divorced a toxic marriage, I successfully left the military, and I moved to another state, and I am evolving into an even more blessed and successful life than I ever had before and she recognized it but instead of acknowledging my strengths she chose to attack them.

She continued on to say, "You think you can run your mouth talking to us like we owe you something and then want to start talking about attorneys when we respond."

I don't talk like they owe me anything because there's nothing they have I can get, sympathy, respect, nothing. They've already shown me that they can't do anything for Mir but lie and pretend they are there for him and some sporadic gifts when they feel like it. I take care of my household and Mir with and without getting child support so for her to say that it's yet another invalid statement filled with anger. I don't bring up attorneys often. The only time I have brought up an attorney or court is when they've been verbally abusive to me and my son as well as when Mack refuses to pay his child support on time and medical expenses as he is responsible for so for her to say I brought it up every time, that's definitely a lie. She ended her message by saying, "No, boo...It doesn't work like that. So go ahead and block us all again and gone. Like you said, I have my other grand babies here and you're disrupting our quality time."

I never mentioned anything directly about the other grand babies they have and the statement she made was so unnecessary which let me know that my words to Correll that favoritism is prevalent amongst this family is correct. She didn't have to go that far but she was attempting to make me jealous or feel some type of way because they had Mack's newest kids around them and not mine. I ended up just ignoring it because honey that karma is going to be something else for her and them and talking to and treating my child like an outcast. Yes, I blocked them because I'm just tired of the drama, unfairness, and the lack of everything to do with Mir. They want to see me fail, they want to see me struggle with Mir so I can break and hand him off to his dad, but I have prevailed and will continue to do so. I will fight for Mir's best interests every time and because of what he's got going on its going to resort in a supervised visitation as it already is especially with this behavior they are displaying.

A few minutes after she sent this text, right before I blocked her she called and hung up and when I asked her why she ignored it. Clearly, she was playing a game on my phone but I blocked her so I no longer have to deal with it. Mack never said anything at all to me which was somewhat surprising but he picks and chooses when he wants to say something to me. A few weeks went by and it was time to celebrate Mir's birthday. I originally planned to have a celebration at LegoLand in Atlanta for his birthday where I would pay for all the guests' admission and the food. They wouldn't have to do anything but show up. Due to the incident that occurred with Mack's family, I figured they wouldn't show up although they previously had stated making plans to make it. After all the disagreement between me and them had nothing to do with them not being there for Mir. It's his birthday and it's all about him. I didn't hear anything from them the day prior or the day of the party. I ended up changing the location of the party to a playground. I was only expecting my parents and a friend who brought her nephew along. The time of the party came and so did the guests. I had pizza, juice, nice decorations, and balloons. I wasn't going to let anything get in the way of Mir's day and just to see the smile on his face when we sang happy birthday to him let all the frustration go away. He opened his gifts and then enjoyed time at the playground.

Later that day when I got home, I happened to be scrolling my emails and I got an email from Mack at 3:51 p.m. I'm thinking he has my phone number to text or call to FaceTime with Mir. In the message he stated, "Hello, I was reaching out for Mir. Please let him know I said Happy Birthday and I hope he has fun and enjoys his day. Also, could you please email me photos of him on his day, thank you?"

I was thinking he is ridiculous. He invited me to the birthday party of a child that he made in our marriage all the way in Virginia knowing I don't get along with the mom and she was also pregnant with his 4th child he wanted me to see to hurt me, yet I invited him to Mir's party and he didn't even show up, nor did his lying mother and father, Tamesha and Correll. It's just beyond ridiculous at this point and its obvious he shows favoritism towards the kids he has with his girlfriend Moesha and she's an enabler that doesn't want him around our son with me around because she can't be involved. I don't respect any woman that doesn't encourage a man to see his kids and honestly it shouldn't even be that way. The man should automatically be in their child's life.

I texted Mack back and said, "The communication on my phone line is still available for you to reach out and see/talk with Mir. I do not check my emails like that so if you ever email and I don't respond that is why."

I was thinking, I'm not telling Mir anything. First off, he hasn't seen Mack in a while so he would be confused as to who I am talking about, secondly, Mack is supposed to be a grown man who can and is able to make a phone call and a visit to see Mir. Third, I don't want this to become a habit that he's sending messages through me to tell Mir because Mir will start questioning why I tell him these things and why he doesn't hear them from his father. It's ridiculous Mack is so bitter he is avoiding his own child, a three year old. I am also not surprised because I remember when him and Bryna weren't getting along for years, I had encouraged him to still contact his daughter and he refused to and stated, "I don't like the person holding the phone" which is just ridiculous so I know for a fact it's the same case for me. He's basically a bitter baby daddy meanwhile myself, I'm just over it. Let's co-parent peacefully without involving Moesha and focus specifically on our son, not the hate you have for me. I dislike him mutually just as much as he dislikes me but I have reason to because of what he's done, he just doesn't like the consequences of his actions and would rather blame me instead of taking accountability that he got caught up. He never responded my email I sent telling him he could reach out to Mir on his birthday.

I sent him a text message saying the same message I sent to his email. I also included in the message to Mack, "Thought you, your family, and the other kids were going to be there however, Mir had an awesome day." I sent along with a couple of pictures of Mir that had a watermark and my name on them for photo credits because I know it's just going to be posted on social media as if his family was present trying to take credit for something I put together, a picture I took, and a celebration they did not partake in. They're social media parents and grandparents as I stated before. I really did not want to send the pictures but of course because everything ends up in court, I did because it would look bad on me even though Mack is very absent and appears and disappears. It's not fair but whatever I'll take it all up in court when the day comes that he decides to start filing motions again playing the blame game for him not seeing Mir. Since Mir's birthday I have not heard a word from Mack. September 30, 2019 officially made a year since he had not seen Mir. At this point, it's on him to reach out. I'm washing my hands of the matter. My main focus is making sure Mir gets all the therapy and treatment he is recommended to have from his autism diagnosis. Anything outside of that is above me and in God's hands. I'm done.

CHAPTER ELEVEN: Reflections

From all I've been through I've learned a vast amount of information about myself and my interactions and experiences with people. To start, a lot of what molded me into who I am today began in my childhood. My father not wanting to spend much of any time with me created insecurity and feelings of abandonment and rejection within me. He was the first man that I was supposed to fall in love with. I resented him for this. My mother and her negative characteristics that she tried to project on me as a child I didn't see anything wrong back then she just was so adamant about me not being pregnant when I would bring up the topic of being interested in boys. The experience my mother had growing up and having a child at 18 years old, she thought was going to be me and it bothered her so much that she had to speak that over My life. I actually surpassed that limit that she placed on me I didn't get pregnant until I was 24 years old. My mother honestly has a lot of childhood trauma. She never got the therapy she needed to cope properly. Instead she projected it on me and made me feel like a troubled child when she placed me under a microscope and onto a pedestal to live her life she wished she had as a child growing up through me. My mother would talk down on me because of my interest in boys as if it was a foreign or forbidden thing. When I got so frustrated that she had a problem with me liking boys I told her what do you want me to do like girls? Okay I'll like girls I got condemned for that as well saying I had better not be dealing with any girls and that it was nasty. She also brought religion into the picture and told me I would be disobeying God. I couldn't win in no way with my mother because she was very stuck in her ways and forgot she too was like me before and her parents didn't treat her the way she treats me. It left me feeling like I was a weird girl and it affected my overall confidence in myself and my natural ability to want a bond with a man. My mother was also a switch sider as well when it came to her relationship with me and my dad. She couldn't balance us two and there were times she made me feel as if I was a burden to her and my dad. I want to make sure I never make my son feel as though he is unimportant or regret just because his dad and I don't see eye to eye. The things I endured in my child hood definitely set the tone for how I turned out and coped as an adult. When I graduated high school, going to college immediately after was not the best thing for me in my opinion. I did not get a chance to celebrate my graduation or be with my friends at all. I was so unfocused I flunked miserably and stopped showing up. I was working at Target as a cashier and I was a production worker at Signature Brands factory where we made popcorn for stores. My parents again made me feel like a burden and a bum and were ready to kick me out of their house because of my interests not being where they wanted them to be. They still wanted to have control of my every movement, limit the amount of fun I have, and make me out to be miserable just like they were. My mom wanted me to also work and give her half of my check which was ridiculous. How was I ever supposed to gain independence if the money I was giving her was to help pay her bills and make it harder for me to get out of the house on my own? Yes my mother was struggling but she acted as if I caused her to struggle as if I asked to be here on Earth. My mother and father overstepped their welcome at my house and violated boundaries that I was not strong enough back then to stand up for myself and create. There was never any need for them to approve or compare my lifestyle. I chose a different path then them both at my age so our story and our journey were to never be a competition. Since I've written this book and discovered where my entire trauma originated, I have minimized the amount of contact I have with my parents. I only talk to them when it involves my son. There is no business of my household that they know or need to know. I had to stand up for myself and set boundaries. I didn't realize how much I haven't had boundaries for several years allowing my parents and others to do and say what they wanted to me. I had to make it clear to them now that I am an adult I am not accepting toxic behaviors or negative energy in regards to my life choices. I had even found a list online as well which I stand by 100%. The list says, "I have rules to dealing with family now that I'm an adult. 1. You will not talk to me or treat me any kind of way just because you're older than me. I'm still an adult. 2. Don't confuse my love for you as weakness. I will cut you off. 3. I don't owe you anything. Anything I do is out of love, not obligation. 4. Respect is a mutual thing. 5. I am not a bad person for calling out toxic people/behaviors just because they've been like that for years. 6. I don't have to tell you my business and if I do it's not yours to tell. And if I do it's not yours to tell. 7. I don't have to consult with you regarding my life choices. 8. If I want your opinion, I will ask for it. Unsolicited advice from people who project their insecurities is the worst. 9. I am not obligated to put up with you because you're family. 10. If family events stress me out, I will not come. You can visit me too. It's important to set boundaries with people in your life, especially family. I love my family, but I also hold them accountable for how they treat me, regardless of who they are. This was not a list I created but it held so much meaning. When I presented it to my mother, she had no clue what it meant. The reason being is she was so used to doing anything and saying anything to me since I was a child that she carried it over into my adulthood and because I was vulnerable, nieve, and unaware I allowed a lot of negative things. It wasn't until I awoke from the hell I've been through to realize what I was really put through. The only thing my mother and father ever do is listen, gather and store information and talk to other family members about it and it gets circled back around to me or when I'm at a high point in my life they'll thrown an ex or a downfall I had in the mix to remind of where I once was and I cannot and will not deal with that. I don't need reminders of my terrible past that I rose from but I do understand with elevation there will be people that cast stones. I also know that it comes with separation. As you graduate to a higher level in life, your interactions with people who are no good for you will change. I'll be honest; I'm still healing from childhood trauma and trying to find a middle ground. I want to make sure that I don't do to my son what was done to me. I don't him to grow up in a sheltered home environment like I was. I want him to have fun, be aware, and experience all life has to offer and I'll stand behind and pray for him when he does. Relationships have been no walk in the park for me. I didn't have that male figure I always wanted in my life to put me on to the game of men. I have experienced the highs and Lows of being in one. I know I've always been a good woman, with a heart of goal, full of empathy and willing to help those closed to me I care about. I am also an independent woman, I don't enter a relationship seeking anything out of a man but protection, love, and reassurance but of course I don't mind him being a provider of other things that are positive. I haven't found or been found by the one who is accepting of all I have to offer. I do realize that I've been a helpmate more than a soul mate. These guys have come into my life with whatever motives they had, played their cards as if they were a good man, accept what I had to offer and leave in a short period of time. Some of them would find a way to blame me, such as if I didn't appreciate a day they went ghost or talked to me any kind of way, or just plain being inconsiderate, as soon as I brought it to their attention, they didn't want to do the work of fixing it, so they would dip. They wanted all a relationship had to offer but, refused to commit and respect my boundaries as well as triggers.

I have contributed to the building up of men such as encouraging them to do something positive or upgrade their life. I'm the woman that'll help a man fill out job applications. The women that'll help you open up a bank account, just to save and help you get on your feet. The woman that'll tell you right from wrong. The women that'll plan things to do just to keep you out the streets, the woman that'll help you go from nothing to something. The woman that'll motivate you and make sure your head is always on straight. The woman that want you to do and be great! Sometimes a man will drain you for everything you have, then play victim. You can be the whole table, but he'll still go and mess around with a napkin! A man deciding to leave or me deciding to cut them off doesn't mean something is wrong with me or them, it's just we were not meant for each other and the one who is meant for me will be there in good and bad times regardless. I'll admit I'm not completely ready for a relationship anymore. I need to rebuild myself love, self-esteem, and establish what real love is and boundaries. I appreciate each one of them for showing me who they are and who they weren't because a lesson was learned in spite of it all. Deciding to go to the military was something I had never thought of. After being in the same city for 23years and growing up with a pretty boring childhood, I decided I didn't want that life anymore. Jobs were dead end, I wasn't in any relationship, and I didn't have kids. I figured it was the perfect time for me to do something out of the ordinary that would benefit me in the long run. I was scared but I stepped out on Faith and signed up. When I started boot camp, I remember being so unfocused. I felt like I was in shock my entire boot camp that I had actually signed up and was doing something I never set out to do so out of desperation and I wasn't sure how it was going to turnout. Swimming was the hardest part for me and in 12 feet of water at that. My past still had control of me. Almost being drowned twice as a child by a couple of family members playing water games had scarred me. My parents had never got me in swim lessons and contributed to me being afraid of water because I didn't get in water much with them. Staying behind in boot camp an extra month and having to go to the pool each day and get in it was mentally tormenting for me. My biggest fear was a reality I had to face to get to the next level. I'll say boot camp. Boot camp was a good and bad experience for me. It allowed me to get out of my comfort zone and see other parts of the world. Some memorable moments for me was going to Chicago, Illinois for boot camp and seeing snow for the first time, going to Meridian, Mississippi for training school, after graduating that school I went to San Diego, California for two weeks before departing on a large aircraft carrier with thousands of people to sail to Busan, South Korea for a port visit where I got a chance to rest and relax before we set sail to my permanent duty station in Yokosuka, Japan and getting a chance to enjoy parts of Japan including my most favorite visit to Tokyo. All of these places I've visited wouldn't have been possible or even a thought in my mind had I not joined the military. Not everyone where I come from can say they've been on a journey like this, but I didn't mind sharing my experiences and photos on social media showing the world my happiest of times. This was truly a blessing I don't take for granted and I cherish the values and success the military has set me up to have the Best for life. In regards to Mack and I's hell, I mean, holy matrimony I got to say what a poor marriage this was. I partially fault myself for being head over heels diving head first into this marriage without completely assessing everything closely and carefully. I partially blame Mack's parents for their example and how he is by exposing him to their toxic relationship for several years, his dad for cheating on his mother several times, and his mother for staying so long for their kids. When Mack grew up, he thought it was okay and did just like his father, cheating, and had babies and expecting them to stay and tolerate his bullshit and when they don't; he is angry and starts chaos. I blame Mack because even if that situation occurred between his mother and father he could've simply chose a different route, he didn't have to follow in their footsteps at all. He could've decided to be the change. If he would take accountability for his actions and be truthful, he would get a lot further in life but because of his deceptions and chaos he can't. He still lives in his childhood where there was a lot of chaos. Mack needs to recognize and take accountability for who he is and the actions he has caused as well as choices he has made.

Second off, he needs to heal his childhood trauma and rise above what his mother and father did and what he saw as a child. He made the choice to continue the behaviors he witnessed instead of saying you know what; I'm going to be better. It appears that as he gets older, his decisions and aging looks get worse. Thirdly, he needs to focus more on himself and not females. He has an extreme drive for females and catering to them for acceptance. He needs to be more career-minded and focus on all of his kids, not the ones that he live with and sleep with the mom or the one that has him on child support. Regardless of everything he has four kids and counting at this point. All of them should have the same treatment but Mir needs a little more care and concern because he is the only one with special needs and it is a serious issues. While this all sounds great, it is nearly impossible for this to happen with Mack being that he displays narcissistic characteristics. He can change for the occasion or situation but he ends up going back to old familiar ways.

Yes Mack was very charming and deceiving but the minute he started coming back and forth with drama before we even got married, that was a sure sign what the rest of our marriage would be like. The fact that he was moving extremely fast not taking caution about all of the possibilities amongst each other showed he was looking for love quick and trying to get over someone or something else. That someone was his first baby mama. He was never over her and honestly not over any of his ex's so to think I could've had a successful marriage with all the baggage he's carrying from each soul he's slept with was darn near impossible. See Mack doesn't take time to heal. He jumps in and out of things very quickly and will play victim all the way. That is not the type of man I should've ever been interested in but I didn't know. The audacity he had to bring his baby mama in my house is beyond me and to think that I wasn't ever going to find out is even more off the wall. He was better off continuously sending Bryna money to hush her mouth and I wouldn't ever found out but I am glad I did, so glad. God knew he didn't want me in that mess but he allowed me to enter in it to show just why it didn't and wouldn't work out. See I'm a woman's woman. I wouldn't have ever done that to another woman period. That's just how much respect for another woman. I'm not eager, jealous, or messy enough to go after what's hers or allow hers to come after me. If anything, I would redirect him to her and go about my business. I wouldn't partake in bragging about being wanted by a married man, it's not cute, and God didn't set us up with other people's spouse. Finding out about Moesha and Mack was just disgusting for me. The amount of karma that occurred was right on time. It's amazing how God works in his timing and in the most mysterious ways. The day I found out about Mack and Moesha's arrest, I knew that it was meant to happen this way. Imagine if I didn't take Mack back, continue to have speculations of him cheating and not having any solid proof while he continued to lie and deceive me. I wouldn't want to live a marriage on the edge or feel like I'm walking on eggshells around my gut feelings. I am glad that I did go through what I went through because not only my eyes were opened but others eyes were too and although he did blame me for getting caught, I didn't have anything to do with it. The investigator and his command had already knew before I even had a thought, they just did not tell me until everything was pieced together. He and Moesha getting together was their karma. They thought it was just going to be peaches and cream living the life together during my marriage while disobeying God's principles of marriage. The best thing I ever did was making the decision to cut him off from having access to me to sleep around with others continuously and come back home with me. I did not want him to pull the same move he did with Bryna with Moesha while I wasn't home. He was angry and punished me with silent treatment when I kicked him out but his mouth and his actions is what did it. I had no idea the amount of drama that was going to stir up from doing so. As far as Moesha goes, I would've respected and possibly been able to deal with her if one, she waited until our divorce was finalized, two she stayed out of our business, and three if she hadn't made a child in the middle of Mack and I still being legally married basically trying to gravitate the attention towards her and her kids so it's away from myself and my son. I also understand that Mack also enabled the actions and behaviors for her to do these things because he did nothing to stop it and I know the amount of control he can have on a female mind. I cannot and will not ever respect a woman, who doesn't respect herself and another woman regardless if she knows her or not to step out and beyond boundaries to hurt another woman whether a man enabled her up to it or not. As women, we have to put ourselves in the other woman's shoes and she didn't. If it was her she would've probably handled things worse than me. All she cared about was having a piece of a man and trying to force him into another marriage while married to me and trapping him with kids. Her self-esteem is low and the level of desperation she has to be with Mack regardless is insane but that's her burden to bear. I learned through my marriage and the divorce that nobody associated with Mack is loyal at all. Not Mack, not his family, not his baby mamas either. They have all played a vital role in why things are the way they were and are. I didn't switch sides and lie and act like or pretend like it was one way when it was really another. I have held the same stance since everything began. They've all flip flopped and not been solid and have been temporarily situationally loyal. I didn't realize until the end that Mack was a pathological liar from the beginning and that I was in love with a complete illusion, a lie, and a fraud. This was the welcoming to me of a narcissistic manipulationship. Mack has brought me so many enemies based off of the lies he told to people naming himself as the victim and me as the perpetrator. Narcissists also like to truncate the story and present only the bit where the aggrieved party reacted to their toxic behavior, framing it as if that's where the story started. They twist it by using euphemisms and deceiving language ("I'm not controlling, I just want what's best for you."). For example, if a narcissist dislikes you and tries to bully you but you stand up for yourself, they will frame it as if they are the ones being a victim of bullying. In their narrative they were just doing their thing or joking around and you started being mean to them. Meanwhile, they simply left out what happened beforehand when they bullied you, so actually you "being mean" to them is a normal response to toxic behavior. Here, by leaving out or downplaying their aggression they simply frame you engaging in self-defense as vile aggression against them. And then they think: "How dare you react or challenge me! You're so sensitive and unfair! That's why you deserve everything that's coming!" Why does Mack lie about things or twist the truth to make him look like the innocent victim? The truth is simply because he fears the outcome. He doesn't want people to know the real him and suffer the injury to his ego by revealing his false self. He knew that the agenda he had would be tarnished if he told the truth, so he lied in hopes I would believe it so he could continue with his misconceptions until he completely destroyed me and my reality of the truth. A majority have never met or personally know me but because he twisted what he did to make himself seem good, I look bad to them but in the beginning I was a beauty being adored by Mack and was groomed me to fit his agenda of marrying in the military to get the extra money benefits and having the house to himself while I was overseas to bring girls galore with ones I never found out. I was sweet and looked at Mack as a faultless and innocent. I honored him as my husband, had his back, and rode for him until the very end while unknowingly destroying my mental health trying to keep him in check. In reality, it was not my job to fix Mack to see life from a logical stand point, because no amount of it would've changed the way he viewed things until he was ready to change himself but with a narcissist being very hard to detect by licensed professionals when placed in front of them, and their viewpoints being based from childhood and the environment they were brought up in its hard and nearly impossible for them to shift their way of thinking. The minute I caught on to the games and decided to not indulge in it I became a beast and I was named as "crazy" by every person in association or relation with Mack. This is at the point where I woke up and started pinpointing every aspect of a narcissistic individual that he exhibited. I even looked up a blog that said signs you are in a relationship or marriage with a narcissist and there was about 15 signs and every last one of them I could relate to. It blew my mind. He kept poking and prodding at me like a bear doing things in a subtle manner, downplaying the abuse. I gave him an inch, he took a mile and then some and as soon as I reacted it was turned against me. In turn, this type of abusive behavior led me to put up a hard outer shell and a wall. I started establishing boundaries and voicing my truths of what I was seeing and hearing and I became an aggressor in his head. Mentally he is ill. Anyone who can do some foul stuff and then play victim is definitely a disturbed individual. I noticed behind closed doors he is a villain and when he's around family, people who are unaware and the courts, he plays victim. Exactly like a Jekyll and Hyde personality. This divorce was greatly needed. I am so glad that everything happened the way it did to reveal everyone true colors and separate myself. I did not deserve any bit of how I was treated. It was the most cruel, cold, and calculated act and person I've ever experience in my life. I am beyond thankful and happy my attorney and the judges were able to see right through Mack. No matter what he said, his actions and lack of evidence spoke the loudest. Honestly, Mack has a lot of childhood trauma and drama with his mother that he tried to take out on me as his eight. They did not have the best relationship at all as he was growing up, according to him. My thoughts are as he got older, the animosity he had for his mother, he projected and used it to exploit women and become a selfish womanizing monster. He was so used to getting what he wanted from his parents and now he seeks the same thing in women. Something's got to be in it for him to play a good role to get what he wants. I don't have any contact with anyone, not Mack's family, Moesha, or Bryna, all of them get along or appear to anyways, befriending each other on social media trying to act as if I'm the only one who doesn't get along, which I am, but I have valid reasons for not wanting anything to do with them being that I experienced a great deal of heartache, drama, and pure craziness from all of them and they treat me like I have wronged them when I haven't and choose to take it out on my son. I have no obligation to cooperate and be civil with anyone but Mack and that's not by choice, that's by court order force for our son only. Besides, if I had bad feelings about someone before, I will always see them as the person they initially showed me. Now that I know better, I wouldn't allow them a chance to show me another side, because honestly true colors come out and no matter how much people act, everything will always.be brought to the light. If the shoe was on their foot, they would feel and act the same way as I did and so I don't know why nor do I care to know why they treat me as if I'm supposed to magically let that go immediately. They don't determine the timing of my healing and whether or not I should reconnect. They can call me crazy, bitter, whatever. I am protecting my peace from those evil people which means I limit the amount of contact I have with them although I still allowed Mir to have contact simply because he can make the decision when he gets older who he wants to disconnect from. Mir eventually will figure the truth out on his own even if Mack tries to lie and cover up or play Mir against me. In reality Mack was no good for me and no good for our son with his back and forth mess. He's not willing to correct Moesha and put her in her place to stay out of his and I business and anything revolving our son but he appears to be of some good to the other baby mamas because they let him manipulate and get over on them, get out of being financially responsible for the kids, and he's slept with them back and forth so they're content and they just love being the favorites to feel like their winning. I don't and he doesn't like that. I don't have anything in common with them anyways but Moesha and Bryna both have in common that they like and have slept with a married man. Like the saying goes, "Birds of a feather flock together" That's why I never fit in. Mack's got everyone thinking I'm such a bad person, this and that, and when I react in a normal way he thinks that proves his point but the problem is, those on the outside only see my reaction, they don't see the damage and deception he's doing or if they do, they choose to turn a blind eye and project me as the problem in front of him so they don't feel his disappearance or wrath. Truth is Moesha and Bryna will dislike me for life all because I had the title. I don't know them and I would have never did such acts to them. I have respect for a woman even if her man doesn't. They wanted my position once upon a time, that's why they never wanted to get along with me except to be petty to prove Mack's stance with them. They'll never admit it but I was and still am a threat to them. The strength I had and how smart I am to overcome Mack is unknown for them, they can't relate, all they know is to give in. While they all want to talk about each other do foul stuff and then come together against me, I don't mind being the one that's counted out. I'm older, I'm different, very set apart and I don't have any of the same morals or standards like any of them have displayed. I do not want to be a part of their dysfunctional relationship nor associate with them. They can continue watching and talking, counting me and my son out. Life goes on and we will still be great. I won't lie; I had murder on my mind for all three of them. To undergo all I had to and suppress it all mentally, I wanted to take their life. . That's just how much everything affected me. I have never and will not ever treat someone the way I've been treated. It's inhumane and insensitive. I've never been like this or had thoughts towards people before but the amount of foulness that went on, I felt like they would've deserved it. So many things could've occurred from them being selfish thinking about their wants only. I could've caught a disease that I would never be able to get rid of, a baby born, things missing or out of order in my place, and just the fact that it was all down right trifling. The only reason I snapped out of carrying out that act is because I have too much to lose. My son, my career, my future, and not being behind bars are important to me. The revenge I wanted wasn't because they took a man who once was married to me, it was simply the disrespect and the fact they thought it was cute to do all the extra messy stuff they did, all of them. They all should be very glad I didn't lose my mind and have a lot to lose because I have no doubt of my capabilities that I would've taken it there without a second thought but reprogramming my mind to know that isn't okay nor will it solve anything was necessary. There are women out here who have been in my shoes and took it to that level and farther so everyday they're alive they need to thank God they're still here on this earth because I definitely had it out for them once upon a time and you just cannot play with everyone's feelings especially when they did nothing to you. Honestly now I have days where I have flashbacks and want to at least fight them both until they're black and blue because of how unfair it is and the fact that myself and my child are affected by it. I'm honest enough to say I haven't been delivered from those thoughts yet, which is another reason I don't want any further contact with them ever in life but I am working against myself and with the help of God that if I ever for some reason come in contact with them, I don't have a flashback and react at that moment. I have to coach myself to snap out of it because my son needs me and none of them are worth it. Mack loves the two baby mamas because they cater to his false ego, the person he wants to be. Me on the other hand, I have always been the truth teller and didn't stroke his ego hoping that he would like or love me more and that's fine. I'm not telling him anything about himself that isn't true based off of my observation and his pattern and the ones who kiss his behind are part of the reason he is the way he is. They enable it and he thinks its okay so those are the ones he loves being around and he will continue to do what he does as long as they give him the okay or sleep with him. Mack is absent because he's trying to make Moesha comfortable with his presence so she doesn't miss anything with him being around me and as long as I don't accept her or tolerate her in my space he won't see our son. It's similar to how I felt about him driving 7 hours to pick up Bryna, not just his daughter while we was married and I was nowhere around to in know what would really go on so I felt uncomfortable but I was his wife so I had all rights to feel that way because I had a hunch in my mind something was going to go down and the way Mack was carrying on about it is what made me have that thought in my mind. If he ever tried to come to Atlanta, Moesha would have a complete fit like she did before when he was sneaking around to see Mir around me. She would break up with him like she did before when she found out so to keep the peace for her sake he stays absent because it's impossible for him to sneak to Atlanta without her knowing of course unless he picks a fight with her, wins, gives silent testament and uses that time to come see him like he was trying to do before and like he has done to me before right before he went to Philadelphia. If he's waiting for me to be cool with her and accept everything done to me with or without an apology, then , he's going to be waiting for a really long time. I can forgive her and still not want to reconnect with her. He should be a father regardless of how she feels. I have not tried to pin my man on him and her but also if I did, that man didn't disrespect him like Mack did to me along with Bryna and Moesha's doings to get to the point of not wanting to see eye to eye. Mack placed Moesha on a pedestal where she acts like herself and the kids they had together after my son have significance and more value because the relationship is still together and because she has that much control over him. I'm pretty sure she has threatened him if he came around me again with our son she would break up with him or put him on child support Mack's biggest fear is child support and she knows that's her leverage that for sure that will keep him away from me and make him cut anything and everybody off so he doesn't go on it again and if that means staying away from me and only caring for their kids he will definitely do it. Bryna and I both can attest to this. Mir will know all of the truth one day. I wrote Moesha off my list as a positive and trustworthy person when she first came into my marriage causing drama and harassing me multiple times as well as calling my job lying on me as well as claiming my baby. I don't ever have anything to say to her in life. I genuinely hope Mack finds a better woman one day who will be a decent stepmother and not on any pettiness to prove her place in my ex's life just to spite me for what Mack says about me which is basically lies to validate her place in his life. I don't have an issue with any other girl as long as she knows her place, treats my son right, and respect boundaries. Overall, no matter how I feel, what they say and what they do, Vengeance is the Lord's and while they laughed and tried to be funny towards me and my storm, there's already and has been brewing. Speaking on motherhood, Becoming a mother to me has been the most rewarding challenge I have ever experienced in life. Since my son has been born, he has given my life a whole new meaning. I couldn't imagine what life would be like if he wasn't here. He has truly been the missing piece in my life and when God removed his father; my son was the better replacement. Even on my hardest days of being a single mother, I wouldn't trade it for anything or anyone in the world. Being in the military added more challenges that I did not want. They wanted me to prioritize the mission of the Navy and I wanted to prioritize my son. I couldn't imagine leaving my son for several months at time to be in the middle of the ocean serving the county. I also couldn't imagine my anxiety being at an all-time high and not being able to focus nor perform being far away from him and being placed into the custody and care of Mack. If Mack was a good father and respectful to me as Mir's mother, I wouldn't have no problem experimenting going on a deployment while leaving him behind for just a little. I didn't have the support or confidence I needed to carry that out. I didn't want my son to not know me or forget who I am and end up in the hands and care of Mack's many girlfriends he likes to have. Telling the Navy my decision wasn't a hard one. After all, I had suffered with my divorce and the entire trauma while in and the last piece of the puzzle was to focus on motherhood after the storm. I began to mentally check out and start acting out because working 10 and 12 hours , 6 and sometimes 7 days out of the week, I just could not do it. Those who had a personal vendetta against me either because of my rank, because I was a strong minded female, or simply because they wanted me to lose it so they could use that against me to gain leverage, none of their attempts worked for long at all. I was constantly on guard, taking notes, documenting everything. By the time I brought up the paperwork to get everything signed off and start the process to get me out, they knew what time it was. I no longer wanted to lash out, or get in trouble, I just needed freedom. Mentally they knew the toll that everything had on me so they attempted to keep me in that circle so I could be miserable. I thank God for the amount of knowledge and strength I had to not give up and continue the fight to win for the best interest of me and my son and I did. I am happy to be out of the military. It was no place for a single mother like me severely attached to my child. I felt bad at first because I only had 6 months left on my contract before I would have completely a total of 4 years but I just knew I wouldn't make it to that point while trying to stay sane. I had a gut feeling that something negative was going to happen before I got discharged so I had to get out as quick as possible. To add to that, Mack didn't show care and compassion for our son and had abandoned him for a female so I didn't believe he would be a good fit to leave my son with while on deployment. Now

I am an advocate and volunteer to help any mother out that doesn't have a support system in the military going through similar. I make myself available for them to talk to and give advice and guidance as well as share my story to empower them to not give up and if need be to get out and I provide them a list of resources that helped my transition go smoothly. As for my move to another state outside of my hometown. I just want to say I love living in Atlanta. It's a huge city and there's room for a lot of growth here. The only thing I hate about it is the traffic. Other than that, there's a lot to do and see. I have seen a few celebrities so far such as Nelly and Benzino. I'm sure I've come across a lot more than I've paid attention too. The weather is great. It's not too cold and not too hot, it's just right. I don't have to deal with snow like I did in Virginia although it was a great experience for Mir and I playing in it. I didn't move back home because there isn't any opportunity, I've outgrown Ocala, and although living there it would've been cheaper but there's nothing positive for my son there. It's a city I feel is best for retirement and people that have families that can't or don't want to make a lot of money. I'm an upcoming young professional and I want to experience a big city life not go back to a small city where I may be prone to pick up old habits and be around the same small minded people I was around before. I just wanted to experience something new and challenging for me and I don't regret it at all. I don't travel to Florida occasionally but I do want to go to Orlando to take my son to the theme parks there. Right now, I am currently searching for a nice house in a good area of Atlanta with a great school system for my son. That is my next big venture and I am so excited for that time to come. Finding out my son has autism has been the hardest thing I've ever had to bare and without the help and understanding of his dad has made it even hard but I'm still making it. I don't know why God placed me in this position; however, I know the purpose is a lot greater than I could ever think of imagine. In spite of it all, Mir is a well-rounded, happy, and smart boy. I am so glad I found out now than later because I couldn't imagine him displaying these characteristics towards others and myself or them not knowing how to deal with it. The biggest fear I have is my son running off and going missing. That is literally the biggest thing for me right along next to someone mistreating him because they don't understand or don't have compassion and patience for him. I would hurt anyone over my son, I don't play about him at all. He recently transitioned from a regular daycare to an autism school that will best fit his needs. He'll get all of therapy and treatment he needs and there will be a lot of progress I'm sure. As far as Mir's granddad calling him crazy, I haven't allowed contact since then because that is a form of verbal abuse that my son will not be subjected to. I haven't heard from Mir's dad because he's busy with his other 3 kids from the other two mothers that love him and put up with all his mess at any cost and as long as he gives his penis and talks negatively about and stays away from me(the ex-wife they are competitive and jealous of) he forgets our son exists until a holiday comes around, if his dad asks him to reach out, or if he wants to prove a point to someone to be in their good graces. When I was on board with his tactics, I was a good woman and the best he's had but when I was not on his side about stuff I know was wrong he said I was against him. It's crazy because I started off amazing to Mack and as I began to discover his character and call it out he became less attracted to me. He felt as if I was attacking him with words when in reality I was telling truths I saw with my eyes and heard out of him with my ears. Narcissists don't want honest relationships, they want cheerleaders. They want people who always give them the right. They want blind loyalty. They want unconditional acceptance, no matter what they do. As long as you don't question anything they do, or give them the wrong on anything, they might just leave you alone. But watch out, if you disagree with them, or go against them in any way, in their eyes this is the deepest betrayal and it never goes unpublished. Narcissists are spiteful and vindictive. I will not sacrifice not getting financial support for Mir and sleep with Mack or let him lie on me in court for my son to have a father. It's wrong and a form of blackmail. I would welcome the relationship between them if it's genuine love and care not situational. I don't want Mir to be treated like a toy because Mack doesn't like his mother. While I don't like Mack at all as a person and his characteristics, I can control my feelings and emotions enough to co-parent but he cannot and refuses to do so. I've completely stopped reaching out to him and put it in God's hands and the courts hands when he decides he wants to go cause chaos there again. I am focused on Mir getting the help he needs. I want Mir to become a healthy person within the environment and grow up to be the successful and smart person I am raising him to be. To sum it up, the biggest lesson I have learned is to be true to myself. I have sacrificed my own values and experiences to please others and I am done with this. Another lesson I learned is to be patient and careful who I lay with, it can truly change your life forever. At this point, I decided I want to be single and focus more on my son and my businesses. Honestly, I kept stacking hurt on top of hurt, setting expectations and when they don't reach the bar, I'm upset, expecting people to have the same heart I do and not recognizing the bad in them, and most importantly taking my time to process everything and heal properly. I'll heal when it's my time. No one can rush that. Although my ex and his family have been trying to rush me to "just get over it" so I can be cool with his mistress not realizing everything I've been through was just as fast as it was foul and realistically I couldn't heal while in the military, I had to hide and suffer in silence and I also couldn't heal being in close vicinity with the perpetrator of everything, Mack. I've been covering those wounds by being in relationships that have similarities to past ones that I didn't pay attention to at first trying to satisfy my flesh and one day when I became awakened to literally everything I said, "I'm done being attracted to toxic, good dick, and what looks good to my eyes and sounds good to my ears. I take full responsibility for allowing abusers to come in my life and diminish my worth because I didn't know it on my own. Moving forward now I know it and I will not stand for abuse anymore."

I decided that from the day I started writing this book and going forward. If God didn't send him, I don't want him. You see the devil knows exactly what you want and he will send one of his people as a distraction that makes you feel like you've found the one, in reality, you've found the one who will make your life a living hell. I just ask of the lord, "Please don't send me another man that's mentally ill, emotionally destroyed, and can't own up to his responsibilities & actions; a man who can't put his foot down to his family or people around him. I don't want it. A man who can't speak for himself or have no control over his life, who don't want help to change for the better because as a woman when you dealing w/ that type of man, You are mentally, emotionally, and physically drained after constantly trying to help the man become a better man. I want that type of man kept away from me." A relationship can come later but it is a must that I secure the bag while I build my empire. I want to thank each and every one of you for reading my memoir and also for your continued love and support throughout my journey. After all I've been through, I could've been out of my mind, prison, or six feet in the ground, or completely broken surrendering my soul to the devil, drugs, and alcohol addiction but I'm not. I've bent a few times, but one thing about it, I did not and will not break.

CHAPTER TWELVE: Healing and Growth

I thank God I do not look like what I've been through. Honestly, I don't know how I've held all this in for several years allowing every bit of it to consume my mind but not enough to make me lose it and I'm thankful for that. I'm one of those people who will suppress and allow things to build up until I get tired and when I finally reach the point where I can no longer hold in my silence, I open my mouth and begin to lash out. That is something I am actively working on and I believe I've gotten a lot better at it over the years. As soon as I recognize something that causes a trigger or a negative reaction to my energy, I may speak on it but I do distance myself and remove it.

One of the things I find that's helping me heal and work towards growth in every aspect of my life is by seeking counseling. Mental health is extremely important and should be our priority to maintain every day in life. It is fine to have a therapist to spill all of your emotions out to. After all, it's their job to listen and help with coping strategies to help bring about better days in life. Don't allow anyone to shame you into the cliché phrase by saying, "You're crazy" for getting mental help.

I never thought I would be talking to a therapist as often as I do but the main reason I am in therapy is because of someone who won't get therapy aka Mack and now because I'm having to cope and deal daily with what my son is going through. Even with therapy, the rate of Mack changing due to his narcissistic character is slim to none. Therefore since I have to deal with him for our son's sake, the only way I'll be able to do so is first by talking to God and secondly a mental health professional because it is a highly conflicting individual. On another note, I love exploring new areas of Atlanta with my son and scouting out a nice area and house for Mir and me to move in. Atlanta is huge and there are so many different beautiful areas of the city so I don't want to limit myself on choices. I also find peace in working out at the gym, listening to Gospel music, retail therapy, going to the gym, eating and learning to cook new foods, as well as ways to develop a successful business. I have a few friends I hang with from time to time and usually we'll do something fun or go out to eat. I am also seeking out new hobbies such as going to the gun range and shooting targets, learning how to dance in different ways, learning more about fashion, painting, bowling, and relearning how to skate.

I also want to gain more confidence in feeling more comfortable with my body and myself as a person so I have decided on taking professional pictures each month to contribute to my confidence. I also enjoy taking walks at the park and driving around the city at night. This gives me a great sense of peace and serenity which is just what I need in this chaotic world. As far as growth goes, I am learning new ways of dealing with my emotions, more effective ways to communicate, and healing my divorce/marriage and childhood trauma. Honestly, it was hard for me to heal in the same environment I got tormented in so moving away was best for me and I am happy I did. I am seeking God in everything because he knows best for my life and I know he's truly got mine and my son's back. My point in sharing my story is to let my readers know that no matter how hard life gets to not give up. As much as I've been through I could definitely been in a padded room, in a jail, on drugs, an alcoholic or even worse, death. Although the things I went through definitely tested me in ways I never thought possible, I didn't give in, I didn't give up. I kept an indomitable spirit and knew that there would be brighter days. Thank you so much for reading and supporting my story. It is truly an honor to be very transparent my journey and hopefully it helps other. As a final tip, I would like to tell you all, trust your gut feeling, it's never wrong, and when things don't add up, make it simple just subtract yourself. Remember to always wear your crown and stand your ground Indomitable Queens and Kings. Sending a lot of love, good vibes, and hugs to you all!

Best Blessings,
Keynu Scott

ABOUT AUTHOR KEYNU SCOTT

Keynu is currently pursuing her studies on her Bachelor's Degree in Criminal Justice with Saint Leo University. She is an honorably discharged; United States Navy Veteran served in the United States Navy for 4 years and has chosen to discontinue service to care for her son. Although her goals did not include writing a book on her shortcomings and risings, her passion to do so has surpassed her expectations. Keynu understands the challenges of dealing with abusive behaviors. Her empathetic persona and pure heart have left a precious mark on all she interacts with. Keynu continues to live her life limitlessly and is striving to live her best and blessed life that God has called her to do.

Made in the USA
Columbia, SC
13 January 2020

86590286R10205